The Gods of Ancient Rome

Religion in Everyday Life from Archaic to Imperial Times

Robert Turcan
Translated by Antonia Nevill

Edinburgh University Press

English edition first published 2000 by
Edinburgh University Press Ltd
22 George Square
Edinburgh
Scotland

Translation © Edinburgh University Press 2000
Guide to Further Reading © J. E. Reeson 2000

First published 1998 by Hachette Littératures
74 rue Bonaparte
75006 Paris
France
© Hachette Littératures 1998

English edition published with the aid of a translation
subvention kindly given by the French Ministry of Culture

Typeset in 11 on 13 pt Goudy Old Style
by Hewer Text Ltd, Edinburgh, and
printed and bound in Great Britain by
The University Press, Cambridge

A CIP Record for this book is available from the British Library

ISBN 0 7486 1389 7 (hardback)
ISBN 0 7486 1390 0 (paperback)

Contents

List of illustrations

1. Funerary relief. Rome. Palazzo Albani del Drago. Photo: German Archaeological Institute, Rome.
2. Marcus Aurelius sacrificing before the temple of Jupiter Capitolinus. Rome, Palazzo dei Conservatori. Photo: Alinari.
3. Sacrifice of a bull. Paris, Louvre Museum. Photo: Giraudon.
4. *Immolatio* of the victim. Rome, Capitoline Museum.
5. Haruspex. Tübingen, University Archaeological Institute.
6. Domestic lararium. Herculanum. Ins. V. 31.
7. Lupercus. Vatican Museum.
8. Augustus as an augur. Florence. Uffizi Museum. Photo: Alinari.
9. Quindecemvir *sacris faciundis*. Paris, Louvre Museum.
10. Banquet of the Vestals. Rome, Museo Nuovo.
11. *Suovetaurilia*. Paris, Louvre Museum.
12. Sacrifice to the Moirai. Coin of Domitian, private collection. Photo: 'Monnaies et Médailles', Basle.
13. The emperor dictating a prayer to the matrons. Coin of Domitian. London, British Museum.
14. Priest of Bellona. Rome, Capitoline Museum.
15. Egyptian festival. Rome, National Museum.
16. Jupiter Dolichenus and his companion. Rome, Capitoline Museum.
17. Sacrifice to the Augustan Lares. Rome, Museo Nuovo.
18. Sacrifice to Nemesis. Rome, Museo Nuovo. Photo: German Archaeological Institute, Rome.

Abbreviations

Marc. = Pro Marcello
Mil. = Pro Milone
Mur. = Pro Murena
ND = de natura deorum
Phil. = Philippics
Quinct. = Pro Quinctio
Rep. = De Republica
Scaur. = Pro Aemilio Scauro
Vat. = In Vatinium
Verr. = In Verrem actiones
Clem. Alex., Protr. = Clement of Alexander, Protreptica
Col. = Columella, De re rustica
C. Th. = Theodosian code (ed. T. Mommsen-P. Meyer, Berlin, 1905; 1962³)
DC = Dio Cassius, Roman History
DH, AR = Dionysius of Halicarnassus, Roman antiquities
Don., Com. = Donatus, Tractatus de comoedia
DS = Diodorus Siculus, The Historical Library
Eur., Bacc. = Euripides, Bacchae
Eus. = Eusebius of Caesarea
    HE = Ecclesiastical History
    VC = Life of Constantine
Fest. = Festus, abbreviator of Verrius Flaccus, De verborum significatione, ed.
        Lindsay, Leipzig, 1913 (Hildesheim, 1965²)
Firm. = Firmicus maternus
    Err. = De errore profanarum religionum
    Math. = Mathesis
Fulg., Serm. = Fabius Planciades Fulgentius, Expositio sermonum antiquorum
Front., Ep. M. Caes. = Fronto, Letters to Marcus Aurelius Caesar
Gell. = Aulus Gelius, Attic nights
Hdn. = Herodian, History of the Roman emperors
Hes., W = Hesiod, Works and Days
Hipp., Ref. = Hippolytus of Rome, Refutation of all heresies
Hor. = Horace
    Ep. = Letters
    Epo. = Epodes
    O= Odes
    S = Satries
Jambal., VP = Jamblichus, Life of Pythagoras
Jer., Ep. = St Jerome, Letters
Jos., AJ = Flavius Josephus, Judaic Antiquities
Jul., Or. = Julian, Speeches

Just., *Apol.* = Justin Martyr, *Apologia*

Juv. = Juvenal, *Satires*

Lact. = Lactantius

  Inst. = *Divinae institutiones*

  Mort. = *De mortibus persecutorum*

Lib., *Or.* = Libanius, *Speeches*

Liv., = Livy, *Roman History*

  Per. = *Periochae* (résumés of lost books)

Luc. = Lucan, *Pharsalia*

Luc. Sam., *Syr.* Lucian of Samosata, *The Syrian Goddess*

Lucr. = Lucretius, *De natura rerum*

Lyd. *Mens.* = Johannes Lydus, *De mensibus*

Macr., *S* = Macrobius, *Saturnalia*

Mart., *Ep.* = Martial, *Epigrams*

Minuc. = Minucius Felix, *Octavius*

Myth. Vat. = Mythographers of the Vatican

Non. = Nonius Marcellus, *De compendiosa doctrina*, ed. Ios. Mercerius, whose pagination is resumed by ed. Lindsay (Leipzig, 1903)

Obseq. = Julius obsequens, *Prodigiorum liber* (Eng. trs. A. C. Schlesinger, following works of Livy, XIV, coll. Loeb, London, 1987)

Olympiod. = Olympiodorus, late Greek historian

Orig., *C. Cels.* = Origen, *Contra Celsum*

Ov. = Ovid

  AA = *Ars Amatoria*

  Am. = *Amores*

  F = *Fasti*

  M = *Metamorphoses*

  Pont. = *Pontics*

  Tr. = *Tristia*

Pers. = Persius, *Satires*

Petr. = Petronius, *Satiricon*

Philost. = Philostorgius, *Ecclesiastical History*

Phot., *Bibl.* = Photius *Biblioteca*

Pl. = Plautus

  Aul. = *Aulularia*

  Capt. = *Captivi*

  Cist. = *Cistellaria*

  Curc. = *Curculio*

  Ep. = *Epidicus*

  Merc. = *Mercator*

  Ps. = *Pseudolus*

Rud. = *Rudens*
Trinum. = *Trinumnus*
Plin., *NH* = Pliny the Elder, *Natural History*
Plin., *Pan.* = Pliny the Younger, *Panegyric of Trajan*
Plut. = Plutarch
  Parallel lives:
  Aem. = *Aemilius Paullus*
  Caes. = *Caesar*
  Cam. = *Camillus*
  Cor. = *Coriolanus*
  Crass. = *Crassus*
  Mar. = *Marius*
  Marc. = *Marcellus*
  Num. = *Numa*
  Pomp. = *Pompey*
  Rom. = *Romulus*
  Sull. = *Sulla*
  Moral works:
  Fort. Rom. = *Fortune of the Romans*
  Par. = *Greek and Roman parallels*
  QR = *Roman Questions*
Pol. = Polybius, *Histories*
Porph. = Porphyrius
  Antr. = *Cavern of the Nymphs*
  V. Pl. = *Life of Plotinus*
Prop. = Propertius, *Elegies*
Prud. = Prudentius
  Apoth. = *Apotheosis*
  C. Symm. = *Against Symmachus*
  Perist. = *Peristephanon* (Book of crowns)
Qunit. = Quintilian
  Decl. = *Declamations* (of the pseudo-Quintilian)
  IO = *Institutio Oratoria*
Ruf., *HE* = Rufinus, *Ecclesiastical History*
Sal. = Sallustius, *Of the gods and the world*
Sall., *Cat.* = Sallust, *Catilina*
Sen. = Seneca the Philosopher
  Clem. = *De clementia*
  Const. = *De constantia sapientis*
  Ep. = *Letters to Lucilius*
  Ir. = *De ira*

Oed. = Oedipus
Tranq. = De tranquillitate animi
VB = De vita beata
Serv. = Servilius, commentaries on Virgil:
  Aen. = on The Aeneid
  B = on the Bucolics
  G = on the Georgics
Serv. Dan. = ancient glosses added to the text of Servius in the edition of P.
    Daniel, Paris, 1600 (= Deutero-Servius)
SHA = Scriptores Historiae Augustae
  A = Aurelianus
  AP = Antonius Pius
  AS = Severus Alexander
  C = Commodus
  Gall. = Gallieni duo
  H = Hadrianus
  Hel. = Heliogabalus
  MA = Marcus Antoninus
  S = Severus
  Tac. = Tacitus
Socr., HE = Socrates (Scholasticus), Historia Ecclesiastica
Sol. = Solinus, Collectanea rerum memorabilium
Suet. = Suetonius, Lives of the twelve Caesars
  Aug. = Augustus
  Caes. = Caesar
  Cal. = Caligula
  Claud. = Claudius
  Dom. = Domitian
  Galb. = Galba
  Ner. = Nero
  Oth. = Otho
  Tib. = Tiberius
  Vesp. = Vespasian
  Vit. = Vitellius
Symm. = Symmachus
  Ep. = Letters
  Rel. = Relationes ad principes
Tac. = Tacitus
  An. = Annals
  H = Histories
Tert. = Tertullian

An. = *De anima*
Apol. = *Apologeticum*
Cor. = *De corona*
Idol. = *De idololatria*
Ieiun. = *De ieiunio*
Mon. = *De monogamia*
Nat. = *Ad Nationes*
Pall. = *De pallio*
Praescr. = *De praescriptione haereticorum*
Spect. = *De spectaculis*
Tib. = Tibullus, *Elegies*
Val. Flacc. = Valerius Flacus, *Argonautica*
Val. Max. = Valerius Maximus, *Memorable deeds and sayings*
Varr. = Varro
  LL = *De lingua Latina*
  RR = *Res rusticae*
Virg. = Virgil
  Aen. = *Aeneid*
  B = *Bucolics*
  G = *Georgics*
Zos. = Zosimus, *New History*

– OTHER ABBREVIATIONS –

ANRW = *Aufstieg und Niedergang der römishcen Welt. Geschichte und Kultur Roms im Spiegel der neueren Forschung*, Berlin-New York, 1972 ff.
BFFAR = *Bibliothèque des écoles françaises d'Athènes et de Rome*
CCID = *Corpus cultus Iovis Dolicheni*, by M. Hörig and E. Schwertheim (*EPRO*, 106), Leiden, 1987
CEFR = *Collection de l'Ecole française de Rome*
CIL = *Corpus inscriptionum Latinarum*
CLE = *Carmina Latina epigraphica* (ed. F. Bücheler)
CRAI = *Comptes rendus de l'Académie des inscriptions et belles-lettres*
EPRO = *Etudes préliminaires aux religions orientales dans l'Empire romain* (ed. M. J. Vermaseren)
IGUR = L. Moretti, *Inscriptiones Graecae Urbis Romae*
ILLR = A. Degrassi, *Inscriptiones Latinae liberae reipublicae*
ILS = H. Dessau, *Inscriptiones Latinae selectae*
Inscr. Ital. = A. Degrassi, *Inscriptiones Italiae*
REL = *Revue des études latines*
RHR = *Revue de l'histoire des religions*

FILIABVS CARISSIMVS

The wretched Europeans preferred to play their Armagnac versus Bourguignon war games, rather than assume throughout the world the great role that the Romans were capable of taking and holding for centuries in the world of their own times. Their numbers and means were nothing compared with ours: but they found more justifiable and logical ideas in their chickens' entrails than are contained in all our political sciences.

Paul Valéry

CHAPTER 1

Introduction: Pietas Romana

This is not a treatise on Roman religion: several justly celebrated works fulfil that function on various counts. My aim is to show the main characteristics of the part played by gods in the lives of Romans, from day to day, in the annual cycle, throughout a lifetime or in the course of history.

I shall therefore emphasise the material aspects of each cult, its ritual forms and practices, rather than concentrate on beliefs or theology. In any case, this approach matches the sense of the Latin *religio*, at least in its original form and in tradition. For Cicero (*ND*, 2, 8), a 'religion' was a way of honouring the gods (*religione, id est cultu deorum*), and God knows there were plenty to honour in pagan Rome! It is important to set out clearly the aspects of this multiform piety in a series such as 'Daily Life', which was inaugurated by a book by Jérôme Carcopino that has become a classic, but in which the religious life of the Romans at the height of the Empire occupies a somewhat limited place. However, in spite of the increase in non-belief or foreign forms of worship, even then the inhabitants of Rome remained loyal to ancestral rites more often than is thought. We must concentrate on the acts and facts of positive religion, especially after half a century of ideological and sometimes immaterial reconstructions.

Roman religion took shape and developed in the course of history, but it is impossible to write a 'history of Roman religion'. With a few rare exceptions, the evidence we have about worship is at best datable to the last two or three centuries BC, even if it refers to earlier times and deeds, and archaeology is grudging with information about its practices. The problem of origins would lead to speculative theorising, and any kind of narrative account would give rise to useless repetition. Moreover, the secret of the way things developed, in both the execution of rituals and the conscious-ness of believers, is bound to elude us; but the inveterate conservatism of the Romans implies and explains certain constants in their attitude to the gods. There is nothing strictly chronological in my account; nevertheless, its three major divisions embrace an overall historical perspective, the religions of the family and the countryside being, so to speak, first or original, whereas the religions of the Empire appeared in Rome only by virtue of a process of political and sociocultural changes marking the end of the city-state's regime.

There was really no such thing as a Roman religion, in the sense that one or another monotheistic faith exists in our own day. Ancient Rome knew about religious procedures or, rather, the processes and formulas required in any given circumstance to ensure the effectiveness of divine assistance. For the Romans, religion was not a belief, a feeling or, *a fortiori* a mystique: it was purely utilitarian practice. Romans lived in obsessive fear of hazards, the occult powers that threatened or hampered human actions, whether as regards subsistence, the daily toil necessary for survival, or the war that must be waged against neighbours to safeguard present or future harvests.

In the first book of his *Antiquities*, Varro notes that it matters little to know that Aesculapius is a god, if one is not aware that he comforts the sick or why one should implore his aid. Life would be impossible without knowing 'who is a smith, who a baker, who a roofer or from whom such and such a utensil is obtainable!' (Aug., CG, 4, 22). Revering the gods is appropriate only on condition that we are duly informed as to their respective powers and understand 'which god to invoke and for what purpose, in order not to be like those buffoons who ask Liber for water and the Nymphs for wine . . .' (ibid). What good are religious ceremonies? To rescue us from danger, affirms Varro (Non., p. 197, 14). We venerate the gods in order to gain some advantage from them (Val. Max., 2, 5, 6). Depending on what one wants, this or that god must be approached. True devotion, the Roman sense of the sacred (*sanctitas*), is 'the knowledge of the regard and consideration due to the gods' (Cic., *ND*, 1, 116), advisedly and keeping to the rules.

Such self-interested realism therefore requires a 'code', and this is the very principle of the *indigitamenta* or prayers appropriate to the different divine powers. 'Frail and suffering, the mortal race, conscious of its own weakness, brought about this division so that each could worship separately wherever his need was greatest', *quisque quo maxime indigeret* (Plin., *NH*, 2, 15). The explanation of *indigitamenta* by way of *indigere* coincides with both the Roman temperament and the concerns of pagans in general. According to Celsius (Orig., *C. Cels.*, 8, 62), demons are honoured 'as long as one has need of them', but without pledging allegiance to their worship, because 'they can do nothing better than heal the body' (ibid., 60). More specifically Roman are the specialisation of the tasks performed by the gods and the promptness of their interventions. Indeed, the names of the gods vary according to the phases of human, animal and plant growth or the circumstances and demands of action to be undertaken. The peasant who knows the cycle of tasks to be done to ensure that the seed germinates, the shoot forms, the ear ripens undamaged, and that the crop is harvested, threshed, garnered and stored, invokes in turn the qualified deities who are appropriate to the successful outcome of each process. Similarly, the conception, gestation, birth and physical and moral development of the child require the successive support of deities, organised as if on a production line.

This religious 'Taylorism' obviously calls for a strict ritualism. It is no good sacrificing just any victim to this or that god, and the methods of killing, the formulas to be uttered and observances of detail to be respected are traditional and invariable. The one making the sacrifice, therefore, magistrate or emperor, who is to be seen in bas relief on public monuments, is never depicted without the scroll (*volumen*) which bears the text of the invocation. 'The sacred language must be as rigidly laid down as the prescribed gestures.' This declaration by Paul Claudel against innovators in liturgical affairs is in fundamental agreement with the Roman point of view.

Usually, 'to prevent any of the terms being skipped or inverted, someone first reads the formula from what is written, while another supervisor has the task of monitoring his accuracy, and yet a third must ensure that silence is observed' (Plin., *NH*, 28, 11). Recalling the disturbing memory of Greeks and Gauls being buried alive in the forum Boarium, Pliny (ibid., 12), although by nature a freethinker on so many other points, does not hesitate to say, 'Whoever reads the prayer of this sacrifice . . . must recognise the power of these incantations, confirmed by 830 years of success.' Indeed, it was to the 'strictest religious practice' (*exactissimo cultu caerimoniarum*) that the Romans ascribed the expansion and preservation of their Empire (Val. Max., 1, 1, 8).

But it often happened that even the priests were unable to determine the name or gender of the god to be invoked. Then the Romans, 'so pious and so prudent' *castissimi cautissimique* (Gell., 2, 28, 2) on the subject of forms of worship, appealed to the necessary deity with circumspection, using the alternative: 'Whether thou art god or goddess.' In the event of an earthquake, for example, they refrained from naming the god who was the object of public prayers 'for fear that, by taking one god for another, the people should be bound by the wrong cult' (ibid.); and if some error compromised the sanctity of the 'feriae' (days of religious festivals) to be celebrated at the time, the expiatory victim was slaughtered *si deo*, *si dea*, whether to god or goddess. The religious code of priestly law might well make provision for a large number of special cases (including for domestic worship), but it also envisaged eventualities in which doubt was permissible. Priests prayed to Jupiter the Most Good and Most Great, adding 'unless you prefer some other name' (Serv. Dan., *Aen.*, 2, 351). The formalism therefore had its share of indecision, because of the very scruples (*religio*) which inspired it, but that by no means allowed the devout to say and do whatever they wished.

The gestures accompanying the words were just as rigorously codified. The cup for libations was not to be held, or the contents poured, in the same way for a god from on high and a god from the underworld. When sacrificing by the *devotio* (see p. 99), 'naming Tellus, one touches the ground; naming Jupiter, one raises one's hands to the sky; making the vow, one touches one's breast with both hands' (Macr., *S*, 3, 9, 12). The deity is greeted by raising the right hand to the lips, as a sign of *adoratio* (Plin., *NH*, 28, 25). For certain sacrifices, the altar must be held (Virg., *Aen.*, 4, 219) or circled (Serv. Dan., *Aen.*, 4).

The gods were to be approached like magistrates, when there was a matter to be settled. The formalism of words and gestures went hand in hand with a strict legalism. 'One could not be a good priest without a knowledge of civil law,' as P. Mucius Scaevola liked to reiterate. Roman religion was wrapped up with judiciary procedure. It was contractual: *do ut des*. One of Plautus's characters puts it crudely (*Curc*)., 531): 'When a man is well in with the gods, they can really do him proud!' If the deity, duly invoked and propitiated by a suitable sacrifice, granted the prayers of the supplicant, the latter could discharge his debt by keeping the promises he had made; but if the gods failed to keep those they were believed to have pledged, they could be treated as faithless betrayers, if need be. Following the death of Germanicus, the outraged populace hurled stones at temples, overturned altars and cast statues of the family Lares into the streets (Suet., *Cal.*, 5, 2). The terms of the contract involved some hard bargaining, even with Jupiter when Numa wanted to expiate and avert the thunderbolt. The king of the gods ordered him to cut off a head. 'Of an onion?' queried Numa. 'No, of a man,' retorted Jupiter. 'Very well, the hair,' said Numa. But the god demanded living creatures. 'Picarel, then,' argued Numa, who would nevertheless be held up as a model of piety (Ov., *F*, 3, 339 ff; Plut., *Num*, 15, 8–9). This bargaining brings to mind the dialogue of Abraham and Yahweh over Sodom (Genesis, 18, 23–32).

As in a lawsuit, or any form of contract, care must be taken with the words uttered. When saying to a god, 'May you be honoured with this wine,' one must specify *inferio* ('which I pour out'), so that the recipient does not claim the entire cellarful, for in fact it is a matter only of what overflows from the cup, no more (Fest., p. 100, 9 f.). Piety is nothing more than 'justice to the gods' (Cic., *ND*, 1, 116). Plato had put it another way. But for a Roman, it was the raison d'être of priestly law. In the formula to be spoken for a sacrifice, it is made plain to the god that the offering is presented 'as you have a right to it', *ut tibi jus est* (Cat., *Agr.*, 139). But the *jus* of humans is matched by the *fas* of the gods; what in their view is permitted or not (*nefas*). Unlike the *jus*, there can be no argument about the *fas*; it is an absolute that belongs to the gods alone, and is the necessary condition of their agreement. *Si fas est*, was said to Jupiter so that he should consent to the appointment of the king Numa Pompilius (Liv., 1, 18, 9). The *jus* may be 'tinkered with', but not the *fas*. It is for doing away with this legal relationship that Aurelius Cotta (Cic., *ND*, 1, 116) reproaches the Epicureans when they reject any kind of community between gods and men. They were deemed to belong to the same city-state (Cic., *Leg.*, 1, 23).

Tertullian (*Praescr.*, 40, 6) compares the minutiae of Roman worship to the demands of the Mosaic law, and in order to accuse the Devil of imitating divine inspiration. But Roman ritualism is derived from the experience of history; it contains procedures applied to manifestations of the divine (*numina*) that have been experienced, which presupposes that they may reoccur in the same forms, but possibly also in unprecedented ways. True piety thus imposes a vigilance that is constantly alert for signs from the gods. As with all empiricism, that of the Romans regarding religion takes account of the changing realities of life. This is what radically distinguishes them from the Jews, at least in the opinion of Tacitus (*H*, 5, 13, 1), when he paradoxically reproves them for being slaves to 'superstition' at the same time as enemies of '*religiones*'. In fact, the Latin historian means that they cling obstinately to their credulity over prophecies instead of keeping on the look-out for the divine warnings manifested by prodigies and other signs from the heavens. Such indifference renders them impious, and Quintilian (*IO*, 3, 7, 2) also taxes them with *superstitio*.

Here we have an idea that is fundamental to the Romans: the 'peace of the gods'. Nothing can be done without them, without their agreement and support, but it is not enough to follow strict observance of the ritual routine that has been hallowed by experience: one must be on one's guard against anything that may denote annoyance or discontent on the part of the *numina*. Warning can be obtained by taking the auspices, or making a fresh sacrifice if the victim's entrails present an unfavourable appearance. But the gods often show their anger without warning, in a dream or an abnormal or supernatural phenomenon: a prodigy, *prodigium*, a word meaning 'predic-tion' according to Festus (p. 254, 14 f.). The various prodigies all indicated either a manifestation (*ostentum*) or a warning (*monstrum*), *omen* being strictly a word for presage. It was then important to consult the priests or the 'Sibylline' books, a collection of oracles attributed to the Sibyl of Cumae which a commission of experts had the task of interpreting, not in order to foresee the future (the Romans had a horror of prophecies which deterred or paralysed action), but to find the solution to a temporary crisis. It was always a matter of diverting threats from the heavens rather than humbly submitting to their effects.

The series of prodigies listed in the priests' annals are both impressive and picturesque. Livy conscientiously transcribed them and, in the fourth century AD, Julius Obsequens gathered them into an edifying collection. A fire, a plague of locusts, an epidemic or an outbreak of animal sickness, lightning (whether striking a man, a herd or a temple), an earthquake (especially if it moved the heads of idols), a crevasse opening, a lake or lagoon overflowing, were prodigies to be 'expiated' by an appropriate ceremonial. Darkness in broad day, or light in the middle of the night, three suns instead of one, two moons, swarms of bees in Rome or on an army's standards, showers of blood, chalk, earth, stones, milk or oil, an incursion of wolves into the city, an ox on a rooftop, a statue that sweated or shed tears, a noise of weapons or trumpets, Mars' lances shaking in the *Regia* (the residence of the king, and later the Chief Priest), doors that opened by themselves: these were all signs to which there must be a ritual response. If an ox, a snake or a dog spoke, if rats gnawed olives on a table or gold in Jupiter's temple, if a bitch had pups on Juno's bed or a dog stole the meal served to the goddess, it was important to ward off these prodigies to make it clear to the gods that their message had been received. There were also 'monsters', properly speaking: hermaphrodites, children without feet, hands, eyes, nose or, on the contrary, born with three or four hands and four feet, four eyes and four ears, two heads or an elephant's head; donkeys or mules with three or five hooves, cocks with four or five feet, calves, lambs or pigs with a human head, a lamb with horse's feet and a monkey's head, a snake with four paws . . . A cock that changed into a hen and vice versa, a woman into a man, a mule that produced young, a colt born of a cow or a snake of a woman, but also and quite simply, triplets, not to mention various accidents that do not seem supernatural to us, all called for a *piaculum*, *piare* meaning to 'appease' (the anger of the gods).

One was never, or at least never sure of being, quits with them. This meticulous concern with the divine earned the Romans the Greek designation *deisidaimon*, which is wrongly translated as 'superstitious', provoking their indignation, for in reality their uneasiness arose from a piety that was constantly mobilised in the expectation of celestial signs. Polybius (6, 56), who was hardly devout, compliments them on it: this *deisidaimonia* 'has developed so greatly and penetrated so profoundly in both their private and public life that anything more is unimaginable.' It curbed the passions of the populace, and that was what gave Rome its strength. The opinion of the Greek historian, friend of the Scipios, matches a thought that was dear to Varro, Horace and Livy who, in a speech against the tribunes of the plebs, reports Appius Claudius Crassus as saying (6, 41, 8): 'What indeed does it matter if the sacred hens do not eat . . . or that a bird has emitted a cry of bad omen? They are mere trifles! But because they did not neglect those trifles, our ancestors built the greatness of the state.'

However, as Cicero writes (*Div.*, 2, 149), if it is necessary to be on one's guard because of some soothsayer, a passing bird, a flash of lightning, thunder, a thunderbolt that has fallen somewhere, in short, about every-thing which cannot fail to occur some day or another, one will never have any peace of mind, and even the night that should be given up to sleep may become a source of torment. Does this mean that the pious Roman was as if paralysed, inhibited by an unhealthy bigotry? Far from it, because – as we have seen – his ritualism and legalism were rooted in an opportunistic realism, concerned first and foremost with obtaining effective results.

He was a man of action who played a close game with the gods – just like Numa with Jupiter – and although he paid heed to their warning signals, he always insisted on maintaining his freedom to act. In the first place, he took the initiative in certain 'necessary' auspices (*impetrativa*), which called for an exact answer and which overrode 'fortuitous' auspices (*oblativa*). Where they were to be observed was clearly defined, and when (a single day, from midnight to midnight). The augur could choose which birds to observe, or ignore a sign simply by saying, *non consulto*. Having made a verbal declaration (*effatio*) of the area or *templum* in his field of vision, he remained the master of his own inner convictions (Liv., 1, 18, 8: *animo finivit*). Later, further auspices could be taken and, if no favourable presages were forth-coming, the mere lack of any that were obviously adverse to the desired action would suffice. As for the fortuitous auspices, it was enough simply not to see them. M. Claudius Marcellus therefore travelled in a closed litter so that his plans should not be upset. In particular, he paid no heed to the flashes of light reflecting from the tips of spears. All this did not prevent him, adds Cicero (*Div.*, 2, 77), from excelling as both a general and an augur. 'Thus we augurs advise unharnessing beasts of burden to avoid the auspice of the yoke' (ibid.): in other words, the evil omen presented to the augur descending from the capitol by the dung of the harnessed animals he might meet. This recommendation is the subject of an archaic inscription on a cippus found not far from the *vicus iugarius*, 'street of the yoke', which goes up to the hill (*ILLR*, 1, 3).

The *omen* could be rejected, or its effects diverted. For instance, Caesar had a fall when he disembarked in Africa; but he immediately turned the accident to his own advantage, by saying, 'Africa, I have you in my grasp' (Suet., *Caes.*, 59, 1). Furthermore, not all prodigies were recorded as such by the Senate; it made a selection favouring those that required a ritual treatment or *procuratio*. For 'to refuse or accept everything that is seen is a matter of our own free will' (Serv., *Aen.*, 5, 230). Pliny the Elder (28, 17) was happy to demonstrate that 'acting on presages lies within our power, and their value depends on the way in which they are interpreted. According to the augural discipline, it is a fact that neither curses nor any auspices affect those who, before an undertaking, declare that they attach no importance to them; the goodness of the gods bestows no greater kindness.' Finally, a single auspice was never sufficient; it was always necessary to wait for the gods to confirm its meaning.

If need be, things could be managed in such a way as to bring about good omens, for example, in the case of the sacred chickens. They ate if the gods were smiling and, in their haste to peck, might even let drop part of their food. To this end, they were kept for a fairly long time shut in the cages of the *pullarius* whose task was to bring them to the magistrate (Fig. 1). At the right moment, their hunger was assuaged with a kind of mash which, falling from their beaks, ensured that the general would have the best possible auguries: *tripudium solistimum* (Cic., *Div.*, 2, 72).

There was nothing more complicated than a Roman sacrifice (Fig. 2). At the outset, there were rules to be observed, whether concerning the kind or sex of the victims, their colour (a bull-calf offered to Jupiter had to have a white blaze on its face), their age or the length of their tail which, in the case of a calf, had to fall to the hock because 'if it were shorter, the gods would not be pleased' (Plin., *NH*, 8, 183). No problem! If a white ox was not available, a piebald animal could always be treated with chalk (Juv., 10, 35). For want of a doe, Diana could make do with a ewe. If a male victim sacrificed to a god had unsatisfactory entrails (*exta*), a female was slaughtered. In any case, priestly law permitted symbolic substitutes in wax or bread dough. Numa played on words when he offered Jupiter fish in place of human lives. Dummies made out of rushes and thrown into the Tiber replaced actual men, and figurines (*oscilla*) fashioned *ad humanam effigiem* were a cheaper way of appeasing the gods of the Underworld (Macr., *S*, 1, 11, 49). Beans offered as food to the spirits presented the same advantage (see p. 32)

If an animal was concerned, the victim had to be 'pure', therefore not blind in one eye or infirm or, in the case of an ox, it must not have been yoked. The *probatio* checked these prior conditions. The animal was prepared for the ceremony: between its gilded horns, from which hung woollen cords, the ox wore a sculpted plaque (Fig. 3) and around its loins an embroidered sash (*dorsuale*), also used on a boar.

After burning incense and making a libation of wine, the officiating priest proceeded to the *immolatio*: he sprinkled the victim with salted flour (*mola salsa*), poured a goblet of wine over its head (Fig. 4) and passed the knife over its back, from the head to the tail (Serv., *Aen.*, 12, 173). But the actual slaughter was the responsibility of the priest's assistants (*popae*). An ox was killed with an axe, a calf with a sledgehammer, smaller animals with a knife. But respect for these imperatives was still not enough: the ritual must be carried out without the slightest unusual or discordant noise or incident; so while the sacramental words were being uttered, a flute-player played loudly enough to cover any other sounds (Plin., *NH*, 28, 11). In the strictly Roman rite, the sacrificer officiated with his head veiled so that he would be spared the sight of any minor, but annoying, incident, such as a passing mouse. For anything could happen . . . So the initiative was taken the day before, by means of a prior sacrifice of atonement (*hostia praecidanea*), to implore divine indulgence for any misdeed or blunder that might be committed on the day of the so-called solemn immolation.

All these precautions did not prevent the worst happening. If the animal was recalcitrant or fled, if it began to limp or had to be carried to the foot of the altar, the sacrifice was a failure. But there were always victims in reserve, and the operation began again. The herald would say to the magistrate, *Hoc age!* (Pay heed to what you are doing!) But if, having duly kept to the ritual, no encouraging sign from the gods could be found in the entrails (the meaning of the word *litare*), there was nothing for it but to begin again. The same sacrifice was repeated up to thirty times (Plut., *Cor.*, 25, 7). Before engaging in the decisive battle at Pydna against Perseus, Aemilius Paullus sacrificed as many as twenty oxen to Hercules without obtaining a favourable omen. 'But at the twenty-first, the signs appeared announcing a victory, if he kept on the defensive. He therefore pledged a hecatomb (huge public sacrifice) and sacred games' (Plut., *Aem.*, 17, 11–12).

The 'entrails' (*exta*) meant the liver, gall, lungs and the membrane enveloping the intestines. The heart was added 'when King Pyrrhus left Italy' (Plin., *NH*, 11, 186), that is, from 275 BC. Previously, the liver was supposed to be the centre of life, but it continued to be of major importance; it was strictly the concern of the haruspex (Fig. 5). If the liver had no protuberance (ibid., 189), or if it had two (sign of division: Sen., *Oed.*, 360;

Luc., 1, 628) or if its 'head' had been accidentally cut (Plin., *NH*, 11, 190); Ov., *M*, 15, 795), it was a bad omen.

Lastly, even the 'cuisine' of the sacrifice had its rules. Depending on the circumstances, the *exta* had to be roasted or boiled (Varr., *LL*, 5, 98); but even boiled in the cooking-pot (*olla*), they could still give rise to anxieties, if, for example, the liver liquefied (Liv., 41, 15, 2). When they had been cooked, the entrails (*prosecta*) were cut up to be presented to the gods on a dish, together with certain parts of the victim (Arn., 7, 24): pieces of the haunch, the neck and the tail, as well as forcemeat and sausages (*farcimina*). All was sprinkled with *mola salsa* and wine (DH, *AR*, 7, 72; Cic., *Div.*, 2, 37). The slightest infringement of the priestly recipe would spoil the gods' feast, and consequently the affairs of Rome.

Just as a sacrifice had to be recommenced, so did processions and games 'if the dancer stopped or the fluteplayer fell suddenly silent, if the child who still had its father and mother living stopped holding the waggon or let go of the strap, if the aedile made a mistake in the formula' (Cic., *Har.*, 23), if one of the horses pulling the ritual floats stumbled or the driver grasped the reins in his left hand (Plut., *Cor.*, 25, 6). This repetition, which at first was valid only once, was soon increased to three, seven or even ten times for the greater enjoyment of the people. Scrupulous regard for formalism, therefore, did not result only in inconvenience.

On the days of religious festivals or 'feriae', no work was done, and priests did not even have the right to watch anyone working. Anyone found guilty had to offer a pig in atonement, as well as pay a fine. But if an ox fell into a hole, or a sheep was sick, or a rafter broke in a roof, such things had to be attended to; so apart from the tasks imposed by the cult, exceptions were made for work of vital usefulness: 'everything that would be harmful if omitted', stated the priest Scaevola (Macr., *S*, 1, 16, 11). The 'feriae' aside, days could be 'fasti' or 'nefasti' (that is to say, those on which it was lawful to transact business and those consecrated to the gods), 'comitial' (when the comitia were convened), and *proeliares* (when battle could be done). 'Interspersed' days (*intercisi*) were 'nefasti' in the morning and evening; but in the interval 'between the slaughter of the victim and the presentation of the entrails' a *fas* or 'leave' could intervene (Varr., *LL*, 6, 31). However, when defending one's life or the public safety, one day was as good as another. At heart, Roman gods were not such bad sorts, and one could often come to some 'arrangement' with them.

For the Romans, this 'good conduct' code, or manual on 'how to get on' with the gods, had nothing at all to do with 'superstition'. *Superstitio* concerned what went beyond the etiquette laid down by priestly law: the exaggerations or aberrations of an uncontrolled mysticism. In Rome, people had always steered clear of imagination and the surge of emotions in religious matters, fringe prophesying and even theology in general, whether human reason applied to the gods was considered pure or impure. Religious legalism had the advantage of curbing the imagination and keeping dread of the supernatural under control. That is why the strictness of Roman ritualism did not rule out free will, even a calm agnosticism. In this respect, the attitude ascribed to Aurelius Cotta by Cicero in his treatise on the *Nature of the gods* is enlightening, and, like so many of his compatriots, Cicero himself adopted it: an attitude that in the end is fairly close to the fideism of Montaigne who, like the Latin orator, considered that we should hold fast to the religion of our native land without ever straying into religious controversy. In a Roman temple one kept quiet, even inwardly: one composed one's 'spirit' (*animos componimus*: Quint., *Decl.*, 265, 12), in order not to reason.

The Romans certainly asked their gods to look favourably upon them, but above all to reassure them in their plans and back them in their actions. The adage 'God helps those who help themselves' exactly suited their inveterate pragmatism. Sallust (*Cat.*, 52, 29) has Cato the Younger make a significant remark: 'It is neither by prayers nor the supplications of women that one obtains the gods' help. Vigilance, action, wise resolutions – these are the means of success.' When a sheep has an ulcer, you must lance its mouth with a knife instead of 'doing nothing and praying to the gods that things will get better' (Virg., *G*, 3, 454 ff.). Romans mistrusted fringe devotions that diverted them from their daily toil. Cato (*Agr.*, 5, 4) did not want his farmer to consult a haruspex, an augur, a diviner or a 'Chaldaean' (astrologer). In the end, *religiones* were useful to give a feeling of security to human undertakings by 'easing the pressure' on the devout person who adhered strictly to the letter of the ritual. By fulfilling these religious 'scruples', one is liberated from them, which is precisely what is implied by an expression such as *religione solvere* (*levare* or *liberare*) which occurs so often in Livy. In short, Roman piety was a form of therapy against superstitious fears, which Lucretius wanted to deal with by means of epicureanism.

Under these circumstances, what was the good of creating a mythology and a corresponding divine iconography? It would be better to avoid doing so. Tradition would have it that the Romans had never put up any statue of a god during the first 170 years of the *Urbs* and, if we are to believe Varro (Aug., *CG*, 4, 31, 2), had they persisted in this aniconism, worship would have remained purer (*castius*). In fact, the Latin antiquary was idealising the ancient Roman religion by modelling it on the Stoics' criticism of the anthropomorphism which, as we know, had worked so well for the Greeks. Etrusco-hellenic influences very quickly introduced images into Latin worship, even if in Rome the strength of Mars was expressed in a spear, or that of Jupiter in a stone, and even if Vesta's fire could do without an idol. But when all that mattered or was evident was the effectiveness of a *numen*, there was no need to imagine or invent stories about his or her love affairs or exploits. Roman gods had neither genealogies nor amorous adventures. A gesture on their part was worth more than some mythical deed. They had no other history than what they had performed in the history of the *Urbs* itself.

Rooted in the family, and having nothing to do with the complexes or inner struggles of the individual, Roman piety was put to the service of the city-state which embraced family hearths and homes. Auspices, said the augur Marcellus (Cic., *Leg.*, 2, 32), were organised 'in the interest of the state' (*ad utilitatem rei publicae*), which suggests any compromises that would be useful to it; so it was impossible to imagine a religion that was distinct from civic-mindedness, and therefore a clergy marginal to the Republic. Members of the big colleges (pontiffs, augurs and the chief priest himself) were elected by the people, as were magistrates – who, moreover, had responsibilities of a religious nature, such as auspices and sacrifices. Priests carried out their religious functions in conjunction with their civic activities, and always in the name of the state. Only the 'king of the sacrifices' was excluded from public duties, and the flamen of Jupiter was subject to 'taboos' which in some respects isolated him from ordinary mortals; but those were exceptions that would disappear in the imperial era. 'Among the divinely inspired institutions of our ancestors, there is none finer than the will to entrust to the same men the worship of the immortal gods and the higher interests of the state' (Cic., *Dom.*, 1): a kind of a secularity, in some ways. Impeccable logic, if public well-being depended on piety. The Romans were so convinced of this that they attributed their universal hegemony to it. 'If we compare our history to that of other nations, we shall see that although we may be equal or even inferior to them in other respects, we outshine them by far in religion, that is to say, in the worship of the gods' (Cic., *ND*, 2, 8).

But Roman religion was the victim of that success as well as of the trials that punctuated its history.

The respectful and vigilant attention paid by the Romans to divine manifestations led them to acknowledge other *numina* than the powers listed by the *indigitamenta* or the great gods who had such an important position in the city. Their prudent realism forced them to take notice of foreign forms of worship and, eventually, appeal to them. While remaining faithful to the formalism of the priestly law, which had proved its worth, but with the pragmatism that inspired its observance, Rome had to incorporate new practices. 'By introducing the rites of all religions, our ancestors' intention was either to thank the gods for favours received, avert the threat of their anger or appease their unleashed fury' (Minuc., 7, 2). It was the result of conquest, but also of earlier contacts with the Hellenic world.

With the *fabulositas* of the Greeks (Plin., *NH*, 4, 1), a whole new world of images obliterated the old Latin foundations. The reactions of the elderly Cato were to no avail. Women and Mediterranean expansion, the world-wide spread of cults, had called the *mos maiorum* into question, and the old ritualism was no longer enough to soothe consciences. 'Believe me, the statues brought from Syracuse into our city came as enemies. I hear all too many people deride the terracotta ornaments of Roman gods' (Cato, in Liv., 34, 4, 4). Greek art seduced and held sway; together with other factors, it contributed to revolutionising attitudes. In Latin literature, humble clay gods continued for a long time to symbolise the simplicity and austerity of a genuine Roman religion as yet unadulterated by the intrusion of mythology or an *externa superstitio*, for Livy (in the time of Augustus) a synonym for a degrading and evil contagion.

Roman piety, therefore, evolved for historical reasons, but also because of its utilitarian concern to conciliate all gods, or at all events other gods than those whose effectiveness was for the time being proving inadequate. Roman polytheism was opportunistic and thus open in advance to possible expansion. Like the English, who would rather make a new law than abolish an old one, the Romans adopted other gods without rejecting any from the old pantheon. We shall see that the imperial cult itself entered the line of Roman traditions, and notably the family religion to which Christian authority would deliver the final blows in order to eradicate its tenacious paganism.

However, in some respects, the Roman attitude continued to impregnate the Catholic religion, at least until the advent of modernism or the Vatican II Council. And, relatively speaking, does not the allocation of their respective powers to the saints remind us of the system of the *indigitamenta*?

CHAPTER 2

Religions of the family and the land

There was nothing more specifically Roman than domestic worship; it was what immediately distinguished Roman religion, for example on Delos, from the Greek environment, in the case of the colonists who lived on the island. A man could not be evicted or have an attempt made on his life 'in the presence of the Lares, gods of the house' (Cic., *Quinct.* 85). 'What is more sacred than each citizen's home? It houses his altars, his hearths, his Penates, his sacrifices; it is the place of his devotions and ritual ceremonies.' Here, Cicero (*Dom.*, 109) was expressing a sentiment that remained very powerful in the consciousness of the ordinary Roman at the end of the Republic. He stressed it again in his treatise on the *Laws* (2, 27): 'Preserving the rites of the family and ancestors – since the Ancients are those closest to the gods – means practising a religion bequeathed in some sort by the gods.' And Varro (*LL*, 7, 88) has the haruspex say, 'Let everyone sacrifice according to his own rites.' But the chief priest kept an eye on private cults (Plut., *Num.*, 9, 8). Certain aspects of public worship would not be comprehensible if that fundamental fact were not recognised. In any case, many of the rites that became public had in fact originated in the family.

A Roman's house was like a temple, and the *paterfamilias* its high priest. His person was sacred: the son who dared to raise a hand against him was consigned to the Manes, or spirits, of the ancestors (Fest., p. 260, 10 ff.). Every part of the house was, so to speak, deified (Serv., *Aen.*, 2, 469). Holy were the threshold protected by Limentinus, the door panels guarded by Forculus and the hinges watched over by Cardea. Mistakenly, but because of a significant tradition, the name 'vestibule' was interpreted in connection with that of Vesta, in an assimilation with the altar and the hearth, for the fire was originally sited at the entrance to the house, as Ovid reminds us (*F*, 6, 302). Fire was part and parcel of the family Lar, and the hearth was used as an altar to the Penates, the household gods who looked after the store room (*penus*) or the interior (*penitus*) of the home where in the past the floor had covered the dead. Those ancestors were still a presence in the form of their wax masks either in the atrium or a reception room, or in a chapel in company with the tutelary gods, in the master bedroom or near the dining room. The table itself was sacred, like the nuptial bed (*lectus genialis*) set up in line with the entrance door. The walls, the furniture, the dishes used for daily food as well as for honouring the gods were equally hallowed. Even workaday tools – broom, pestle, axe – had their own familiar demon: Deverra, Pilumnus, Intercidona.

Pliny the Elder (28, 27) reminds us of those old Romans 'who believed the gods were involved in all our actions and at all times' of our life, those gods who 'despite our vices have maintained their benevolence towards us'. Every instant of the domestic day was thus governed by a ritual that was still observed in certain rural and even urban circles in the imperial era.

– DAILY RITUALS –

On waking, the Roman's first act was to ponder over his dreams, in case the gods had sent him a warning: 'The human race, doomed to worry, averts the night's presages by a pious offering of flour and crackling salt' (Tib., 3, 4, 10). It was also important to know whether lightning or any other imperfection required prompt expiation.

At dawn (for Romans rose early), the master of the house was greeted by his children and servants, which meant that prayers were said aloud invoking the family's protective gods. Horace (O, 4, 5, 33–40) and Ovid (*Pont.*, 4, 9, 111 f.) invoked them every morning, together with the living or deceased emperor, burning incense on the Lares' hearth. The presence of a lararium in the bedroom of emperors (Suet., *Aug.*, 7, 2; *Dom.*, 17, 5; see SHA, AS, 29, 2) suggests that morning prayers were said there. Anyway, these were celebrated by making a sacrifice at the altar of the family hearth for the Penates, Lares and tutelary deities whom the master worshipped especially, for personal or circumstantial reasons, if not professional ones: Luck (*Fortuna*), Venus, Apollo, Mercury or Minerva, for instance. If, in exceptional conditions, an animal victim was offered, an inspection of the entrails enabled one to verify whether on that particular day the gods were propitious or not. Possibly a technical expert might be called in – the haruspex.

In the beginning, it was mainly a Lar that was invoked, the *Lar familiaris*, a kind of demon of the ancestors and the continuity of the tribe as well as being the familiar spirit of the household. He presented himself like this in Plautus's *Aulularia* (3–25):

I have had my establishment and my residence in this house for many years now. I was already here in the time of the present occupant's father and grandfather. Now, the grandfather once secretly entrusted me with a great treasure: he hid it in the middle of the hearth, praying to me, imploring me to look after it for him.

The grandfather dies saying nothing to his son who, having no respect whatever for the *Lars familiaris*, dies as poor and 'back at square one' as before. The grandson, Euclion, is scarcely more attentive; but he has an only daughter. 'She, on the other hand, brings me offerings every day of incense, wine, or some little thing. She garlands me with flowers.' As a result, the Lar enables Euclion to discover the treasure so that he can marry off his daughter honourably. The story has a moral: homage must be paid daily to the Lar, otherwise he may become troublesome, even threatening. For there is a mysterious, but certain, link with the spirits of the dead.

The Lar was always greeted before crossing the threshold (right foot first), and upon returning home (*redire ad Larem suum*). He was invoked before one left on a journey or on campaign. When a long-lost relation reappeared, a sacrifice of thanksgiving was made to the Lar (Pl., *Rud.*, 1206 f.). When one returned from war, he was offered part of the booty (Prop., 2, 30, 23). The soldier rejoining the army promised to sacrifice a sow if he returned safe and sound (Tib., 1, 10, 25 ff.). If one moved house, the *Lar familiaris* was invoked on behalf of those who stayed (Pl., *Merc.*, 834 f.). When one saw a friend who had escaped from a shipwreck, thanks were rendered to the 'paternal Lares' (Juv., 12, 89) as well as to Jupiter.

In the classical era, the Lar was duplicated and the Lares became rather confused, or at least associated, with the Penates, who appear in the lararia of Pompeii in the form of gods for whom the master of the house had a fondness. As for the two Lares, they are shown as two young people, their heads crowned with flowers, pouring the contents of a rhyton into a situla or libation patera. They flank Vesta or the domestic 'Genius' or spirit, thus setting an example of sacrificial piety. They are also to be found in the company of Mercury, Venus, Bacchus or other deities dear to the paterfamilias. The one or two snakes associated with the *Genius*, or shown below the Lares (sometimes entwined around the altar where the *Genius* sacrifices) appear to be the guardians of the place as well as an expression of the vital, if not genetic, force of the family. When Aeneas pays homage to the Manes of his father (Virg., *Aen.*, 5, 84 ff.), a serpent appears and, slithering among the paterae and vessels, 'tastes the sacred food' (*libavit dapes*), before returning to the depths of the tomb. And the pious Aeneas wonders, 'The Spirit of the place or my father's servant?' Ancestors indeed are present at family meals.

According to Pseudo-Quintilian (*Decl.*, 301, 10), the gods were invoked before one went to the table. Traditionally, the family gathered, together with the servants, facing the fire of the lararium, which was originally in the atrium, but at Pompeii is to be found in the kitchen or sometimes against a garden wall. For Columella (11, 1, 19) in the first century AD, it was still important to eat in the presence of the servants before the 'Lar of the master and the family hearth'. Pliny the Elder (28, 24) thought that at that time the act of removing one's ring was a ritual, but did not elucidate its meaning. If a piece of food was let drop, one must not blow on it to clean it; it had to be replaced on the table before being burnt in front of the Lar (ibid., 27).

After the first course, a religious silence was observed before offering the gods the first choice pickings of the meal: a piece of meat (Varro in *Non.*, p. 554, 1–2) with *mola salsa* – roasted wheat flour with added salt – was thrown into the fire (Serv. Dan., *Aen.*, 1, 730). This was done using a *patella* (Ov., F, 2, 633) or ritual dish and a salt-cellar; hence the name *patellarii* that Plautus (*Cist.*, 522) gives to the gods of the hearth. Salt was sacred, and sanctified the table. The *patella* and *salinum* were the two items that the Roman of the pioneering days held above everything to be the *deorum causa* (Liv., 26, 36, 6). They were the only two items of tableware that the generals of that time took with them on campaign (Plin., *NH*, 33, 153). The gods demanded no more sumptuous signs of regard; but the Lar was always appreciative of his share of roast meat and tasty fruit. Valerius Maximus (2, 5, 5), however, in the early decades of the first century AD, already speaks of it in the past tense: 'In the beginning, men appeased the gods with the first-offerings of their food; offerings that were all the more effectual (*efficacius*) because they were simpler.'

The mistress of the house took part with her slaves in the domestic worship (DH, *AR*, 4, 2; Plut., *Fort. Rom.*, 10, 323 *b*), but drank no wine except on the fairly rare occasion of certain ceremonies (Serv., *Aen.*, 1, 737). In the fire of the lararium, where the gods' share was consumed, legends concerning the birth of Romulus, Servius Tullius or the Praenestine hero Caeculus recognised an image of the procreative power, so often linked with the cult of ancestors (DH, *AR*, 4, 2; Plut., *Rom.*, 2, 4; Serv., *Aen.*, 7, 678):

> O, divine nights and meals where we eat, my family and I, before the Lar of my own home . . . (Hor., S, 2, 6, 65)
> What joy to see slaves who were born in the household at table around the resplendent Lar! (Id., *Epo*, 2, 65 f.)

If people were gathered away from the fire, statuettes of the Lar or Lares were brought to the table and a slave passed round a patera of wine, saying,

'Propitious Gods!' In the imperial period, libations were poured in homage to the Spirit of Augustus, with cries of 'Long live the emperor, father of the homeland!' (Petr., 60, 7). For the emperor was indeed the *paterfamilias* of the great Roman family.

Lamps were not left burning on the table when dinner was over; before going to bed, the mistress of the house – who had a part to play in family priestly duties – saw to it that the house was swept, the lararium and the hearth carefully cleaned. The embers were contained under ashes so that the fire should last till the morning (Cat., *Agr.*, 144, 2). 'Let the fire burn in the hearth and never go out' (Tib., 1, 1, 6). The presence of lararia in some bedrooms gives reason to suppose that before going to sleep prayers were again offered to the gods. An idol of *Fortuna* (SHA, AP, 12, 5; S, 23, 5) watched over the sleep of the emperors. In his bedroom, Augustus also had a portrait of his great-grandson as Cupid, on which he would bestow a kiss each night when he entered (Suet., *Cal.*, 7). In every home, the dead surrounded the living.

When night had fallen, if the master had to take auspices requiring total silence, he waited until everything seemed quiet. If a slave or servant-girl whispered or made any sound under the blanket, it mattered little provided that the *paterfamilias* heard, or pretended to hear, nothing, according to old Cato (Fest., p. 268, 16–20).

– FROM THE CRADLE TO THE GRAVE –

Life has its high points which, as such, were strictly ritualised. The most critical was birth, attended by a whole crowd of 'good fairies'. For, in keeping with the division of labour implied by the *indigitamenta*, there was no phase of the genital, natal and postnatal process that did not have its own tutelary deity.

Jugatinus catered for the union of the man and woman; but Cinxia or Virginensis loosened the bride's girdle, Subigus handed her over to her husband, Prema supervised the embrace, Inuus (Tutunus or Mutunus) and Pertunda put an end to her virginity (Aug., CG. 6, 9, 3). Janus, the god of gateways, opened up access to the generative seed which was provided by Saturn, but its emission was favoured by Liber Pater (ibid., 7, 2). With Juno, Mena ensured the future mother's menstrual flow (ibid.). Once conceived, the child needed Fluonia or Fluvionia, a Juno who controlled the nourishing blood (Tert., *Nat.*, 2, 11, 3), but it was more precisely Alemona (Tert., *An.* 37, 1) who intervened to feed the embryo. Finally, Nona and Decima brought her successfully to term in the ninth or tenth month. In the eyes of the Romans, these were the divine attentions called for by intra-uterine life.

Postverta and Prosa were invoked in order to avert the dangers of a breech birth. Sacrifices were also made to the nymph Egeria, who was deemed to 'bring out' (*egerere*) the baby without difficulty from its mother's belly (Fest., p. 67, 25 f.). The birth itself was presided over by Parca, according to Varro (Gell., 3, 16, 10), Partula, according to Tertullian (*An.*, 37, 1); but it was Vitumnus who imparted life, and Sentinus sensibility (Aug., CG, 7, 3, 1). In fact, supplications must go first and foremost to Juno, in the form of Lucina, she who gives the light of day (*lux*):

> I beg thee, Good Lucina, spare pregnant women, and when the fruit of their womb comes to maturity, deliver them gently. (Ov., F, 2, 451 f.)

Women did not pray to her until they had loosened their hair (ibid., 3, 257), 'so that in her turn the goddess should gently pluck the child-fruit'. Sterile women or those with childbirth sicknesses also resorted to Lucina. Diana of Nemi could equally well be approached, as she was said to ensure an easy birth. 'The long hedges are festooned with small strips of cloth, and many ex-votos are offered to the goddess in sign of gratitude,' says Ovid clearly (F, 3, 267 ff.). Circlets on their heads, women whose prayers had been answered brought her lighted torches from Rome.

For the birth of every male child, a coin was offered to Lucina in her Esquiline temple (DH, AR, 4, 15). But every birth imposed certain purifications, and it was Juno again, under the name *Februa* or *Februalis* (*Februlis*), who delivered women in childbirth of the placenta (Myth. Vat., 3, 4, 3).

Around the new mother, three deities mounted guard against the dreaded violence of Silvanus, that 'fierce, terrifying, rough' demon of the woods (Aug., CG, 6, 9, 2): they were Intercidona (for without the blade of the axe one cannot cut trees *intercidere*); Pilumnus (for without the pestle one cannot make flour), and Deverra (for without the broom one cannot pile up the grain). Thus, in their name three men made the nightly rounds of the house and struck the threshold with an axe and then a pestle, before sweeping it (ibid.). A bed was set up in the atrium for Pilumnus and Picumnus or for Juno, and a table for Hercules (Serv. Dan., B, 4, 62; Aen., 10, 76). There also had to be an offerings table on which the female friends who came to congratulate the fortunate mother sacrificed to the gods (Non., p. 312, 11–13). The detail and very meaning of these *primordia* of the first few days elude us, and it would appear that they eluded the ancients even then. But the cutting blade goes hand in hand with sweeping, using the twigs of the branch that becomes a pestle. It is a matter of dispossessing Silvanus of his wood to turn it into a tool that is necessary for getting food. Deverra is also concerned with purification following the birth. As for Juno in her bed, she represents the nursing mother, and Hercules is the child she is supposed to be feeding. 'Idolatry is the midwife of the newborn' (Tert., *An.*, 39, 2).

With the help of the goddess Levana, the midwife lifted the baby, which had first been laid on the ground for the umbilical cord to be cut, and presented it to the mother (as can be seen on sarcophagi). A grandmother or maternal aunt took the infant in her arms and rubbed its forehead and lips with her finger covered with 'lustral' saliva, which was wonderful for 'warding off the burn of the evil eye' (Pers., 2, 31–4). It was then the father's turn to acknowledge the baby and show his intention of bringing it up by holding it upright. Statina (Statilina, Statinus or Statilinus) helped it to keep itself straight (Tert., *An.*, 39, 2; Aug., *CG*, 4, 21). If the baby was born a monster or sickly, it was drowned or smothered (Sen., *Ir.*, 1, 15, 2). Others were exposed before the temple of *Pietas* (destroyed by Caesar for the construction of a theatre that would become Marcellus's), at the foot of a column known as 'lacteal' (Fest., p. 105, 13 f.).

The baby's first cry had the patronage of Vaticanus (Gell., 16, 17, 2). For girls, on the eighth day, for boys, on the ninth, the child was 'purified' and given a name. This purification day or *dies lustricus* was rendered divine by Nundina (Macr., *S*, 1, 16, 36). At that point the 'Carmentes' (Aug., *CG*, 4, 11) also intervened, or the *Fata Scribunda* (Tert., *An.*, 39, 2), kinds of 'fairies' confused with the Parcae, who ordained the child's future. A thunderbolt that fell on the day of the birth was equally valid as a presage for its entire life (Plin., *NH*, 2, 139). As well as the signs sent by the gods, the bestowing of a name was a religious act, which was always connected with its destiny (Suet., *Ner.*, 6, 3).

Meanwhile, the baby had to suckle, and this was in the care of Rumina (Aug., *CG*, 4, 11; 21; 34; 7, 11), to whom libations of milk were always made (Plut., *Rom.*, 4, 1). Edula (Edulia, Educa or Edusa) taught it to eat, Potina (Potica or Potua) to drink (Aug., *CG*, 4, 11 and 34; 6, 9, 1). Ossipago (Ossipagina) strengthened its bones, Carna its muscles (but Carna was also supposed to defend its intestines against witches or 'strigae'). Cunina kept watch over its cradle and fended off evil spells (Lact., *Inst.*, 1, 20, 36). Cuba took over from her when the baby was weaned, and went from the cradle to a bed. Paventia or Paventina drove out its fears, and Peta watched over its first wants (Arn., 4, 7).

When it learned to walk, the presence of Adeona and Abeona was necessary to its goings and comings, like that of Iterduca and Domiduca for leaving and returning to the house (Aug., *CG*, 4, 21; Tert., *Nat.*, 2, 11, 9). Farinus loosened its tongue, Fabulinus made it say its first words, Locutius its first sentences (ibid., 7; Non., p. 532, 22). Mens gave it intelligence,

Volumnus or Volumna the will for good (Aug., CG, 4, 21). It wore the toga praetexta, the purple band resembling that worn by priests and magistrates, which rendered it holy: *Maxima debetur puero reverentia*, said Juvenal (14, 47). This purple acted as a kind of safeguard: *custos . . . purpura* (Pers., 5, 30). Round its neck hung a gold ball enclosing a talisman 'against envy' (Macr., S, 1, 6, 9) to which an amulet or holy image was sometimes attached.

The child grew, and Numeria taught it to count, Camena to sing (Aug., CG, 4, 11). In the imperial period, epitaphs and sarcophagi of children show us their early receptivity to the favours of the nine Muses who nurtured them with science and great literature. Religious instruction was given at home. Together with their mother, children helped their father in acts of family worship, like the *camilli* (or choirboys) in public ceremonies. They might possibly be initiated into certain priestly tasks, if not to the mysteries. But whatever the role of parents could and must be in such circumstances, these offices were connected with collective forms of worship.

Most often around the age of seventeen, but sometimes earlier (notably for members of the imperial family), the *puer* consecrated his transition to the status of young man or, rather, junior (*juvenis*): this was the second high point of his existence. He abandoned the toga praetexta for the toga virilis, or toga of manhood. He hung his golden bulla on its chain on the statue of the Lares (Hor., S, 1, 5, 65; Pers., 5, 31); the Lares were thus known as *bullati* (Petr., 60, 8). He would then go to the Capitol with his parents and family friends. Sacrifices were made to Jupiter and Juventas, the goddess of Youth who, with the god Terminus, had refused to yield the site of her temple to the king of the gods, who was honoured in fact in this chapel under the name *Juvenis*. Good wishes were made for the new citizen, who placed a coin in the collection box of Juventas. Sometimes *Spes*, 'Hope', was also invoked. The ceremony often took place on 17 March, on the occasion of the *Liberalia*, festival of the god of seed and puberty (Liber Pater) which came under the *sacra publica*. According to Tertullian (*Apol.*, 42, 5), the families then went to table in the street, probably at the entrance to the house.

It was *Fortuna Barbata* (Aug., CG, 4, 11) who caused the young man's beard to sprout. When it was cut for the first time, these 'first fruits' were offered to the gods, and this again was the occasion for a family festival, *Barbatoria* (Petr., 73, 6), which would become a public one when it involved a prince of the imperial house. In the lararium of Trimalchio (ibid., 29, 8), a gold pyx is the receptacle for the master's first downy hairs, alongside his silver Lares and a statuette of Venus. Nero had his beard cut for the first time 'with all the pomp of a hecatomb' (Suet., *Ner.*, 12, 9) and, like Trimalchio, placed the hairs in a gold box set with pearls, that he dedicated at the Capitol. At the time he instituted a great festival of youth (*Juvenalia*), not without provoking some scandals. First hair-cuttings were also offered to the gods (Cens., 1, 10).

The third high point in life was marriage, at least in the old tradition, for by Cicero's time it had already lost much of its sanctity.

Of the three forms of union, by *coemptio* (or fictitious purchase of the young girl from her father), by *usus* (or cohabitation) or by *confarreatio*, only the last was of interest to the gods. It consisted of the couple eating a wheaten cake together: hence their title of *farreati*. 'Among religious rites, there was none more sacred' (Plin., *NH*, 18, 10: *nihil religiosius*). The bride who was thus married entered into a share of possessions and *religiones* (DH, AR, 2, 25). But it had been a privilege of patrician families, which in the imperial era they scarcely claimed any more, mainly because of its ritual demands. Certain public priests (king of sacrifices and major flamines) had to conform, and themselves be the sons of *farreati*, which posed recruitment problems. As plebeian families knew nothing of this sacred marriage, legislation was forced to recognise *coemptio* and *usus*; but even these two methods ultimately fell into disuse, and a ritual was imposed that gave the gods their part by incorporating certain traditional aspects.

Marriage was so sacred that it could not be celebrated on just any day or month of the year. May was ruled out, because it was the month of the old (*maiores*): 'Who marries then has not long to live' (Ov., *F*, 5, 488); the 9, 11 and 13 were in any case devoted to the dead. This prohibition was still observed not long ago in Provence. Also ruled out were the first fortnight of March (season of war: Ov., *F*, 3, 395) and June (before the 'purification' of Vesta's temple). Naturally excluded were the days known as *religiosi*, since they were dedicated to the gods of the underworld (*Parentales* or *Ferales* from 13–21 February, opening of the aperture giving access to the Manes on 24 August, 5 October and 8 November), or consecrated the memory of an unfortunate event (defeat of the Allia, 18 July), all the days of great public festivals, together with the calends, nones and ides, and the day that followed each, which were 'black' (*atri*), days when 'religious law forbade sacred acts' (Macr., *S*, 1, 15, 22).

On her wedding eve, the maiden dedicated her toga praetexta to Fortuna Virginalis (Arn., 2, 67), her child's attire and her dolls to the Lares, Penates or Venus. In this circumstance the support of the household gods was of great importance. Even the miserly Euclion bought a pinch of incense and some floral headdresses: 'We will lay them on the hearth in homage to our Lar, so that he will grant my daughter a happy marriage' (Pl., *Aul.*, 386 f.). The bride-to-be donned a vertically woven tunic (*recta*) in the old style and with no hem, *ominis causa* wrote Festus (p. 364, 24), so by way of a good omen. She wore a red snood on her hair, and would replace it on her wedding day with a flame red veil (*flammeum*).

On that day, with a curved-back spearhead, her hair would be divided into six tresses bound with strips of cloth, 'the emblem of modesty' (Ov., *AA*, 1, 31; *Pont.*, 3, 3, 52), therefore with a prophylactic function. She wore a circlet of marjoram, verbena, myrtle and other auspicious herbs that she had gathered with her own hands (Fest., p. 56, 1–2).

White was worn for weddings. Under the straight tunic of the bride, a girdle of wool was tied round her waist with a 'herculean' knot (with four turns?), which was deemed not only to protect her from the evil eye but also to ensure that she would have many children, 'like Hercules, who had seventy' (Fest., p. 55, 18). At dawn the auspices were taken, and a sacrifice would confirm the fortunate auguries, by means of an examination of the victim's entrails performed by a haruspex. The augur would announce to those present that the gods were favourable, and the contract was then concluded and sealed by ten witnesses. A matron, the *Pronuba*, who must not have been married more than once, joined the right hands of the newly-weds (*dextrarum junctio*), as a sign of fidelity. The one who took the auspices (*auspex nuptiarum*) invoked the gods. An ox, pig or sheep was sacrificed. Good wishes were expressed and a vibrant *feliciter* was the prelude to the wedding feast.

In marriage by *confarreatio*, offerings were made to Jupiter (in the presence of his flamen and the chief priest) of fruit and the wheaten cake which the couple shared with each other and the god. Prayers were also said to Juno, Tellus, Pilumnus and Picumnus, for whom a bed would be set up on the day when the bride gave birth. Bride and groom took their place on two seats that were joined together and covered with the fleece of a sacrificed sheep (a magico-religious practice deemed to transmit the divine fluid). During the invocation, they walked clockwise round the altar (Val. Flac., 8, 246) to salute the gods (Pl., *Curc.*, 70), preceded by a *camillus* armed with a receptacle (*cumerum/cumera*) apparently containing certain votive articles (Fest., p. 43, 25 and 55, 24).

Escorted by female friends bearing the distaff and spindle (Plin., *NH*, 8, 194), the bride was led to her husband's house (*domum deductio*) in a noisy and joyful procession with the added sounds of flute-players and 'fescen-nine' songs (which were believed to be specially effective in warding off the *fascinum* or what Neapolitans call the *iettatura*). There were shouts of 'thalassa', a mysterious word of Etruscan origin (?). Nuts were thrown, a supposed agent of fertility. Three boys who still had their father and mother living (*patrimi et matrimi*) accompanied the bride, and one of them lit her way with a hawthorn torch, the wood that is 'the best augury for nuptial torches' (Plin., *NH*, 16, 75). Having reached the marital home, she anointed the doorposts with the fat of a pig or wolf and crowned them with wool, for a 'religious power' was attributed to wool (Plin., *NH*, 29, 30). *Ubi tu Gaius, ego Gaia*, she would say to her husband, who lifted her in his arms to cross the threshold, in memory (so it was believed) of the rape of the Sabines, but doubtless also because the threshold was sacred: it was the god Limentinus.

The bride presented her husband with water and fire, whose union was believed to condition the birth of beings (Varr., *LL*, 5, 61), but which were both a necessity of life (Fest., p. 3, 2–3). In line with the entrance door, they found their marriage bed which had been prepared by the *Pronuba*. Brought into the presence of the lararium and the gods of her new family, the bride addressed an invocation to them. She brought three *as* coins: in her hand the first, which she gave to her husband; on her foot the second, which she placed on the hearth of the Lares, and the third in a purse which she offered at the altar of the neighbouring crossroads (Non., p. 531, 12 ff.). The following day, a meal renewed the banquet of the day before for the relatives of the bride, who then celebrated her first sacrifice to the household gods. Naturally, special deities attended the handing over of the dowry (Afferenda), the arrival at the house (Domiducus), the installation of the bride (Domitius), her joining her husband (Manturna), the completion of the marriage (Perfica), and we have already seen the requisite *indigitamenta* for the conjugal act (Tert., *Nat.*, 2, 11, 12; Arn., 4, 7 and 11; Aug., *CG*, 6, 9, 3).

Originally, marriage by *confarreatio* had been indissoluble and – besides the complicated rites – it is thought that this indissolubility had encouraged the other forms of the *usus* and *coemptio*. However, a procedure did exist (of necessity religious) for breaking its binding effects: the *diffarreatio*. Another wheaten cake was made, but the husband and wife, now at loggerheads, cast it away in the sight of the priest, perhaps exchanging curses; but we are rather poorly informed about about these exceptional methods. Fustel de Coulanges rightly remarked: 'This religion taught men that conjugal union was something more than a sexual relationship and a fleeting affection, and united two spouses by the powerful bond of the same cult and the same beliefs.' That thought had already struck Dionysius of Halicarnassus (*AR*, 2, 25).

Needless to say, it did not rule out domestic quarrels, but when a tiff broke out between husband and wife, they both went to the temple of Viriplaca on the Palatine. After arguing matters out before the goddess who 'calms husbands', they would go home reconciled: *concordes* (Val. Max., 2, 1, 6). To turn wives away from vice or bring them back into the path of virtue, a Venus who 'changes hearts' (*Verticordia*) would be addressed. There is, however, no evidence that, for their part, betrayed wives could have recourse to a god who restored fidelity. Anyway, the husband who repudiated his wife had to make a personal sacrifice to the gods of the underworld in order to redeem himself (Plut., *Rom.*, 22, 3).

From the moment a man became head of a family, he assumed all the religious responsibilities involved in the life of the household. He must at once watch out for all the signs from the gods. The first that exploded for the new *paterfamilias* were known as 'family thunderbolts' and were 'fateful for the whole of his existence' (Plin., *NH*, 2, 139). If need be, he could then consult an expert in 'brontoscopy', the Etruscan science of interpreting thunder.

Life had its hard times. Illness and epidemics provoked reactions that sometimes affected the whole city, upsetting morale and even calling ancestral piety into question. In the hearts of families and individuals a crisis of confidence towards gods who had been entreated in vain could jeopardise loyalty to the *mos maiorum*, thus opening the door to occult superstitions and foreign forms of worship. But here again, tradition had its specific *indigitamenta*. Against the tertian ague, one appealed to the compassion of Dea Tertiana; against the quartan ague, to Quartana; against unhealthy effluvia to Mefitis and, more generally, Febris, whom the Christians laughed to scorn, little knowing that in the Vatican quarter their fellow-Christians would one day honour a 'Madonna delle Febbri'. This goddess of Fever still had three temples in the first century AD. Remedies or amulets that had eased the sufferings of the sick were placed there as ex-voto offerings (Val. Max., 2, 5, 6).

Romans willingly resorted to popular magic. 'Knocking in an iron nail on the spot where a person falling in an epileptic fit first hits his head is said to be a definitive cure for that illness' (Plin., *NH*, 28, 63). We shall see that resorting to a nail was equally effective in cases of epidemics or public calamities. To restore the health of his mistress, Tibullus (1, 5, 11–12) circulated purifying sulphur around her, 'after an old woman had uttered spells'.

In some respects, dreams were a part of human ailments, when they were not actually provoking illnesses because they were thought to predict them. It was important to avert the ill effects of bad dreams, 'warding them off with the pious offering, thrice made, of wheat and salt' (Tib., 1, 5, 13–14); and Tibullus himself confesses that nine times in the silence of the night, veiled in linen and clad in a beltless tunic (so as not to impede the benefits of the divine influence), he made supplications on behalf of his mistress to the Triple Hecate (see ibid., 3, 4, 10). It was a service that could be rendered to a friend if the need arose. Every morning, Nasidienus related his dreams of bad omen to Martial (*Ep.*, 7, 54). The poet made one sacrifice after another:

he even appealed to a sorceress who was the ruin of him in bribes (Fr. *pots de vin*, jugs of wine) in the literal sense of the term. But the gods, too, needed a lot of persuasion: 'I have used up my salted cakes and heaps of incense, my herds are depleted (. . .) I have neither pigs nor poultry nor eggs left!'

The last important point in family life was death. 'May the dues of the Manes gods be sacred' (Cic., *Leg.*, 2, 22). These Manes were present in the house through the images of the ancestors, or in the tutelary powers of the Lares. They mysteriously survived in order to help the living, provided that on their death they had received the *justa*, or ritual honours that were their due; for as long as those *justa* were unfulfilled, the family was as if tainted by the *funus*: *funesta*.

Having closed the eyes of the deceased, whose sight was extinguished by Caeculus and whose soul was separated from his body by Viduus (Tert., *Nat.*, 2, 15, 2), they called to him (*conclamatio*), to make sure that he was well and truly dead, or rather to assure him that he would not undergo the sad fate of the *insepulti*, and this farewell was repeated until the end of the funeral. The corpse was laid on the ground, washed with hot water, perfumed with oil of cedar, honey, myrrh (even though the Twelve Tables prohibited its use as a luxury article too dearly purchased from the Carthaginians) and other unguents. The dead man was adorned with the insignia of his rank or a costly garment; but most often he was dressed in a Roman toga, which in the imperial era became a ceremonial costume worn only on one's death, so Juvenal tells us (3, 172). Charon's obol was placed in the corpse's mouth, intended to pay for his crossing of the Styx. He was put on view on a bed adorned with flowers and garlands. While incense burned, women mourners marked the rhythm of their lament by beating their breasts, sometimes accompanied by the sound of flutes. Nenia presided over the chanted lamentations for the funerals of the old, which prompted St Augustine (CG, 6, 9, 5) to say that as a good theologian of the *indigitamenta* Varro pursued man to his final decrepitude.

In the early days, care was taken to make a wax death mask of the dead man, and that *imago* was placed under a wooden canopy 'in the most conspicuous spot in the house' (Pol., 6, 53), sometimes in company with the family gods.

One week after death, the body was carried to the funeral pyre, for cremation was the dominant rite until the second century AD (only the *Cornelii* buried their dead up to the time of the dictator Sulla, who wanted to be burnt for fear that his body would be violated). To 'purify' the family, a sow was sacrificed to Ceres, and a portion of the sacrifice (we do not know which) was made in the presence of the deceased (Fest., p. 298, 1–4), that is, either before the burial, or in front of his *imago* (?). The house was ritually cleaned with a special broom to get rid of all taint and soiling: *exuerriae, extra verrendo* (Fest., p. 68, 8–13).

The funeral procession proceeded with music at its head, the sons being veiled, the daughters bareheaded (Plut., *QR*, 14, 267 *b*), all clad in black. According to Polybius (6, 53), men wore the masks of their ancestors and donned the toga praetexta of consuls or praetors, the purple robe of censors or the gold of triumphant victors. They led the cortège in chariots, with the fasces, axes and all the insignia of the magistracies that the ancestors had held. The deceased himself figured in effigy (with his mask) on the funeral bed borne by a carriage preceded by torch-bearers. Thus the dead escorted the deceased to his last resting-place, after protecting him while he was alive. Distinguished people, men in the public eye, were entitled to a funerary eulogy in the Forum, and the representatives of his ancestors took their places to listen to it, seated on ivory chairs, beside the deceased.

With a few notable exceptions (Vestals and certain eminent people), the remains of the dead were entombed only outside the city after the law of the Twelve Tables. The cremation of the dead person with his personal effects and the animals he had been fond of – which had had their throats cut beforehand – was most frequently carried out at the place of burial, on a pyre of precious wood on which those present threw foodstuffs, clothing, jewels, incense and costly perfumes. The eyes of the deceased were re-opened, 'religion not allowing them not to be revealed to the heavens' (Plin., *NH*, 11, 150). After one last call, the fire was ignited with the torches that had accompanied the cortège. Once the fire was over, the chief mourner dismissed those attending with an *ilicet* (=*ire licet*, 'you may go'), the funerary equivalent of an *ite missa est*. People said 'Goodbye!' or 'Farewell!' to the departed. Their hands bathed in purifying water, the family members gathered up the calcined bones in the folds of their black garments, then sprinkled them with wine and milk, dried them with fine linen before enclosing them in a marble urn (Tib., 3, 2, 16–22). In memory of the time when burial was performed, a finger severed before the body was burnt was buried separately, and a handful of earth was thrown three times on this *os resectum*. Also buried, chiefly at night and by torchlight, were infants who had died before the age of seven months and cutting their first teeth.

According to Plutarch (*loc. cit.*), the mourners circled the tomb which was honoured as if it were a temple, and when the first homage was paid to the departed after the funeral, it was to declare that he had become a god. As often, in this instance Plutarch draws his inspiration from Varro.

On returning from the funeral, those attending were purified (Serv.,

Aen., 6, 229) with water, fire and sulphur (*suffitio*). A ram was sacrificed to the family Lar. A meal (*silicernium*) was shared, its menu set by tradition: eggs, broad beans, lentils and poultry. But funeral banquets tended at times to border on a debauch, and the Fathers of the Church would waste much breath damning Christians who stayed loyal to this custom. Moreover, food was left for the deceased on his tomb (or it was burnt on the pyre), and it was not wasted on everyone; some people managed to live on it: the *bustirapi* (Pl., *Ps.*, 361). Rufa who, according to Catullus (59, 2–3), stole her dinner *de rogo* in the cemeteries apparently had no fear of the vengeful Manes!

Then began a period of 'days off', which would not have been holidays, wrote Cicero (*Leg.*, 2, 55), 'if our ancestors had not wished to number among the gods those who had departed this life'. During these *dies denicales*, even the animals stopped work. On the ninth day after the funeral (*novemdial*), the Manes were offered a sacrifice with libations of undiluted wine and milk, as if to nourish and strengthen them, the wine being a substitute for blood. This sacrifice was followed by a meal, where mourning garments were laid aside, and funeral games were held for which originally gladiators, *bustuarii*, were engaged (Serv., *Aen.*, 10, 519). We know that the funerals of popes also included a novena which kept its Roman name *novemdiale*, 'for prayers for the soul'.

When a man was murdered and thrown into the sea, his heir was obliged to sacrifice a sow (*porca*), observe three days of mourning and 'expiation' by sacrificing a young female pig (*porcus femina*); the sow alone was sufficient for a drowned person (Cic., *Leg.*, 2, 57). According to Varro (Non., p. 163, 20 ff.), in any case, for one who died without burial, the sacrifice of a 'preliminary sow' (*porca praecidanea*) had to be made to Tellus and Ceres. The site of a cenotaph was *religiosus*. Three times the Manes of the deceased were summoned (Virg., *Aen.*, 6, 506), in order to enclose his wandering soul in it: *animamque sepulcro condimus* (ibid., 3, 67 f.).

A mysterious deity formed the link between birth and death: Genita Mana, to whom small dogs were sacrificed (Plin., *NH*, 29, 58), the type of animal that was associated with the Lares, and sacrificed on the occasion of the Lupercalia, a rite of purification and fecundation. The idea that with Mania, the mother of the Lares (Varr., *LL*, 9, 61; Macr., *S*, 1, 7, 35), the Manes as Genii of the human race governed family procreation, remained fundamental to Roman religious thinking.

But what could Orbona do, when invoked by parents who had been 'orphaned' of their offspring (Arn., 4, 7)? She had a chapel, or at least an altar, near the temple of the Lares (Cic., *ND*, 3, 63; Plin., *NH*, 2, 16), and this vicinity could not have been without some significance.

– SPECIAL RITES, DUTIES AND SOLEMN OCCASIONS –

Within the home there were periodic rites that were common to all families. Others, and important ones at that, recurred annually, but were specific to each family. There were also occasional rites, such as those which, as we have seen, sanctified the good and bad times in life. Some were performed in the town, others had their place in the countryside and agricultural life.

– DOMESTIC CEREMONIES –

From earliest times, the rite of homage to the family Lares had been laid down. Every month, at the calends (new moon), the nones (first quarter) and the ides (full moon), the mistress of the house hung a garland of flowers round the hearth and accompanied her prayers with a suitable offering, depending on her means or the season. That lunar rhythm was eventually reduced to the monthly cycle of the calends (Prop., 4, 3, 53):

> If only I could once again celebrate the Penates of my ancestors, and each month pay homage of incense to the ancient Lar! (Tib., 1, 3, 33 f.)

The Lar was offered the first-fruits of the month (Hor., S, 2, 5, 14), a bunch of grapes, cakes, a honeycomb. His sacred head was crowned with a wreath of ears of corn. On occasion, he was propitiated by the sacrifice of a ewe-lamb (Tib., 1, 1, 23) or a 'voracious sow' (Hor., 0, 3, 23, 4). Virgil (B, 1, 43) mentions this sacrifice, associating the future Augustus with the Lares.

In the lararia, these gods of the hearth flanked the *Genius* of the family, notably of the master of the house. the 'Genius' was a kind of guardian angel, but one who, being born with us to perpetuate the race (whence his intervention in the *lectus genialis*), accompanies or, rather, lives within us until the end of our days (Cens., 3, 1–5). From him proceeded the tutelary Genii of the male members of the household, whose anniversary was celebrated with sacrifices and banquets. Similarly, that of the wife or other women and girls was also celebrated; they had their *Juno*:

> Mark this day, Macrinus, with a favourable stone which, if it is white, will secure the passing years for you. Pour out wine to your Genius . . . (Pers., 2, 1–3)

For the occasion the altar was encircled with verbena and a garland of flowers:

> May the Genius himself be there to contemplate the honours rendered to him! (Tib., 2, 2, 5)

Garlands adorned his sacred hair, 'drops of pure nard run down his temples. His hunger is satisfied with a cake, and he is sprinkled with undiluted wine' (ibid., 6, 8).

The officiant was the one whose *natalicium* or birthday was being celebrated. Wearing a white garment, like that of the *Genius*, he came forward, together with his family, and invoked the god following a hallowed formula, mingled with personal prayers and vows, *bona verba*. Then, taking grains of incense presented to him by a child, he made three libations of undiluted wine

which, as it spread, crackled on the sacred fire. (Ov., *Tr.*, 5, 5, 12)

For her birthday, a woman honoured her *natalis Juno* (Tib., 4, 6, 14):

Here is a triple offering of cakes, chaste goddess, a triple offering of pure wine.

These sacred cakes (*liba*) were made of boiled salted wheat (Plin., *NH*, 18, 84).

Varro (Cens., 2, 2) justified the consecration of wine by recalling that the ancestors, to fulfil their annual duty to their Genius, avoided soiling their hands by a bloody killing, 'for on the day when they had received life, they did not want to deprive another of it'. Children whose birth was being commemorated received symbolic presents that acted as talismans. Thus, in Plautus (*Ep.*, 639 f.), Telestis received a gold crescent and a little ring of the same metal.

The dead, too, had a right to personal and regular celebrations; the anniversary of their death was not forgotten. Exactly one year after the death of Anchises, Aeneas honoured his father by sacrifices to which the Trojan Penates were invited. His head wreathed with myrtle, he went to the tomb, poured two goblets of pure wine on the ground, two more of fresh milk, then another two of the blood of victims slaughtered on the burial mound. He also threw down brilliant red flowers – a *rosatio* – before saluting 'the paternal shades'. At that point a snake appeared 'emerging from the holy depths of the sepulchre'. Aeneas therefore resumed the sacrifice he had begun by killing two sheep, two pigs, two bull-calves with a black back (as was suitable to the Manes). His companions brought along further victims which they sacrificed, before roasting on a spit over live embers the meat to be consumed in the presence of the dead man (Virg., *Aen.*, 5, 55–103). At the end of nine days, games were offered to him. The poet is transposing and enlarging upon a ritual which, generally speaking, was performed more modestly; but the wine and milk (considered to feed the deceased), the flowers that associated him with the annual renewal of plant life, and symbolically (through the red of the roses) with invigorating blood, had to conform to custom. Sometimes honey was also offered, and oil or, simply, water: we know the importance that the *refrigerium animae* would retain in Christian tradition.

It would appear that in certain instances the anniversary of the deceased's birthday was celebrated; the kind of homage varied according to the family rites or following the fixed solemn occasions in the calendar, some honouring their dead every two months, others four times a year, that is – besides the two anniversaries mentioned – on the day of roses (23 May) and of violets (22 March), that were common to all families. Wreaths of flowers were then laid down, a joint offering to the Manes and the Lares (P., *NH*, 21, 11). This kind of obligation could extend to dead people who were unknown to you. If, for example, you bought a piece of land in which a dead person was interred, you had to pay him suitable homage every year: by doing so you were guaranteed his protection – always useful (Mart., *Ep.*, 10, 61, 5).

The ceremony of the *Lemuria* (9, 11 and 13 May) was carried out in the house and concerned only the *paterfamilias*. Who were the *Lemuria*?

> Among these Lemuria, wrote Apuleius (*Socr.*, 152–3), one having been allotted the task of watching over his descendants looked after the household with his benevolent and serene divinity: he was known as the family *Lar*; another, because of his misdeeds, remained homeless, condemned to wander at random as in a kind of exile: an empty scarecrow for good people, but a scourge for the bad, this kind was generally considered to be one of the Larvae, or bogeymen.

It was therefore an ambiguous category, but more precisely belonging to those whom E. Jobbé-Duval called the 'malevolent dead': *nigri Lemures* (Pers., 5, 185), *nocturnos Lemures* (Hor., *S*, 2, 2, 209), black spectres of the night.

Just three nights were given over to them, during the hours favoured by wandering souls. When the shadows were deepest,

> when the dogs are silent and you too, many-coloured birds, the man who is faithful to the ancient rite, he who fears the gods, rises and both his feet are free of all bonds. (Ov., *F*, 5, 429 ff.)

This barefootedness was part of the rules laid down for whoever came into contact with the sacred. His thumb between the closed fingers of his hand, he made an obscene gesture, 'for fear that some fleeting shadow might meet him during his silent walk'. It was an apotropaic sign, always used against the evil eye. The father of the family then washed his hands in water from a fountain and, armed with black beans, he moved forward and threw them down, turning his eyes aside and saying, 'By these beans I redeem both myself and my family.' He repeated this nine times without looking behind him. It is known that beans were the subject of an orphico-pythagorean prohibition, because of certain 'sacred reasons concerning souls' (Jambl., VP, 109). They were believed to be imbued with life, and to give them as food to the dead was to spare the living who were threatened by the Lemuria. 'It is thought that the shade gathers up the beans and follows the man unseen' (Ov., F, 5, 439 f.). The master then washed again and, to the sound of brass, ordered the shade to depart from the premises. When he had said nine times, 'Manes of our forefathers, go hence', he looked behind him, convinced that he had fulfilled the rites in a holy manner (ibid., 441–3).

This 'redemption' through the beans originally involved human sacrifice. In former times infants were sacrificed to Mania, the mother of the Lares, 'to safeguard the members of the family' (Macr., S, 1, 7, 35). Brutus, the founder of the Republic in 509 BC, was said to have substituted garlic and poppy heads. When any danger threatened a family, an image of Mania was hung over the door (but perhaps this was a sacrifice in effigy).

More serene and less charged with magico-religious thrills were the *Parentales* in February (from 13 to 21):

> The Manes do not ask for much: piety is more pleasing to them than rich gifts . . .
> A tile wreathed with votive garlands, corn scattered with a few grains of salt, the
> wheat of Ceres soaked in undiluted wine, strewn violets: that is all they need. Let
> a shard laid in the middle of the road receive these offerings. (Ov., F, 2, 535–40)

During this novena, the dead wandered freely (and quite harmlessly) outside their tombs to enjoy the food offerings that had been left for them. But the temples kept their doors closed: 'No incense on the altars, no fire in the hearths' (ibid., 664).

On 21 February (*Feralia*), as well as the last dishes served to the dead, some smaller livestock might be slaughtered. Ovid (ibid., 573–81) also speaks of an old woman surrounded by young girls, when she officiated at this time for Tacita, the 'Mute':

> With three fingers, she places three grains of incense on the threshold, at the
> point where a mouse has made itself a secret passage, then she attaches enchanted
> threads with blackish lead and turns seven black beans in her mouth; she sews up
> and roasts over the fire a fish-head which she has smeared with pitch and pierced
> with a bronze needle; she also pours a few drops of wine over it. 'We have tied

enemy tongues and hostile mouths,' says the old woman, who departs in a state of inebriation.

Here we again find the beans and the fish that Numa substituted for men. The 'Mute' thus propitiated is identified, according to Ovid (ibid., 615 f.), with the mother of the Lares, whom we always meet when the dead are involved, and in fact it seems that this act of witchcraft was to protect the household.

Certain families observed another calendar of funeral homage. The *Junii* kept the February rites in December, perhaps in connection with the *Larentalia* of 23 December. But on that day a public funerary sacrifice was offered to Acca Larentia, the nurse of the city's founding twins, and a sacrifice 'to the Manes of slaves' (Varr., *LL*, 6, 24). This Acca Larentia has been confused with Larunda and Mania, the subject of the ritual described by Ovid.

After the *dies Parentales*, the *Caristia* of 22 February sanctified the reconciliation of families (Val. Max., 2, 1, 8). People met to share a meal and together honour the tutelary Lares at the same time as the ancestors:

Offer incense, virtuous relatives, to the family gods (*dis generis*) . . . Offer also part of your food, so that, as a token of the worship that is pleasing to them, the dish placed before them (*missa patella*) may feed the short-robed Lares deities. (Ov., F, 2, 631–4)

Once night had fallen, the head of the family took a goblet and said, as he poured the wine on the altar, 'Good health, O Lares, and likewise to you, Caesar, father of our country!' Concord among the living and loyalty to the head of the Roman community were thus rooted in homage to the dead, the cult of the 'father' gods (*di parentes* or *patrii*) being the religious foundation of veneration for the *pater patriae*.

This festival of the *Cara cognatio* or 'beloved kin' (Tert., *Idol.*, 10, 3) was too popular to be eradicated from Roman customs; so it was Christianised under the name of 'Chair of St Peter', the *cathedra Petri* always recalling the chair on which one participated seated (and not reclining) at the funeral meal with the dead. In 567, the Council of Tours (Mansi, IX, 790) still expelled from the Church those who, at St Peter's festival, offered food to the dead and who, after the mass, ate meat dedicated to the 'demon'.

– COLLECTIVE LITURGIES –

Other festivals concerning all families as such recurred on a fixed date in the official calendar.

This was notably the case of the *Matronalia* on 1 March, 'the calends of the women' (Juv., 9, 53), a solemn occasion said to have been instituted in honour of the Sabine women and the anniversary of the temple dedicated to Juno Lucina in 375 BC. It was, in fact, a kind of mothers' day when their daughters, and also their husbands, gave them presents (even lovers offered gifts to their mistresses, as if in anticipation: Tib., 3, 1, 1). Later, the emperor Vespasian – so stingy in other ways – gave presents to matrons on this date. This solemnity therefore had public aspects. Women brought flowers to Juno and wore circlets on their heads to invoke her in her sanctuary on the Esquiline. But sacrifices were also offered in every home for the good fortune of the household, and mothers treated their slaves as their husbands did at the time of the Saturnalia. The festival thus sanctified conjugal, parental and domestic cohesiveness, with this simple and Roman concept that family life formed an indivisible whole with the state.

Quite different was the solemn occasion of the *Matralia* (11 June) which in fact involved only certain secondary aspects of family relationships. Their name is linked with Mater Matuta, the goddess of the Dawn, who had been identified with Ino Leucothea, the wet-nurse of Bacchus after the death of Semele. The festival gave rise to peculiar ceremonies which even then confounded the wisdom of the ancients. It concerned matrons, but only once-married wives (*univirae*) had the right to crown the statue of the goddess, which prompted Tertullian to say (*Mon.*, 17, 3), 'Monogamy and solitude meet in the service of the idols.' Mater Matuta was offered crusty, golden buns (*testuacia*), specially cooked in an earthenware utensil called a *testu*. Access to her temple was prohibited to female slaves, with the exception of a single one who was driven out, being slapped on the cheeks and beaten with canes; after which the matrons gathered their sisters' children in their arms (as Ino had for Dionysus). They pretended to make a fuss of them, at the same time invoking for them the kindnesses of the goddess. On the same day, they went to pray to Fortuna, whose temple was like the twin of Mater Matuta's (excavations of the *area* of Sant' Omobono revealed both on their common podium). The idol of Fortuna was on view there, covered by two togas, one on top of the other, which almost completely hid her (Ov., F, 6, 570: Non., p. 189, 26 s.). It may be supposed that after propitiating the maternal Aurora on behalf of their nephews and nieces, the matrons commended their future to the 'Fortuna' who had favoured Servius Tullius, born of a female slave in union with the fertilising fire of the royal hearth (above, p. 17). As for the ritual of the *Matralia*, it can be explained in connection with the attributes of the sister-godmother, *matertera*, the aunt (who, it would appear, is called 'Matuta' in Romanian). She took the mother's place, not only if the latter died, but also during the days when, after the birth, she underwent a 'quarantine' of purification. The slave driven from the temple personified the shadows before the dawn of the birth, that was eventually accomplished by 'luminous' Juno (Lucina).

The matrons met again on 7 July, but this time in company with their slaves and outside the town, at the foot of a wild fig tree, to sacrifice to Juno 'Caprotina'. This goat-goddess probably had the goatskin worn by Juno Sospita ('the Preserver') of Lanuvium, connected with the generative power of a he-goat god, Faunus Lupercus, who was honoured at the Lupercalia at the same time as Juno Februata, protectress of births, who was also distinguished by a *februum* (or goatskin). The fig tree whose 'milk' was offered ritually to Juno represented the reproductive he-goat, and a branch of the tree was probably used in a mock act of fertilisation. For the occasion, maidservants donned the *stola* or garment worn by free women and feasted merrily with their mistresses. These 'Caprotine Nones' were historicised by relating them to the disappearance of Romulus in the marshes 'of the goat', or to an episode of the war against the Latins who were claiming the right to marry Roman women (Plut., *Rom.*, 29, 2, 11: *Cam.*, 33, 7–10): the female slaves were said to have been prepared to yield themselves in order to deceive the enemy; during their wedding night, they handed their sleeping supposed husbands over to the soldiers alerted by Tutela, who was perched on the fig tree. A simulated fight may have recalled the happening. At all events, the festival was important to the fertility of the matrons as well as to their solidarity with all the women in the *familia*.

Prior to 154 BC, when the year commenced on 1 March, both public and private sacrifices were made in the first month perhaps on 5 March) to Anna Perenna, in order to have a good year and perpetuate (or render 'perennial') its satisfactory aspects (Macr., *S*, 1, 12, 6). Later, people remained faithful to this tradition, which was repeated on the calends of January, after which the Saturnalia consecrated the close of the annual cycle in both state and family.

On 17 December, a dawn bath was taken (Tert., *Apol.*, 42, 4), and a suckling pig was sacrificed on the family altar:

> Tomorrow you will tend your Genius with undiluted wine and a two-month old piglet, with your servants freed from work. (Hor., *0*, 3, 17, 14–16)

Not only did slaves have time off, but they were treated as guests:

> On this festive day, households faithful to the rites honour their slaves by serving them dishes first as if they were the masters. Only after this is the ceremony of the meal repeated for the heads of families. (Macr., *S*, 1, 24, 23)

This tradition was held to be retraceable to Saturn, the god of a golden age when all men lived as happily as the Immortals, 'their hearts free of care, far from sorrows and misfortunes' (Hes., *W*, 112 f.).

Until 23 December people passed the days in relaxation and feasting. Schools closed, and so did he courts, the punishment of culprits being postponed until later. Life was peaceful, so as to reflect the time when Saturn reigned over the world. People played with dice or walnuts, exchanged presents, especially wax candles (to ward off the anxieties of the solstice before the rebirth of the sun, *Natalis Solis*, which would become Christmas). They also presented one another with clay figurines (*sigillaria*) 'in a sacrifice of atonement for oneself and one's family to Saturn instead of Dis', the god of the dead (Macr., *S*, 1, 11, 49). The truth is that the Manes were never forgotten!

Many public solemn occasions had been the *feriae familiares* spoken of by Cato (*Agr.*, 140) and in fact still were, emerging into collective demonstrations, because families celebrated them on the same day. The very strong civic and rural community spirit in no way diminished the fundamental role of the *domus* for the master and his nearest and dearest. This balance explains the vitality of Roman traditions in the heart of Italy.

In Rome itself, the organisation of the thirty curiae institutionalised the equilibrium that was so necessary to national cohesiveness. Indeed, the curiae assembled families who observed the same domestic worship. At first reserved for the patrician *gentes*, they were subsequently opened to the plebeians. The 'curio' (priest of the curia) took the role of the *paterfamilias* in every household; but, for certain sacrifices, he was assisted by a curial flamen (Fest., p. 56, 7), and all the curiones were responsible to a *maximus curio* (ibid., p. 113, 29). In parallel with the rites of the daily family meal, certain feast days were regularly celebrated in the curia by all eating together at a communal table, and a communal hearth imitated the family lararium. Dionysius of Halicarnassus (*AR*, 2, 23) tells us in the time of Augustus of his admiration for Roman fidelity to ancestral to ancestral traditions:

> For each curia a room for feasting had been provided, and it was there – on the lines of Greek prytanea – that a table had been set aside for all members of the curia . . . In any case, I have seen with my own eyes, in these holy buildings, meals laid out for the gods on antique wooden tables, in baskets and little clay dishes; bread and barley cakes, wheat cakes, early fruits and other similar eatables, all simple, inexpensive and unostentatious. I also saw the wine for libations mixed not in gold or silver vessels, but in small goblets, terracotta ewers, and I marvelled at the sight of these men who were preserving intact the customs of their ancestors, without changing anything or introducing an empty lavishness.

The Romans had originally made their bread themselves, and each family had its oven for roasting the grain before cooking their cob-loaves in it. For the *Forcanalia,* a sacrifice was made in front of the oven, before sharing a meal like the one described by Dionysius. That feast in fact became a curial solemn occasion which was celebrated in February. The curiae solemn occasion which a kind of projection of domestic worship in the state and for the well-being of the state. Besides Vesta and very probably the public Lares, the Juno of the curiae *Curitis* was honoured there (DH, *AR,* 2, 50; Fest., p. 56, 21 f.).

– CULTS OF THE LAND –

In rural circles, the rites celebrated on each of the estates were also very often connected to a collective festival; but household gods remained pre-eminent.

When the head of the family paid a visit to his tenant farmer, he began by saluting the *Lars familiaris* (Cat., *Agr.,* 2, 1) before making his tour of inspection. The same duty was imposed on the farmer at the place of the Penates gods (Col., 1, 8, 20). Every day, in his master's absence, he took his place in the convivial homage to the protectors of the home, but ate only when seated, excepting on feast days, when he dined reclining on his table-couch (ibid., 11, 1, 19). Apart from the worship given to the sacred fire and the Lares of the crossroads (Cat., *Agr.,* 5, 3), he sacrificed only on his master's orders, and had to eject witches or haruspices (ibid., 4; Col., 1, 8, 6). The ploughshare of the plough that had traced the first furrow of the year was burnt on the Lares' hearth: 'As long as this rite is observed, a wolf will attack no animal in this field' (Plin., *NH,* 28, 267). Nailed to the farm door, a dried wolf's head was also believed to protect from evil (ibid., 157).

Outside the house, a 'pig shining with grease' was sacrificed to the crossroads Lares (Prop., 4, 1, 23). The gods were omnipresent, whether presiding over crops, harvests or hunts or, like the god Terminus, watching over the boundaries of the land (Ov., *F,* 2, 639 ff.; DH, *AR,* 2, 74). Tibullus (1, 1, 11–18) expresses the townsman's sense of religion towards the countryside:

> I devoutly revere a tree stump in the depths of the countryside or an ancient stone garlanded with flowers where paths cross. And the first-fruits of all that spring brings me are the offering placed at the feet of the rustic god. For you, fair Ceres, a wreath of corn-ears from my property will hang at the gates of the temple. In my orchard, I will place the idol of a rubicund Priapus, whose cruel billhook will frighten the birds . . .

Taking another view, Apuleius (*Apol.*, 56, 5–6) denounces his wife's brother-in-law as a typical scoundrel:

> Even to the rural deities who give him food and clothing he never once offers the first-fruits of his crops, his vines or his herds. On his lands there is not a single sanctuary or holy site or wood! And why mention groves or chapels? Those who have been at his place declare they have never seen so much as a stone anointed with oil or a branch adorned with a garland anywhere on his estate.

Elsewhere, the author of the *Florides* (1, 3–4) evokes this sanctification of the landscape:

> An altar wreathed with flowers, a grotto shaded with foliage, an oak hung with horns, a beech with animal skins or a consecrated knoll surrounded by a fence, a tree trunk in which a hatchet has carved a divine effigy, a patch of turf sprinkled with libations, a stone anointed with scented oil . . .

Every place had its Genius (*genius loci*) or its own god. Plains were attributed to Rusina, hilly crests to the god Jugatinus, hills to Collatina and valleys to Vallonia (Aug., CG, 4, 8).

Here again, the Roman sense of operational realism made use of the *indigitamenta*; one therefore had to pray to Sterculinius for animal manure, Vervactor for turning over fallow land, Redarator for the second ploughing, Imporcitor for the third, Obarator for a new turning of the soil, Occator for harrowing, Sarritor for weeding, Seia for the germination of seed, Segetia for the corn to grow, Nodutus for the stem to have nodes, Volutina for the sheath of the corn-ear, Patellana for it to open, Hostilina for the corn to be of the same height (to make harvesting easier), Lacturnus for the ears to be milky, Runcina for killing the weeds, Matuta for the ripening, Messia for the harvesting, Convector for loading, Noduterensis for threshing, Condito for garnering, even Promitor for taking the grain from the granary, but chiefly Tutilina for preserving it (Aug., CG., 4, 8; Serv., G, 1, 21). Even this list is by no means exhaustive.

Cato enumerated the rites to be observed so that the estate should suffer no harm. To keep oxen in good health, an offering must be made in daylight to Mars and Silvanus, in the forest, of three pounds of wheat, four-and-a-half each of bacon and fresh meat, and three pints of wine for every animal. Once the sacrifice had been performed, the components to which man was entitled had to be eaten on the spot. A slave could officiate, but not a woman, who did not even have the right to be present (Cat., *Agr.*, 83). For these same oxen (so indispensable for working the fields), the gods were served with food 'when the pear trees blossomed'. At that time a goblet of wine was offered to Jupiter *Dapalis* (from *daps*, the sacred food). He was invoked to be presented with the offering, after washing one's hands, and was entreated to accept the meal, which comprised roast meat and an urn of wine. He could be associated with Vesta, the guardian of the home. That done, two kinds of millet were sown, together with garlic and lentils (ibid., 132).

Before harvesting, a preliminary (*praecidanea*) pig had to be sacrificed, and Janus, Jupiter and Juno invoked. Janus was offered a *strues* (a cake resembling the clenched fingers of a hand), with a prayer for oneself, the children, the home and the entire household. Jupiter was presented with a *fertum* (another type of sacred pastry). Both Janus and Jupiter were entitled to a libation of wine accompanied by the appropriate invocation to each; but only the wine that overflowed the vessel belonged to the gods. Only then was a sow sacrificed to Ceres, its entrails subjected to a ritual dissection (*prosecta*) before being offered to the goddess with some wine (ibid., 134). That particular day was a holiday for the oxen, the herdsmen and all the employees taking part in the ceremony.

The forest belonged to the gods. To the ancients it gave that frisson of the supernatural, even when traditional religion was tending to collapse. 'Faced with an ancient stand of tall trees (. . .) the grandeur of the trees, the mystery of the place, the impressive view of such dense shade (. . .) you are inspired with faith in a divine presence,' wrote Seneca (*Ep.*, 41, 3), who quotes a line of Virgil (*Aen.*, 8, 352) on a sacred grove that formerly crowned the Capitol: 'A god lives there: who? A god, anyway.'

Cato (*Agr.*, 139) had the same respectful uncertainty. When a wood had to be cleared, the crime constituted by such an attempt on divine property had in some way to be expiated, by means of a *piaculum*: the sacrifice of a pig accompanied by a prayer whose recipient remained anonymous (*si deus, si dea*). The god of the forest was thus propitiated for the family and the whole household.

If a site had to be dug over in order to grow crops on it, another expiatory sacrifice was required, and had to be renewed each day everywhere that work was going on (ibid., 140). For to make holes in the earth was to rape it! The Romans had scruples about violating or disfiguring the landscape: their *religio* had aspects that today we would call 'ecological'. That did not prevent their undertaking large-scale works, but always with the approval of the gods.

Treatises on agronomy contained a number of 'recipes' that had more to do with traditional magic than religion strictly speaking, but were often closely connected with worship. To protect young shoots against harmful insects, Columella (10, 354) advises 'feeding them with the black ash from the family Lar'. To prevent Rubigo ('rust') attacking plants that were beginning to turn green, she was to be appeased with the blood and entrails of an unweaned puppy (ibid., 342 f.). To calm bad weather or the fury of squalls, says Columella again (ibid., 340 f.), one should proceed to make 'Tuscan' sacrifices: what did that mean? The Etruscans were said to have the secret of warding off thunderbolts, but we know nothing of the sacred procedures to which the agronomist alludes. At the beginning of the twentieth century, prayers were still said in Umbria against storms and hail. At all events, if lightning or a thunderbolt struck anywhere on the estate, its mark had to be expiated by surrounding it with a ritual fence. Any tree that had been struck required a special sacrifice, with the offering of a sacred cake (*fertum*) of the same kind as that offered to Jupiter for the health of the oxen. A 'technical expert', the *strufertarius*, had to carry out this office (Fest., p. 376, 12–20; 377, 2–3).

Several special ceremonies to which the state resorted in cases of dire distress were of rural origin; for example, the *petra manalis*, a stone which was kept in a field and had to be rolled like a cylinder in times of drought to obtain rain from the gods (Fulg., *Serm.*, p. 112, 14 f. Helm).

All working of the land required an appeal to the gods. 'Among the ancients,' Deutero-Servius reminds us (*Aen.*, 3, 136), 'one could neither marry nor plough a field without carrying out sacrifices.' *In primis venerare deos*:

> First and foremost, revere the gods, and each year renew your offerings to the fair Ceres. Let all the youth of the countryside adore Ceres in your company! In her honour, mix honeycombs in milk and the sweet liquor of Bacchus. Let the victim make the beneficent circuit of the new crops, escorted by the whole chorus of jubilant companions . . . Let no one scythe the ripe corn-ears unless his head is bound with oak-leaves in honour of Ceres. (Virg., G, 1, 338–49)

In this enthusiastic and synthesised evocation, the poet is associating with the *Cerialia* of April the Ambarvales (the purification of the fields that was originally applied to one's own estate) and a harvest ritual celebrated in July. Tibullus (2, 1, 15–26) devoted just as vibrant a poem to the purification of the crops and fields, which remained a family festival, or one for the families connected with the land:

> See how the consecrated lamb goes to the resplendent altars, followed by the crowd wearing white and crowned with olive! Gods of our fathers, we purify our land, we purify our country folk: you, for your part, drive all evils from our borders, so that the treacherous shoots do not betray the hopes of a good harvest, and the sheep that has lingered may not have to fear the speed of wolves! Then

the peasant in his festive attire, secure in the richness of his glebe, will bring plenty of wood to the blazing fire, and the band of slaves born in the household – a good sign, bearing witness to a prosperous peasant – will play games and build cabins of branches. My prayer will be answered; do you not see how, in the propitious entrails, the prophetic fibre means that the gods will look kindly upon us? (An allusion to the examination of the sacrificed lamb's liver.)

The estate was purified by a ritual of circumambulation by the three kinds of victim sacrificed to Rome for the ending of the census: a boar, a ram and a bull (*suovetaurilia*). Cato (*Agr.*, 141) preserves for us the precise and detailed formulary of this *lustratio agri*. Following a prayer to Janus and Jupiter, who were propitiated with wine, Mars had to be addressed in these terms:

Father Mars, I pray and implore you to be benevolent and propitious towards me, my household and all my people, to which end I have ordered the suovetaurilia to go round our fields, lands and estate, so that you will banish, repel and drive away (*averrunces*) all visible and invisible maladies, dearth and desolation, calamities and bad weather.

This negative prayer was followed by the positive invocation:

And so that you will allow crops, corn, vines and young shoots to grow and ripen well, that you keep safe shepherds and their flocks, and that you safeguard and grant good health to myself, our household and people: to these ends, to purify estate, land and fields, for their purification, as I have said, receive the sacrifice of these suovetaurilia, which are still unweaned.

This was therefore a preventive ritual, to some extent prophylactic but also for the promotion of growth and prosperity. Here Mars takes on the three functions (religious, warlike and productive) of Indo-european society, since he exorcises, drives out, evil 'by sweeping' (*averrunces*: Averruncus was yet another of those *indigitamenta* protecting the crops), before ensuring abundance and good health. After the invocation, sacred cakes were presented with the hope that the god would accept the sacrifice. If an examination of the entrails proved unfavourable, he was asked to accept the sacrifice by way of expiation.

Tibullus (1, 1, 19–24) mentions a kind of ritual redemption of the flocks which are saved by consecrating one animal to the gods of the estate:

You also, guardians of a once rich, now impoverished land, you have your presents, Lares gods! Then, a slaughtered heifer served to purify innumerable bulls. Now, a ewe-lamb is the modest victim for a smallholding: a ewe-lamb will fall victim for you, and may the young rustics gathered around her cry: Io! give us good harvests and good wines.

The poet still had his little sheepfold and, every year, he was in the habit of 'purifying' his shepherd, but also of sprinkling milk over an idol of Pales, the protectress of pastoral activities against thieves and wolves (ibid., 33–6). She was feted at the *Palilia*, on 21 April.

Ovid (F, 4, 735 ff.) is more precise and detailed. Out in the fields, he invites the shepherd to purify his sheep in the first moments of morning half-light:

Let water first sprinkle the ground and a broom sweep it, let foliage and branches decorate the sheep pen, let garlands cover and adorn its doors! Let the blue smoke rise from the cleansing sulphur, let the ewe bleat as the sulphur smoke touches it! Burn the wood of a male olive tree, resinous pine, Sabine herbs (juniper). Let laurel crackle in the heart of the flames! A basket of millet will accompany millet cakes: that is the food which delights the rustic goddess. Mix the food and the milk she loves in her milking-pail and, when the meal has been served, pray to Pales, the friend of the woods, offering her warm milk. Say to her: Watch over both the flock and the masters of the flock. Drive all harm far away from my cowsheds. If I have grazed my herd in a holy place, if I have sat beneath a holy tree and if, unknowingly, my sheep has browsed on the grass of tombs, or I have entered a forbidden wood, if my gaze has put to flight the Nymphs and the half-goat god (Faunus), if my billhook has despoiled a sacred wood of a shady branch to make a bed of foliage for a sick sheep: forgive me my fault and do not be angry with me for having sheltered my flock in a rustic temple to keep them from a hailstorm. May I not suffer for having disturbed the ponds: forgive me, O Nymphs, if the animals' hooves muddied their waters. You, O goddess, on our behalf, please appease the springs and their deities, and the gods scattered throughout the woods. May we not see either the Dryads or Diana bathing, or Faunus when he is abed at midday in the fields . . .

There follows a series of invocations for men, sheep, dogs; for plentiful milk and cheese; for the vigour of the ram, the litters of the females, the quality of a wool soft enough not to 'hurt the young girls' and which is 'fit for the most delicate hands'. This long prayer had to be recited four times, facing the rising sun. One then had to wash one's hands in running water, before drinking from a bowl of 'snowy milk with crimson cooked wine'. Lastly, fires of straw were lit and everyone jumped joyfully on the crackling heaps. In Rome, the *Palilia* (whose date coincided with the city's anniversary) were marked by other rites of importance to the entire state. But even reinterpreted by the poet, this prayer conveys intensely the major concerns of the peasant trying to survive and, at the same time, the religious scruples of the Roman who senses everywhere the disturbing and hidden power of divine beings.

But were all these rites enough to ward off in advance a spell or curse put upon crops (Plin., *NH*, 28, 17)? At all events, there was great haste to consecrate the first golden ears of corn to Ceres (Ov., M, 10, 433: *F*, 2, 520), the first samplings of must to Liber Pater (Plin., *NH*, 18, 8; Fest., p. 423, 1 f.) and, in general, the first ripe fruits to the gods (Plin., *NH*, 28, 23; Cens., 1, 9–10). Grape harvests were the occasion for traditional and popular rural and family festivals. A he-goat was sacrificed to Bacchus, and its fat entrails grilled on hazel spits; the peasants decked themselves out with masks cut from the bark to exchange unbridled badinage in improvised sketches, as in the commedia dell'arte (Virg., G, 2, 385–96). Clay effigies (*oscilla*) with an apotropaic function were hung on pine trees. In the imperial era they were made of marble, with Dionysian profiles (Satyrs, Maenads, Silenuses or Pans) to protect inner gardens from the evil eye. The redoubtable Messalina made use of the grape-harvesting festivities to celebrate her Bacchic marriage to the handsome Silius (Tac., *An.*, 11, 31, 4–5).

On 11 October, for the *Meditrinalia*, the must was treated with old wine, in homage to Jupiter, although a goddess, Meditrina, was dreamed up, who was not otherwise known. Tasting the brew, one said by way of good omen (*ominis gratia*): 'New, old, I drink the wine; new, old, I cure my ill', *morbo medeor* (Varr., *LL*, 6, 21; Fest., p. 110, 21–3). The *Meditrinalia* therefore consecrated the blood of the vine as preventive medication, but the name was originally applied to the treatment of the must by a specific *medicamen*.

The following year, the *Vinalia priora* of 23 April also honoured Jupiter, since libations were made to him with the new wine, which on this occasion was called *calpar*, the name of the earthenware jar from which it was taken *sacrificii causa* (Fest., p. 40, 27 and 57, 16–18).

These were the ordinary and extraordinary offices that had to be fulfilled in the lives of families, who often foregathered for this purpose in both town and countryside. But other and different ceremonies survived which were peculiar to this or that *gens* or 'clan', even if some were eventually incorporated into the holiday calendar of the state. To these we now turn.

– GENTILITIAL OR 'CLAN' CULTS –

Assuming the role of *paterfamilias* from then on implied shouldering all its religious obligations or *sacra*, and that was sometimes an onerous duty. It was impossible to inherit possessions without also inheriting gods. In his treatise on *Laws* (2, 45–53), Cicero holds forth at length on the methods applicable to different cases. According to certain specialists in priestly law, such as Scaevola or Coruncanius, one need have only a share of the inheritance in order to be subject to the *sacra*. Conversely, when passing from one *gens* to another by adoption or 'adrogation' (a procedure peculiar to citizens dependent only on themselves), at the same stroke the person involved renounced these of the religious duties (*detestatio sacrorum*) only to assume those of the family into which he was entering. Thus we see Cicero blaming Clodius for 'upsetting' the *sacra* and debasing the families, the one he was leaving and the one he was dishonouring by violating 'the law of the Quirites' (*Dom.*, 35), when he consecrated the lower part of his house (stolen from Cicero) *genti Clodiae* (ibid., 116). This overturning of gentilitial cults compromised the well-being of the state itself.

So the expression 'an inheritance without *sacra*' became a proverb to mean absolute and unadulterated happiness (Pl., *Capt.*, 775; *Trin.*, 484). 'Our ancestors did not want a family's religion to die' together with its head, explains Cicero (*Mur.*, 27). However, if a *gens* died out, in theory its cults disappeared with it; but the state made efforts to preserve at least some of those whose celebration was important to the Roman people (who were always concerned to treat the most minor deities tactfully) by entrusting them to an association (*sodalitas*).

Certain obligations fell upon on this or that member of the *gens* in particular. Among the recognised excuses of citizens who failed to respond to military conscription, Cincius Alimentus (praetor in 210 BC) noted chiefly: funeral of a relative, 'denicalis' holy days (to purify the survivors from the taint of death) . . ., 'an augury that cannot be neglected without committing sacrilege, an anniversary sacrifice which can be carried out only by the man in question on that day and in that place' (Gell., 16, 4, 4). Cato the Elder confiscated L. Veturius's horse because he had failed in the strict fulfilment of his religious duties.

In the early fifth century AD, Macrobius (S, 1, 16, 7) comments that the *Claudii, Aemilii, Julii* and *Cornelii* still had their own ritual festivals. There were others which each family celebrated 'according to the tradition of domestic solemnities'. We know nothing about the special *sacra* of the *Aemilii* or *Cornelii*, though it is known that the *Julii* paid special honour to Apollo and Venus, but evidence of this devotion appeared belatedly and not without some political ulterior motive. They had a family sanctuary at *Bovillae*, where Vejovis seems to have been the object of a gentilitial cult (CIL, I^2, 1439; 14, 2387); but Vejovis also had worshippers among the *Caesii*, the *Licinii* and the *Fonteii*, at least judging by the *denarii* struck in their name.

We know a little more about the *Claudii*. Originating from the Sabine region, the *Appii Claudii* distinguished themselves very early on (in the fifth century BC) by a strong and proud attachment to their religious traditions. The surname *Nero* peculiar to this *gens* recalls the name of the goddess *Nerio*, who was called Bellona in Rome. In an unfortunately mutilated text, Festus (p. 462, 28 ff.) records a dispute setting a Claudius against the chief priest Metellus on the subject of Saturn, to whom supplications had to be made bareheaded (*capite aperto*). A special feature of the Claudian cult was the sacrifice of the *porcus propudialis* or 'pig of shame', which was slaughtered by way of atonement to pay for the disgrace incurred by neglecting ritual obligations (Fest., p. 274, 29–32).

We have seen that the Junii were in the habit of rendering homage to their dead in December rather than in February, probably on the occasion of the *Larentalia* (23 December), the festival of Acca Larentia, whose effigy occupied the obverse of the coins of P. Accoleius Lariscolus around 37 BC. But in the *Curia Accoleia*, it was Angerona – the goddess of the distress (*angor*) caused by the shortening of the days at the winter solstice – who was celebrated two days earlier, on 21 December. The specific attributions of these gentilitial cults elude us, and some families must have taken responsibility for them on their own account or have inherited them.

The *Aurelii*, of Sabine origin like the *Claudii*, had charge of the cult of the Sun, to whom they owed their name (*Ausel* which harked back in fact to the Etruscan *Usil*) and to whom the family sacrificed in the name of the Roman people (Fest., p. 22, 5–8). As we know, the emperor Aurelian once more took up the torch of this centuries-old calling when he made the adoration of *Sol Invictus* official in AD 274. But in republican coinage, it was the *Aquilii* or the *Mussidii* who devoted the obverse of their *denarii* to the Sun. And current tradition ascribed the introduction of *Sol* and *Luna* into the Roman pantheon to Sabinus Tatius (Varr., *LL*, 5, 74, 3; DH, *AR*, 2, 50; Aug., *CG*, 4, 23, 1).

It was believed that the celebration of the Secular games, which had become a public liturgy, was due to the *Valerii*. Their function was periodically to render to the Roman people the health inherent in the very name (*valere*) of the family. It was recounted that a certain Valesius, whose daughter and two sons were ill, had placed some hot water on his hearth at the same time entreating the Lares to divert the danger threatening his family on to himself. These gods advised him to go and get some water at the altar of Dis Pater and Proserpine, following the course of the Tiber as far as *Tarentum* (where, on the Campus Martius, the *ludi Terentini* or Secular games would be held). Valesius carried the water from the river to a spot where the soil was smoking; there, he heated it and gave it to his children to drink. Healed, they said they had seen in a dream a god sponging their bodies, ordering the sacrifice to Dis and Proserpine of black victims on the altar from where the water had been brought, and there to celebrate lectisternia and nocturnal games. Returning to the place, the father had the foundations of an altar dug out, but found one already there precisely dedicated to the two underworld deities. This archaeology legitimised a gentilitial cult, and Valerius Publicola (consul with Brutus in 509 BC) was supposed to have been the first to apply its benefit to the Roman people. But, significantly, Valerius Maximus (2, 4, 5) ascribes the first link in the chain of this process to the family Lares, who sent the man concerned to the gods of the dead . . .

To the same *gens Valeria* belonged one L. Valerius Acisculus Soranus who, around 45 BC, had some coins struck with the effigy of Apollo Soranus and others with that of Valeria Luperca, carried off by the heifer of her legend (Plut., *Par.*, 35, 314 *c-d*). This is again a story of health, but one which concerned Falerii, the heroine having cured the sick of the plague with a little hammer (*acisculus*, the nickname of the magistrate responsible for currency). Other coins of L. Valerius Acisculus show the Sibyl, which brings us back to the Secular games, since a L. Valerius in 76 BC had brought back certain oracles from Erythrae to replace those which had been lost seven years earlier when fire consumed the Capitol. Soranus, another nickname of Valerius, was the one used to invoke an Apollo of the Soracte, honoured every year by the *Hirpi Sorani* or 'wolves of the Soracte', who propitiated him by running over a bed of hot coals. They were 'families' (Plin., *NH*, 7, 19) exempted for this reason by a decree of the Senate from military service and all other duties.

The typology of their coinage attests the devotion of the *Petronii* to Liber Pater and Feronia, the *Gellii* to Mars, the *Renii* to Juno Caprotina. Originally from Tusculum, the *Fonteii* promoted the image of the Dioscuri. The *Papii*, *Procilii*, *Roscii* and *Thorii* boasted of Juno Sospita of Lanuvium, who had her temple in Rome at the 'vegetable market' (*forum Holitorium*), where today S Nicola in Carcere occupies the site of its *cella*.

The *Servilii* observed a bizarre custom: they possessed a third of a copper *as* to which they offered an annual sacrifice 'with extreme attention and magnificence' (Plin., *NH*, 34, 137). It seems that it could be seen to grow or dwindle to presage the greatness or decline of the family. Certain trees also foretold the future, such as the old oak whose branches predicted the destiny of each child of the *Flavii* (Suet., *Vesp.*, 5, 2), or the cypress on the family land which, having fallen, grew again more strongly than ever to guarantee Vespasian his imperial future (ibid., 7), then crashed before Domitian's death (Suet., *Dom.*, 15, 5). Here we have examples of prophetic signs, of which the city's religions offer us further instances: the myrtles of the temple of Quirinus, one 'patrician', the other 'plebeian', their vigour varying according to the waxing or waning of one or other class (Plin., *NH*, 15, 120), and above all the Ruminal fig-tree, foster-parent of Romulus (ibid., 77; Tac., *An.*, 13, 58).

Like the Secular Games, many public liturgies evolved from family traditions.

The rite of the *Tigillum Sororium* was traced back to the story of Horatius, who killed his sister Camilla, a wooden beam, under which his father made him pass with his head veiled, as if under a yoke. Every 1 October, a sacrifice was offered to Juno *Sororia* and Janus *Curiatius*, two alternative names which have set imaginations working. It could in fact be a matter of a rite of passage to adulthood, for both girls (Juno) and boys (Janus) incorporated into the curiae (*Curiatius*). Each autumn, too, warriors had to be reinstated into the civic community. It was originally a gentilitial ceremony, *genti Horatiae* (Liv., 1, 26, 13). Hence the role of the father who presided over the ritual in the case of the conqueror and killer of the three Curiatii (ibid., 12), a ritual of expiation in the view of the ancients (DH, *AR*, 3, 22, 7; Fest., p. 380, 18–25; 399, 2–4). The regional records or guides of Rome in the fourth century AD still mention the *Tigillum*, which was situated north-west of the Colosseum, at the corner of the Colosseo and G. Agnesi streets.

In 312 BC, the censor Appius Claudius made another private cult public: that of Hercules at the Great Altar (*Ara Maxima*), where Virgil (*Aen.*, 8, 102 ff.) portrays Evander presiding over the annual festival. It was the responsibility of the *Potitii* and *Pinarii* families, following tradition. The former were the more important, while the latter had to help them and serve the festive meal subsequent to the sacrifice (DH, *AR.*, 1, 40; Fest., p. 270, 5–16; Serv., *Aen.*, 8, 269). If the names of these two *gentes* were not contrived after the event, as J. Carcopino conjectured, their origin remains uncertain, even though Plutarch (*Num.*, 21, 3) makes the *Pinarii* descendants of a certain Pinus, son of Numa. The *Potitii* were said to have ceded their rights to public slaves by financial means – a payment of 50,000 asses (Fest., p. 270, 10–11) – which scarcely does them credit and, moreover, was not at all in keeping with priestly law.

The Lupercalia was another liturgy that finally came under state control, judging by the two teams of *Quinctiales* (or *Quinctilii*) and *Fabiani*, derived from the *Quinctii* for the first, and the *Fabii* for the second. Ovid (*F*, 2, 375 ff.) explains this duality by a competition between the *Fabii* of Remus and the *Quinctilii* of Romulus who arrived at the post-sacrificial feast too late to find anything left except the bones of the goat sacrificed to Faunus. The forename *Kaeso* is not found attributed to any other than the members of these two families, and apparently concerns the action of *caedere* (hitting, striking) which characterises the Luperci (Fig. 7) using their strips of goathide (*februa*) to lash the backs of women wanting to become pregnant.

The *Fabii* had other ritual obligations. During the siege of the Capitol, Cn. Fabius Dorso girded up his toga and, his head enveloped in a fold of this ample garment, went through the Gaulish advance posts to the heights of the Quirinal, where he fulfilled a traditional family solemn ceremony. Later, when the Romans wanted to emigrate to Veii, Camillus invokes this notable example:

> What? Private cults, even in time of war, must not be interrupted, but public worship and the gods of Rome can be abandoned, even in time of peace? And pontiffs, flamines, have more right to neglect official ceremonies than a private individual his gentilitial cult? (Liv., 5, 52, 4)

There could be no better expression of the fundamental solidarity between the religions of the family and the city.

It is verified chiefly in the case of Vesta, whose temple housed in an inner sanctum, unseen by the eyes of the profane, an idol of Minerva: the famous *Palladium* which Ulysses and Diomedes were supposed to have stolen from Ilium; but according to Actinos of Miletus, it was a copy made to deceive the Greeks (DH, *AR*, 1, 69), and it was Aeneas who was said to have carried off the genuine and precious *xoanon*. It was among the 'pledges of well-being and empire', kinds of fetishes guaranteeing Rome's eternity (Cic., *Scaur.*, 48; *Phil.*, 11, 10, 24). However, tradition would have it that this *Palladium* had been rescued by the Trojan priest of Pallas, a certain Nautes (Serv., *Aen.*, 2, 166; 5, 704) or Nautios (DH, *AR*, 6, 69), a companion of Aeneas and ancestor of the *Nautii*. In the fifth century BC, this family claimed to preserve the idol and render it homage of gentilitial nature. As the *Julii* claimed Aeneas as a distant ancestor, there had been a tendency to obscure or reinterpret this story. But the *Nautii* had been bequeathed the cult of Minerva (Serv., *Aen.*, 5, 704), and Virgil himself makes the old Nautes the accredited spokesman for the goddess (*Aen.*, 5, 704 ff.). Varro spoke of it in his work on *The Trojan Families* and Festus (p. 164, 25 f.) reports a bronze statue of Minerva which the *Nautii* were in the habit of supplicating in their own fashion. According to Dionysius of Halicarnassus (*loc. cit.*), the members of the *gens* took it in turns to ensure that the appropriate offices were carried out. It may be that other families practised the same kind of take-over; but in the time of Augustus, there were no longer any *Nautii* to assert these sacred rights.

With the disappearance of the great Roman families under the Empire, gentilitial cults as such fell into disuse, either because they had been incorporated into the calendar of the *sacra publica*, or because associations had taken over from the *gentes*, but including other devotions. Similarly, where families had formerly honoured their dead, henceforward funeral colleges often regrouped subscribers under names that no longer had anything to do with the disparate identities of their members.

Nevertheless, family gods in general held their ground, as did rural gods, right up to the period when government became Christian. In the early fifth century, in his commentaries on *Isaiah* (57), St Jerome bears witness to what he saw in Rome several years before. Like Tertullian in his *De idololatria*, he deplores the fact that nowhere escaped paganism. No sooner had one crossed the threshold of a house than one saw the idols of the domestic Lares, 'as they say!' In many towns, the religious weight of the past remained a major preoccupation for the translator of the Bible:

> Rome, master of the world, venerates in every house, in every dwelling, a statue of Tutela with lamps and candles. She is entreated for the safety of the home and, both entering and leaving, the inhabitants are recalled to their inveterate error . . .

Around the same period, Prudentius reproaches pagans for allocating their Genius to doors, to houses, to baths, to stables, and imagining them in their thousands in every part of the town 'so that no nook or cranny lacks its phantom' (*C. Symm.*, 2, 446–9).

On 8 November 392, a law of Theodosius, known as 'the Great', (*C. Th.*, 16, 10, 12) condemned the kind of clandestine sacrilege (*secretiore piaculo*) which worshipped the god Lar with fire, the *Genius* with libations of undiluted wine, the Penates with the aroma of roast meat (*nidore*). It forbade the lighting of torches, the burning of grains of incense and garlanding with flowers. All these precise details corresponded to the rites which were practised at that time and would continue to be practised for a long while to come, despite the bishops and saints and their brutal activism. Nowadays in the small shops and houses of Rome images of the Virgin or patron saints lit by a tiny light replace the ancient tutelary Spirits which formerly aroused such indignation in the Fathers of the Church. As for the horde of minor gods who respectively watched over every stage of life and work, 'we believe that the angels carry out their duties,' said Tertullian (*An.*, 37, 1).

But in Rome as elsewhere, whatever religious changes occurred, the cult of the dead who 'rule the living' (Auguste Comte) was the one thing that did not perish. And the agnostic Alain, twenty centuries after Cicero, echoed his *Laws* (2, 55) when he wrote: 'The dead are superhuman (. . .) Our natural gods are our dead, magnified and purified.'

CHAPTER 3

Religions of the city

Like every family, Rome had its Lares, Penates and focal hearth, but it needed a sacerdotal organisation and suitable places of worship. Temples or simple sacred areas, like the Volcanal at the foot of the Capitol, established a different form of piety from that of the domestic hearth, and involved the solidarity of the Romans in a ritual which, without upsetting that of the *gens*, transcended it to the benefit of national well-being.

After being the jealous custodians of the 'auspices', the patricians had had to share them with the plebeians. In 304 BC, the aedile Cn. Flavius made public the 'Fasti' or pontifical calendar and the secrets of civil law, which were linked with religion. Correspondingly, around 300 BC, the Ogulnian law granted the plebeians access to the augurship and priesthood.

Every *paterfamilias* was a conscientious citizen of the state. It irked St Augustine (CG, 6, 4, 1–2) that Varro put human affairs before divine ones, for – the Latin antiquary explained – cities had existed before religious institutions, 'as the artist exists before the picture and the architect before the building'. Such an attitude was typical of a Roman, for whom religion was not a matter of personal devotion, but concerned a collective interest. The pontiff Scaevola (Aug., CG, 4, 27) and Varro (ibid., 6, 5, 1) were indebted to the Stoic doctrinaires for the famous distinction between three 'theologies': poetical, philosophical and political or 'civil'. Their preference was obviously for the last: 'Gods can be found whom everyone must honour publicly, and with which rites and sacrifices' (ibid., 3).

Cicero (*ND*, 1, 3–4) challenges the disinterested piety of Epicurus; for 'if the gods cannot and will not help us, if they are not in the least concerned about us, if there is nothing on their side that touches our life, what reason have we to devote worship, honours and prayers to them?' There could be no society that lacked the 'good faith' of the oath that called on the gods as witnesses. Polybius (6, 56, 14) hails this basis of Roman *fides* as a capital asset, and at the same time, fear of the gods as a means of curbing the passions of the people (ibid., 11–12). 'May the well-being of the people be the supreme law' (Cic., *Leg.*, 3, 8). That well-being depended on the gods; so life in Rome could be 'regarded as an immense permanent liturgy' (Georges Dumezil).

– ORGANISATION OF THE PRIESTHOOD –

Although every Roman was obliged to be alert to divine manifestations (*numina*), the fulfilment of rites called for rather specialised skills and therefore men who were able to perform them.

As Athens had its archon-'king', so Rome had its 'king of sacrifices' (*rex sacrorum* or *sacrificulus*) who, in 509 BC, had inherited some of the prerogatives pertaining to the abolished monarchy (Liv., 2, 2, 1). He was patrician, married by *confarreatio*, the son of *confarreati*. Together with his wife, 'queen of sacrifices', he lived in the *Regia* which would become the official residence of the chief priest. Although subordinate to the latter, he retained precedence, before the major flamines and the very *pontifex maximus* who had chosen him (Fest., p. 198, 30 ff.). At a sacred banquet, he reclined above the flamen of Jupiter (Gell., 10, 15, 21). His primacy matched that of Janus, the god of beginnings, to whom in January the *rex* sacrificed a ram, who also walked at the head of the flock. This priestly royalty barely survived the last years of the Republic, and under the Empire no longer interested anyone but the scholarly.

With the *rex*, the three major flamines (of Jupiter, Mars and Quirinus) and the Vestals shared the privilege of being taken by carriage to the *sacra publica*. The name *flamen* cannot be likened to that of Brahman without phonetic difficulties. Like a Brahman, a flamen sacrificed, but was not the only one to do so, not even the *flamen Dialis*. The three major flamines were patrician, and Jupiter's was married by *confarreatio* and was the son of *confarreati*; hence the recruitment problems in the time when the liberalisation of customs made even the sons of illustrious families resistant to a 'rebarbative antiquity' (Tac., *An.*, 4, 16, 3). With their innate pragmatism, the Romans proceeded to make adjustments; but the *flamen Dialis* remained subject to a series of taboos which did not make life easy for this man *quotidie feriatus* (Gell., 10, 15, 16), for whom no day was ever 'profane'.

He could not swear, ride a horse, wear a ring (unless open and hollow) or any knot at his belt or on his head, touch a dog, a horse, a she-goat, fermented flour or raw flesh, ivy or broad beans, or pass under the shoots of vines stretched overhead, stay away from home three nights in a row, or leave the house without his headdress, which was cut from the white skin of a victim sacrificed to Jupiter and topped by an olive wood wand enveloped in woollen thread (*filum*), to which the *flamen* perhaps owed his name. He must never go where a dead person was being burnt, or touch a corpse. The feet of his bed had to be smeared with mud, and no one but he had the right to sleep in it. His nail clippings and hair cuttings had to be buried at the foot of a 'lucky' tree (dear to the gods, and fruit-bearing). A thick woollen cloak (*laena*) woven by his wife distinguished him when he sacrificed. If he lost his wife (the flaminica), he lost his priesthood, which was matrimonial. His person was sacred, and if one who had been sentenced to a flogging begged him on his knees, the punishment could not be carried out that day (in eighteenth-century papal Rome, prelates were confined to their quarters on execution days, for if the man being led to his doom begged for mercy, they could not deny him). The flaminica, a devotee of the cult of Juno, never went out unless wearing a long garment of purple wool. A veil similar to the *flammeum* of a young bride shrouded her hair, which was braided and dressed high to form a (conical?) *tutulus*. Her shoes were made from the leather of sacrificed animals.

It is understandable that such a priesthood remained seventy-five years without a holder, from 87 BC to the day when Augustus became the chief priest (12 BC) and appointed a new one. Unlike the *Dialis*, the flamines of Mars and Quirinus, could undertake public duties. They were not compelled to observe such restrictive *religiones* (Serv. Dan., *Aen.*, 8, 552).

Of the twelve minor flamines, whose recruitment was open to plebeians, we know only those of Vulcan, Volturnus, Palatua (the local goddess of the Palatine), Furrina (another local goddess, but of a sacred wood on the Janiculum), Flora, Carmenta (the 'Prophetess'), Portunus, Falacer (?) and Pomona. The imperial cult would also have its provincial and municipal flamines. Whether they were major, minor or 'augustal', the flamines therefore had prerogatives that bound them to the service of a particular deity.

Both the *rex* and the *Dialis* could be replaced in their office by pontiffs with a broader, universal authority over the religions of the city, governed by priestly law under the supreme responsibility of the *pontifex maximus*. They formed a college of fifteen members whose duty was, as their name implies, to 'create a bridge' linking the city-state to the surrounding world, or rather to open a ritual path to divine peace. In fact, they controlled the whole of Roman piety, and the chief priest was a kind of 'pope' who very quickly acquired the prerogatives of the *rex*. Thus in 12 BC Augustus assumed its title and attributes. Custodian of the sacred law, formularies, the calendar, the statutes pertaining to the different temples, he had a hand in all acts of public or private worship. It was he who 'inaugurated' the king of sacrifices, settled matters regarding wills and adoption (with the passage from one family to another and thus repudiation of gentilitial cults), presided over marriage by *confarreatio*, chose or 'acquired' the major flamines and the Vestals. He had a privileged link with the 'great Vestal': 'as long as the priest together with the silent virgin goes up to the Capitol,' wrote Horace (0, 3, 30, 8 f.), meaning that Rome's eternal existence depended on their vigilance. Did priestly ritualism contribute to the 'demythifying' of Roman religion? At all events, the pontiffs were the epitome of attachment to the letter of the law regarding ritual procedures and had overall authority over domestic, family and official state worship; in the priestly *ordo* they were always at the head of the four great colleges.

In their wake, the augurs had scarcely less considerable prestige and responsibility. An augural law governed their practice, which rested on the tradition laid down in the *libri augurales*. To endorse any undertaking in the name of the state, the augurs' task was to consult the gods by observing the sky, birds, their flight and their cries, but also lightning and thunder. Their number had grown: from three under Romulus or Numa (according to tradition) to over fifteen from the time of Caesar. Their name had the root of the verb *augere*, meaning 'to increase', the augur reinforcing men's actions by giving them the weight of divine approval. Their insignia was a short, smooth, crook-handled staff (Fig. 8), the *lituus* used for marking out and dividing the areas of the *templum* corresponding to the visual field of observation:

> May the public augurs, interpreters for Jupiter Most Good, Most Great, discern the future by signs and auspices. (Cic., *Leg.*, 2, 20)

Whether one's occupation was war or government, one would therefore be warned of the auspice and have to conform to it. The augurs had to recognise the signs of divine wrath and make provision for it: *Divorumque iras providento* (ibid., 21).

The *duoviri sacris faciundis*, who would become ten, then fifteen, were the guardians of various 'prophecies' attributed to the soothsayer Marcius, but chiefly to the Sibyl of Cumae who was supposed to have sold three books of oracles to Tarquin the Proud, after proposing nine at the same price and burning the six others (Gell., 1, 19). The *quindecemviri sacris faciundi* were the only ones officially allowed to consult them when the peace of the gods was in jeopardy. Their title means that they recommended 'the sacred acts to be carried out', by virtue of the oracles enclosed in a stone casket beneath the temple of Jupiter Capitolinus (DH, *AR*, 4, 62) until the fire of 83 BC which completely destroyed them. About a thousand lines of them were reconstructed, by means of research everywhere that the Sibyls had prophesied (Samos, Ilium, Erythrae and elsewhere in Africa and Sicily). During the disturbed period preceding the Empire, there were swarms of apocryphal oracles. Augustus had 2,000 of them burnt, and ordered the quindecemvirs to review the genuine maxims, transcribing them in their own hand. The official manuscript was kept in two gilded cabinets constructed below the idol of the Palatine Apollo. The college especially intervened when it was necessary to appeal to gods other than those of the strictly Roman rite. So through Apollo they were concerned with the *ritus graecus* and contributed to the naturalisation of foreign cults, over which they retained control. They wore the Greek cloak (Fig. 9) and a laurel wreath. Their symbols were the tripod (*cortina*) of the Sibyl, the dolphin and the crow of Apollo.

The fourth and last major college was that of the 'epulones', at first three, then seven and finally ten under Caesar, though that did nothing to change their title of *septemviri epulones*, whose task was to feed (*epulari*) Jupiter, together with Juno and Minerva on the Capitol, a feast to which senators were invited. At first linked with the Plebeian games, under the Empire this solemnity was extended to other games.

The order of the six priestesses of Vesta was a very conspicuous special feature of Roman religion, and that singularity confirmed its roots in the family cult. Recruited at a tender age, between six and ten years old, by the high priest who 'selected' them from among patrician daughters whose parents were both still living (and married by *confarreatio*), they had to be neither deaf nor dumb, and with no bodily defects; they lived under the supervision of the priest who exercised the authority of a father over them. They also had some connection with the *rex*, but we do not know why on a certain day of the year they had to say to him: 'Are you vigilant, king? Be vigilant.' For their 'inauguration', their hair was cut to be hung from a lotus-tree.

They lived in the temple annex, where they devoted ten years to being educated, another ten to officiating and yet another ten to instructing new recruits. They ensured the upkeep of the public hearth under the authority of their most senior member, the great Vestal (*Virgo Vestalis Maxima*). Besides guarding the flame, they prepared the brine (*muries*) that seasoned the flour to be sprinkled on victims (*mola salsa*). Pounded in a mortar, the coarse salt was poured into an earthenware pot that was placed on the fire under a lid of gypsum. It was next cut up with a saw, before being thrown into a large jar (*seria*) with the addition of running water or, at least, water that did not pass through pipes (Fest., p. 152, 5–12). In May, the Vestals roasted ears of wheat, before grinding them to make the flour which, three times a year, they used for *mola salsa* (Serv. Dan., *B.*, 8, 82). With the ashes of calf embryos burnt at the *Fordicidia*, horse blood and bean stalks, they also concocted the mixture for the purifying fumigations (*suffimina*).

Their vow of chastity (*castus*) was temporary, because after thirty years of priesthood they could marry. But, if they betrayed their *castus*, they were buried alive in the 'Field of Crime' (*Campus Sceleratus*). There was 'no more terrifying spectacle, no more dismal day for the city' (Plut., *Num.*, 10, 11). The Vestal was carried in a litter closed with straps, which were untied once the place of execution was reached. The chief priest pronounced a secret prayer, raising his hands to the heavens, before the fatal moment. The veiled guilty woman was brought out of the litter and put on the ladder leading to the bottom of the pit. There she found a bed with a blanket, a lighted lamp, a little bread and water, milk and oil, 'as if the Romans felt some compunction about causing the death of a person who had been consecrated by the most august ceremonies' (ibid., 9). In fact, her fate was left to the gods of the underworld. After drawing up the ladder, the opening was stopped up with a great deal of soil to level the ground, so that no trace of the atonement remained evident. Woe also to the virgins who let the flame go out: the chief priest would have them flogged until the blood ran.

Their forehead adorned with a bandeau, the Vestals wore a white veil fastened under their throat by a brooch (*suffibulum*). Their person was sacred, like that of the *flamen Dialis*. If, when walking in the street preceded by a lictor, they met a condemned man, he had to be pardoned. They took part in the great public ceremonies, especially liturgical banquets (Fig. 10).

Like other peoples in ancient Italy, Rome had a college of fetials, 'a holy institution if ever there was one, which shames Christians, in whom a god who came into the world to bring peace to all things was unable to inspire charity and peace' (Bossuet, *Disc. sur l'hist. univ.*, 3, 6). In fact, the fetials who, like the pontiffs and augurs, had a special authority (*jus fetiale*) demanded the ultimate reparations before declaring war. But they also sanctified peace; thus the Greeks called them 'judges of peace' (εἰρηνοδίκι) 'guardians of peace' (εἰρηνοφύλακες) or 'peacemakers'. Twenty in number, they were recruited by co-option. If intervention was necessary, one of them, bearing the title *pater patratus*, was spokesman on behalf of the Roman people, either to demand reparations from the enemy, or to give him satisfaction by handing over a guilty party, or to negotiate and conclude an alliance by way of the appropriate rites. He was accompanied by the *verbenarius*, the bearer of the sacred herbs (*sagmina*) that had been used to consecrate him as 'officiating father'. The name fetial is derived from a root **dhe* – found in the Greek θέμιζ and the Latin *fas*: it indicates the divine foundation guaranteeing a just peace after a just war.

War and peace also dominated the function of the Salians, 'leaping' and singing priests grouped in two sodalities: twelve Salians of Mars and twelve of Quirinus, who respectively opened and closed the season, the first in March, the second in October, under the common protection of Jupiter, Mars and Quirinus. Clad, under the ceremonial toga, in a short tunic fastened at the waist with a broad bronze plaque, and helmeted, they leaped about striking with their swords the holy 'ancilia', 'figure-of-eight' shields, twelve copies of an original that had miraculously fallen from the sky. Their procession ended in a banquet whose reputation is proverbial. Together with the priests, the *tribuni celerum* – formerly officers of the royal guard – were present at this armed 'dance'.

Lastly, the brotherhood of the Arvals, whose foundation dated back to Romulus and Acca Larentia (his nurse), a group of twelve members whose duty was ritually to promote the crop fertility of the arable fields or *arva*. The Arval Brothers therefore wore as their major insignia a crown of wheat-ears bound by a white ribbon. Their leader was a *magister* or president, replaced on occasion by a *promagister*. They chiefly celebrated Dea Dia in May.

Other priests did not have the same authority in the city.

Expert in examining entrails of sacrificed animals, but also in interpreting prodigies and lightning, the haruspices were for a long time the custodians of an Etruscan science resorted to only in exceptional circumstances. They formed an official college of sixty members only from the time of the emperor Claudius (41–54), who was, as we know, passionately interested in Etruscology. There is a familiar witticism of Cato, expressing surprise that one haruspex could look at another without laughing (Cic., *Div.*, 2, 51). In his *Agriculture* (5, 4), this same Cato warns people to be on their guard against every 'haruspex, augur, soothsayer and Chaldaean' (astrologer). Here we can recognise the old Roman who does not want to be hindered in his daily activities.

We know almost nothing of the *Sodales Titii*, said to have been instituted by T. Tatius to preserve the religious traditions of the Sabines (Tac., *An.*, 1, 54, 1). We saw earlier that certain liturgical teams (Luperci, *Potitii* and *Pinarii*) seemed to have had a family origin. Other sodalities were created to cope with the ceremonial obligations of cults imported into the *Urbs*, at the same time that priests were assigned to the service of the foreign gods.

As may be seen, the majority of public priesthoods had a collegial structure; they acted under the control of the Senate until the imperial era. All had their own jurisprudence based on the records of proceedings (*acta*) or *commentarii* that preserved the component elements of a long tradition.

– PERIODIC RITUALS –

The personnel and authority of this sacerdotal apparatus in the service of the city-state enabled them to cater for repeated ceremonies as well as the variations depending on circumstance of the 'permanent liturgy' described so aptly by Georges Dumézil, with which Roman life was so heavily preoccupied. That liturgy was largely of a festive nature. Games and feasting, amusements and merriment tempered the rigours of a ritualism that was strict yet necessary for maintaining mental equilibrium. Regular repetition had its virtues that were based on the constancy of the *mos maiorum*. The city's collective rites were complemented by the solemnities of trades and districts, besides those of the curiae already mentioned.

– PAGAN DAILY RITUAL –

Like the family, the city had its daily religious acts, whether the days were 'fasti', 'nefasti' or 'comitial'. For instance, the Vestals, first and foremost, who in certain respects publicly recreated the matrons' responsibility for the domestic hearth. Unlike what happened in Greece, the civic flame was tended by virgins and not married women, for 'fire is without blemish as the virgin is without stain' (DH, *AR*, 2, 66) or 'fire, being sterile and infertile, has affinities with virginity' (Plut., *Num.*, 9, 10).

The Vestals had a liturgy of the sacred fire which called for their vigilance day and night, so we must suppose there was a continuous relay system. They did not feed the fire with just any kind of wood. If the virgin on guard let the fire die out, it was a prodigy of bad omen to be expiated, according to the rules, by flogging the culprit, unless she was lucky enough to have a miracle, like Aemilia who revived the fire by spreading her veil over the hot embers (Val. Max., 1, 1, 7; DH, *AR*, 2, 68). The flame was relit by briskly boring a piece of wood taken from a 'lucky' (or fruit-bearing) tree, and the fire was carried to the temple in a bronze sieve (Fest., p. 94, 1–4). At all events, a new fire had to be lit each year, on 1 March, using the same procedure.

As in every family, each day the hearth was the object of careful attention, and the fire of an assiduous cult; bloodless offerings were made to it. Water was also part of the daily ritual; the Vestals went to fetch it either from the spring of Egeria or the Camenae (near to the Porta Capena, where Rhea Silvia met the god Mars to conceive the twin founders), or like Tarpeia, at the foot of the Capitol (Prop., 4, 4, 15 f.). This water was used for the needs of the cult, to wash holy objects (Ov., F, 3, 12) and to clean the temple (Plut., *Num.*, 13, 4).

For Numa (Plut., *Cam.*, 20, 5), Vesta's perpetual fire was to be 'the image of the eternal power that governs universal order'. But the Vestals also had custody of mysterious fetishes which were considered to be the sacred pledges of Roman hegemony (*pignora imperii*), hidden in the strongroom of the temple or *penus Vestae*. The eternity of Vesta's hearth was thus associated with the eternity of Rome: *aeternos ignes et conditum in penetrali fatale pignus imperii Romani* (Liv., 26, 27, 14; *cf.* 5. 52. 7: *aeternis Vestae ignibus . . . imperii pignus*). and when the *Augustan history* (Hel., 6, 7) accuses Heliogabalus of having wanted to extinguish the 'perpetual fire', it tends to impute the end of Rome to him, perhaps not without having the Christian emperors in mind. Among the *pignora imperii* were the idol of Pallas and the Penates brought (so it was believed) from Troy by Aeneas. Those sacred objects were accessible to the Vestals alone, and even the chief priest Metellus, who saw them only when saving them from a fire, was said to have been stricken with blindness as a result (Cic., *Scaur.*, 48; Ov., F, 6, 439–52).

Every day in 'ceremonial' state (*quotidie feriatus*, as Aulus Gellius expressed it), Jupiter's flamen observed a daily ritual, like the Vestals. He had his sacred fire, to which he sacrificed every day, and his table was never empty (Serv. Dan., *Aen.*, 1, 706): it was known as an *adsidela* (Fest., p. 18, 8), for he officiated while seated at it. Even at night, while he slept, the *flamen Dialis* was supposed to be attending to his divine service, for a receptacle containing sacred cakes was at the foot of his bed (Gell., 10, 15, 14).

Hardly a day passed when the Roman in Rome had no civic or judiciary obligations in which the gods had a share. When he passed in front of a temple or divine idol, he raised his hand to his lips and imprinted a kiss on it (Plin., NH, 28, 25; Minuc., 2, 4), if he did not kiss the statue itself, to the point of wearing it away (Cic., *Verr.*, 4, 94; Lucr., 1, 314 f.), as pilgrims today touch the foot of the first pope in St Peter's in Rome. To make a special appeal to a god, a person's prayer was written on a wax-coated tablet and placed on the knees of the idol being invoked (Juv., 10, 55; Prud., *Apoth.*, 457). An oath was sworn only with one's hand on the altar of the god taken as witness (Pl., *Rud.*, 336; Cic., *Flacc.*, 90; Virg., *Aen.*, 12, 201). A magistrate would not address the people without first pronouncing a solemn prayer (Liv., 39, 15, 1).

Apparently, a daily ceremonial took place in certain temples after the opening of the gates, whereas others remained closed (like many churches in present-day Rome) until a visitor's request to the doorkeeper (Sen., *Ep.*, 41, 1). In the mornings, a crowd besieging the Capitoline forecourt saluted

Jupiter *Imperator* (Plin., *Pan.*, 5, 4). After deploring these imitations of Egyptian religion, Seneca shows his indignation on the subject of ordinary Roman worship:

> However, this delirium (of Isiac followers) has only a limited period. To go mad once a year is tolerable. But go up to the Capitol! You will blush to see the madness in everything that empty folly thinks it a duty to perform. One person submits names to Jupiter, another tells him the time; another is his masseur, yet another his perfumer who, by the empty movement of his arms, simulates rubbing. Women arrange the hair of Juno and Minerva (keeping at a distance not only from the idol but from the temple, they move their fingers like hairdressers); others present a mirror . . . A supremely expert mime, already a decrepit old man, used to act out his role daily at the Capitol . . . Workmen of every trade spend their time there labouring for the immortal gods! (from Aug., CG, 6, 10, 2)

This testimony has been related to the feast of Jupiter, which was the responsibility of the *septemviri epulones*. But Seneca here denounces a daily ritual. It would appear that every guardian or sacristan (*aedituus*) of a chapel or temple had to ensure its maintenance and see to the toilette of the deity, without the stage setting or mimes of which Seneca speaks. But the face of Jupiter Capitolinus was made up with red lead paint only on feast days (Plin., *NH*, 33, 111). With the success of oriental religions, we shall see Rome's pagan diurnal reinforced by rites that were foreign to tradition.

– THE LITURGICAL YEAR –

Four types of holidays may be distinguished: fixed (*stativae*), movable (*conceptivae*), for special circumstances (*imperativae*) as well as market days (*nundinae*), which occurred every ninth day to mark a kind of week, their periodicity being thus fixed (but some people deny them the title 'feriae'). To begin with, we shall concentrate only on the first two categories which come under the annual heading.

The history of the Roman calendar that we have inherited is complicated. The lunar year of Romulus comprised ten months, or 304 days, as well as an intercalary month every second year, of either twenty-two or twenty-three days. This month was inserted after the *Terminalia* of 23 February and included the five remaining days of the month. As such a system gave the years on average one day too many, they had to be grouped in series of twenty-four, inserting sixty-six days in the last eight instead of ninety (from the fifth century BC onwards).

By catching up with the solar cycle, this lunar year preserved the rhythm of lunar months, with the calends marking the beginning, the nones the first quarter and the ides the full moon. 'The first day of the month was called calends, because it was the day when the nones of the month, whether they should fall on the fifth or the seventh, were proclaimed (*calantur*) by the priests on the Capitol, in the *Curia Calabra*' (Varr., *LL*, 6, 27). In theory, the nones fell on the fifth of the month, but the seventh in March, May, July and October. According to circumstances, they said five or seven times: 'I proclaim, Juno Covella', using a mysterious invocation which people have tried to relate to the waning crescent moon. On the nones of February the pontiffs had to announce the intercalary period and its duration; but towards the end of the Republic they took liberties with tradition for electoral and political reasons that had nothing to do with the sun's revolution. Disorder reached the point where harvest festivals no longer occurred in summer, nor grape harvests in autumn (Suet., *Caes.*, 40, 1). Caesar put the clocks right, so to speak, for a calendar by which we still live, through the reform of Pope Gregory XIII (in 1582), with a system of bissextile (leap) years: one day is inserted every four years after 24 February, the sixth day (*sextus*) before the calends of March. In fact, before the self-interested manipulations of the regime in its decline, adjustments ensured from year to year, if not day to day, that holidays would coincide with their seasonal raison d'être.

D. Sabbatucci was able to write a *Religione di Roma antica* (*Religion in Ancient Rome*, 1988) based on the calendar alone, which in real time ritualised a cosmic order and a certain representation of humankind in the world. Above all, it ritualised a way of life which was fairly typical of the ploughman-soldier that every true Roman remained at heart. Rather than theorising about his ways of thinking, it is more important to enter into the annual cycle of the acts that sanctified tasks and days.

Some sacrifices belonged to a fixed date:

> The cult of Juno demands the ausonian calends; on the ides, a white ewe, of good size, falls in honour of Jupiter; the nones have no tutelary deity. (Ov., *F*, 1, 55–7)

The sacrifice on the calends ritualised the announcement of the nones in the name of Juno Covella by a pontiff in association with the king of sacrifices who honoured Janus, the god 'of beginnings'. On the ides, it was Jupiter's flamen who officiated, with the ewe known as *idulis*, led to the capitol along the Sacred Way (Fest., p. 372, 10–12). The day following these days was 'black'.

As soon as they took up office, the consuls fixed the date of the Feriae Latinae, which linked Romans and Latins for the sacrifice of a white bull to Jupiter Latiaris in the sanctuary of Mons Albanus. There the thirty towns forming the confederation partook of the victims' meat. In Rome itself, chariot races were held; the victor was entitled to a goblet of absinthe which was supposed to guarantee his health (Plin., *NH*, 27, 45). The Feriae extended in duration to four days, usually in May or June. Like praetors or dictators, consuls neither assumed nor left office without going to sacrifice to Vesta and the Penates of Lavinium, the sacred cradle of the *Urbs*.

In these temples was celebrated the anniversary (*natalis*) of their dedication (today we would say their 'inauguration'). This commemoration, whose tradition is perpetuated by the Catholic church, was solemnised by ceremonies we know little about, sometimes even being unable to locate the exact site of the temple concerned. Unless there is some useful exception, I will therefore leave them aside.

Every month had its 'fasti', most frequently linked with seasonal cycles.

The first in the civilian year (from 154 BC) connected the empty part of the winter following the Saturnalia to the month of the final purifications, *Terminalia* in February, before the return of the traditional liturgical year in March. Janus, who was rightly *bifrons* (two-faced), was therefore the patron of a month (*Januarius*) which, at the meeting of the two years, looked – like the god himself – simultaneously both forward and backward. To Ovid (*F*, 1, 149 ff.), surprised that time does not recommence in spring, Janus replies that 'the winter solstice is the first day of the new sun and the last of the old' (ibid., 163).

As it is for us, 1 January was a day of good wishes and new year's gifts, when only words of good omen had to be spoken (ibid., 71):

> Do you see how the air is brilliant with scented fires and how Cilician saffron crackles on the hearths? The brightness of the flame strikes the gold of the temples and spreads its flickering light to the rooftop of the sanctuary. In spotless garments, we make our way to the Tarpeian citadel. (ibid., 75–9)

The consuls started their magistracy by the sacrifice to Jupiter Capitolinus of 'bull-calves that had never known the yoke and had been fed on the grass of Faliscan meadows' (ibid., 83 f.). We know that the waters of Falerii were supposed to whiten the hides of animals that grazed there (Plin., *NH*, 2, 230). The colours of the victims and the festive clothing were pleasing to Jupiter, god of the luminous sky. But Janus, who was the god of the first month, and challenged Jupiter, the sovereign god (*summa*: Aug., *CG*, 7, 9, 1), was present, not only through the offering of the *rex*, but on the coins that were given on the occasion (Ov., *F*, 1, 230). It was also the day when, on the island in the Tiber, the temple of Vejovis was celebrated, a kind of anti-Jupiter whom it was important to propitiate in order to give the year a good start (Gell., 5, 12, 9), and also of Aesculapius, the god of health, whose favour was just as opportune on the first day of January.

From 3 to 5 January in the imperial era, but in republican times only on the day fixed by the praetor, celebrations were held at the crossroads in the city, as in the countryside, to the Lares who were the district's protectors, under the presidency of the *magistri vicorum* (heads of residential blocks) who organised sacrifices and sports competitions: it was a very popular festival, which the Caesars would make use of to the advantage of their cult.

In this month, which on the whole was not over-endowed with religious 'fasti', we find Janus again on the 9 for the *Agonia* (or *Agonalia*), when the king of sacrifices offered him a ram in the *Regia*, that is, in the trapezoidal area to the east of Caesar's temple, *atrium regium* communicating with the chapels of Mars (where the shields of the Salians were kept) and Ops Consiva, the goddess of national 'financial resources'. Two days later, the 11, it was the festival of the *Carmentes* who presided at births: Porrima and Postverta, according to whether the baby arrived head or tail first (Gell., 16, 16, 4). But Ovid (F, 1, 635 f.) and others see them as the goddesses of destiny, one of whom sees the past and the other the future, which ties them in with the cycle of Janus (Macr., S, 1, 7, 20). In fact, two feast days fixed with a day's interval were normally complementary in the Roman calendar, simply because the gods liked uneven days and the day following a ferial day was 'black'. However, Ovid (F, 1, 628 ff.) relates the *Carmentalia* to the concerns of pregnant women, recalling the banning of leather in the sanctuary, 'so that dead things shall not sully the chaste altars'. On that day, the 'Carmental' flamen sacrificed in a chapel neighbouring on the Carmental Gate, at the foot of the Capitol; but priests attended the ceremony.

On that same 11 January, water supply workers celebrated the anniversary of the temple of Juturna (Diuturna) on the Campus Martius (as distinct from the complex linked with the 'lake' of the goddess on the Forum). But we know absolutely nothing of the forms which these 'Juturnales' took.

A movable seedtime festival (*Sementivae*) was celebrated around the end of January in rural areas. Cakes were offered on the hearths of the village. The Earth and Ceres were propitiated by the entrails of a pregnant sow, as well as the ritual wheat. They were entreated to protect the seed against birds and ants, the shoots against icy cold spells, 'rust', bad weather and rye grass.

February was the month of atonement and, as we have seen, the dead. The first day, in fact, linked the anniversary of Juno Sospita (on the Palatine) with the cult of Helernus. This was the Juno of Lavinium, wearing a garment and headgear made of goatskin (*februum*) or instrument of purification to which the month owed its name, and which we shall see again at the Lupercalia. As for Helernus, he was the father of Carna who protected the intestines of children against vampires, a god linked with the shadowy world (since a black ox was sacrificed to him: see Fest., p. 83, 1), as well as with the beans with which the dead were exorcised in May. On that day the priests asked the king of sacrifices and the flamen of Jupiter for the wool also called *februa*. This was the designation for the 'instruments of purification used by the lictor in houses sullied by a murder' (Ov., F, 2, 19 ff.), like the grilled wheat and grains of salt (the latter having remained symbols of protective purity even today) or the branch of a 'lucky' tree. People assembled in the sacred wood of Helernus, not far from the mouth of the Tiber. A two-year-old ewe was sacrificed in the atrium of Vesta, then to Jupiter Tonans and Jupiter Capitolinus (ibid., 67–70).

On 13 February, these ides consecrated to Jupiter also honoured Faunus in his sanctuary on the island in the Tiber and in country areas:

> Today we must sacrifice to Faunus in his shady groves the ewe-lamb he demands or, if he prefers, a kid. (Hor., 0, 1, 4, 11 f.)

The god of woods and flocks, Faunus deifies the forces of nature which the peasant both fears and entreats. So in this instance he was propitiated on the fringes of the city and civilised life, in a temple built with the product of fines inflicted on farmers of public grazing land. There was often a connection between the financing of sacred buildings and the sphere of authority of their occupants; thus Venus had the benefit of a large temple near the Circus Maximus thanks to the money of adulterous matrons, and on several occasions dishonest moneylenders had to provide the where-withal to embellish the temple of Jupiter, the guarantor and guardian of oaths.

The 15, day of the Lupercalia, was the *dies februatus* par excellence (Varr., LL, 6, 13 and 34), under the patronage of Faunus, on the next day but one after his festival: here we see again the rhythm of duplications on odd-numbered days. We saw earlier that the brotherhoods of the Luperci, or wolf-men, had originally been gentilitial groups. The ceremony commenced at the Lupercal, a grotto at the south-west corner of the Palatine which was supposed to have sheltered the twins Romulus and Remus. There, goats and a dog were sacrificed, and the bloody knife used in the slaughter marked the forehead of two young men of noble family, the traces being wiped away with a woollen cloth soaked in milk, whereupon the two youths had to burst out laughing: was it the simulation of a human sacrifice, or perhaps an apotropaic rite?

After a banquet where the flesh of the victims was eaten, the Luperci cut from the hide of the sacrificed male or female goats the *februa* or 'purificatory' strips, and set off at a run, using the straps to hit women who wanted to become mothers or to have a satisfactory birth. Girt about with goatskins, they probably circled the Palatine, and it was chiefly on the Via Sacra (Aug., *CD*, 18, 12) that they whipped the backs of barren women. These wolf-men exorcised the enemy of the flock, at the same time assuming the powers of Faunus (goat-god identified with the Greeks' Pan) by the very attributes of the animal that made the flock prolific. Apparently, the Lupercalia had the ultimate aim of promoting both human and animal fertility in the agro-urban community. The flamen of Jupiter took part in the office, and Juno was not neglected, for the purifying leather had the name *amiculum Junonis* (Fest., p. 76, 1), and Ovid (*F*, 2, 429–46) explains the Lupercalia on the strength of an oracle of the *Juno sub Esquilio*, reputed to have said to Romans who were worried about their population numbers: 'Let the sacred he-goat penetrate the matrons of Italy!' In AD 494, Pope Gelasius I christianised the Lupercalia to celebrate the purification of the Virgin.

The *Quirinalia* of 17 February are identified with the 'Festival of the Mad', when people who did not know to which curia they belonged to celebrate Fornax finally had to face up to their obligations by means of an expiatory sacrifice (Ov., *F*, 2, 513 ff.). In Quirinus, the god of the curiae was honoured.

After the family solemn occasion of the *Caristia*, the *Terminalia* chiefly concerned Terminus, the god of boundaries in the countryside. His idol was 'sprinkled with the blood of a sacrificed lamb; but he does not complain if offered a suckling pig' (ibid., 655 f.) or a 'kid snatched from the wolf' (Hor., *Epo.*, 2, 60). Terminus was also another aspect of Jupiter, who had had to agree to cohabit with the god of boundaries in a temple whose roof had a hole in it, as sacrifices could be made to him only in the open air (Serv., *Aen.*, 9, 446), which was true for the majority of public cults. On the edge of the ancient *ager Romanus*, at the sixth 'milestone' on the Laurentine Way, the god Terminus was offered the heart, liver, lungs and spleen of a lamb (Ov., *F*, 2, 681).

At the end of this lengthy bimestrial 'welding' of the last and first month of Romulus, there occurred the very curious ferial day of 24 February, called the *Regifugium*, which was exceptional in that it fell on an even day – like the *Equirria* in March – and all in all ritualised the final departure from the past year. We do not not know its details, only that after an (expiatory?) sacrifice at the Comitium, the king of sacrifices simulated a flight to the Forum (Plut., *QR*, 63) and the Salians took part in the ceremony. The 24 February was the first of the five intercalary days corresponding to the lull of an interregnum. The king stepped aside and, while awaiting 1 March, this vacancy seemed to sanctify the chaos following a time gone by. The Ancients thus linked the *Regifugium* with the expulsion of Tarquin the Proud and the abolition of royalty, in keeping with their historicising reinterpretation of the *religiones*.

On 27 February, chariot races (*Equirria*) enlivened the Campus Martius in homage to its god, the father of Romulus who instituted them; but this month was also marked by the purifications prior to the agricultural and military year. After the *Feralia* mentioned earlier there reigned (says Ovid, F, 2, 33) 'a time of purity, when the dead in their tombs had been pacified'.

March opened the war season as well as that of plant renewal and procreation. In this first month of the Romulan calendar, a new fire was lit in Vesta's hearth; the withered laurel was replaced and fresh branches fixed before the *Regia*, the former Curia and the house of the flamines. Significantly, too, the first day of the month was devoted to Mars and Juno Lucina, whose cult Ovid (F, 3, 205 ff.) links with the story of the Sabines separating the combatants of the war provoked by their abduction. The *Matronalia* were celebrated at that time. All soldiers have a mother, and the poet compares the service of the matrons to a *militia* (ibid., 244).

At this time also the Salians carried the shields of Mars in their triple-time dance (*tripudium*), hymning Mamurius who made twelve copies of the shield that fell from the skies. Their procession included places to lay down their shields, and lavish banquets. We find them again at the 'Quinquatria' (19) for the purification of those same shields, before the priests and the *tribuni celerum*. Two days earlier (17), however, boys donned the 'manly toga' which turned them into citizens fit for military service. During these *Liberalia*, old women sold their honey cakes, grilled over stoves, for Liber Pater was the god of sacred cakes (*liba*) and libations (*libamina*). But chiefly he looked after the seed of human generation. On the same day, the *rex sacrificulus* sacrificed to Mars (*agonium Martiale*).

After thanksgiving to Vesta on 6 March and 'placing incense on her Iliac hearth' (Ov., F, 3, 418), the anniversary of Vejovis was celebrated on the nones in his Capitoline temple. Once again, on 14, Mars was offered horse races (*Equirria*), but the next day (15) Jupiter had to share the ides with Anna Perenna, who deified the intifinitely renewable year, in popular rejoicings near the banks of the Tiber. People made huts of foliage or set up tents by hanging their togas on reed stalks; they ate and drank on the grass, wishing one another as many years as goblets could be drained. There was singing, and dancing, and everyone performed his own 'party piece' with appropriate gestures; the young maidens sang saucy ditties. They all staggered home in the evening and, as at today's Roman New Year's Eve, the roisterers were showered with congratulations (ibid., 523–42).

On 16 and 17 March, with her hair in disarray (thus as a sign of mourning), the flaminica of Jupiter took part in the procession of the Argei, from one temporary altar to the next: twenty-seven chapels housing the sacred model figures which would be thrown into the Tiber two months later. The number twenty-seven recurs often enough in Roman worship to rule out the hypothesis of thirty original altars matching the thirty curiae, but with three units severed after the Servian reorganisation of the *Urbs* into four tribes.

The Quinquatria (so named because they coincided with the fifth day after the ides) concerned not only the Salians; it was the anniversary of the temple of Minerva on the Aventine. But *Minerva Medica* (on the Esquiline) was associated with it to celebrate arts and trades, including professions connected with health: four days of sacrifices and competitions, mainly gladiatorial, for 'the warrior goddess likes unsheathed swords' (Ov., F, 3, 814). Spinners and weavers, fullers and dyers, shoemakers, carpenters, painters and sculptors, schoolmasters too (who then received the bonus title of *minerval*, before giving their students a few days' holiday) thoroughly enjoyed themselves. At that time, too, women created a masterpiece in homage to the divine patroness of the textile industry, whose activities are celebrated on the frieze in Nerva's forum.

On 23 March, there was the purification of the trumpets (*tubilustrium*) in the atrium 'of the shoemakers' (Fest., p. 480, 25 ff.; Varr., *LL*, 6, 14). These were the trumpets sounded on certain ceremonial occasions, and had probably originally had an apotropaic intent. But Lydus (*Mens.*, 4, 60) bears witness that they were associated with the shields of Mars, which would refer us to the war trumpet. A ewe was sacrificed at this time to the 'Strength of Mars' (*Nerio Martis*), which Ovid (F, 3, 850) calls *fortis dea*.

The month came to a close on the Aventine with the *natalis* of the temple of the Moon, dedicated in the past by the king Servius Tullius. Lucina was identified with Diana, and the moon was deemed to favour childbirth. In this regard, the end of March rejoined its beginning. But on the whole, this month was male dominated, with corresponding and complementary female connotations.

No less evident was feminine pre-eminence in the following month. Indeed, April was devoted to Venus and Ovid at once invokes this goddess in the fourth book of the *Fasti*. *Aprilis* may even have emerged from the Etruscan *Aphru*, which transcribes the Greek name Aphrodite. At all events, the first day of the month concerned women, who honoured Venus at the same time as 'Virile' Fortune. In 114 BC, a young girl on horseback was struck by lightning, which stripped her bare and tore out her tongue (a prodigy connected with the fornication of three Vestals), and this prompted the building of a temple to Venus 'who changes hearts' (*Verticordia*), who already had an official idol. On 1 April, therefore, both matrons and courtesans bathed the goddess, not before they had removed her 'gold necklace and rich jewellery' (Ov., *F*, 4, 135 f.). After this ritual toilette, her finery was restored and roses offered to her.

The women also bathed, crowned with myrtle wreaths: this was a plant consecrated to the goddess of love, and thought to have cathartic rather than strictly aphrodisiac powers. But, according to Lydus (*Mens.*, 4, 65) and the Praenestine Fasti (*CIL*, 1^2, p. 314), it was more precisely the women of the ordinary populace who took a dip in homage to Virile Fortune in the men's baths, which perhaps aimed at promoting sexual union. By means of the incense offered to this 'Luck', the goddess concealed from men the defects of the naked bodies in the bath . . . (Ov., *F*, 4, 147 ff.). Women were recommended a mixture of poppies crushed in milk with honey:

> As soon as she had been brought to her ardent husband, Venus drank some and then she became his wife. (ibid., 153 f.)

Fortuna reappeared on 5 April for the festival of her temple on the Quirinal, but then it was a matter of 'Public Fortune'. We find Venus again on 23, the very day when, for the *Vinalia priora*, the wine made the year before was tasted, with libations to Jupiter. Wine was associated with love. Aeneas, the son of Venus, had once offered the vineyards of Latium to the sovereign of the gods in order to conquer the impious Mezentius (Ov., *F*, 4, 894). Wine which was a *venenum* was not unknown to Venus's powers. On 23 April, honour was paid also to the goddess of love who had temple prostitutes on Mount Eryx, and whose grace and favour had been won by dedicating a temple to her on the Capitol, then another at the Colline Gate:

> Celebrate, courtesans, the powers of Venus: Venus enriches those who promise much (. . .) Offering her incense, ask her for beauty and the favour of the people! Ask her for seductiveness and the art of pleasing words! With her myrtle, give your patroness the mint that pleases her, garlands of rushes with roses entwined. (ibid., 865 ff.)

Other goddesses had their place in April, starting (from 4 to 10) with the Anatolian Great Mother, whom I will mention again, and whose arrival in the *Urbs* in 204 BC was said to have brought immediate benefit to the harvests. But Ceres and Earth were chiefly honoured, with Pales. From 12 to 19, Ceres's games (*Cerialia*) were celebrated with chariot races in the Circus Maximus. To the goddess who made cereal crops germinate and grow, wheat and crackling salt were offered, and 'a few grains of incense on ancient hearths' (ibid., 409 f.). If no incense was available, resinous torches were burnt. The sacrifice was not the ox which ploughed the fields but the 'lazy sow' (ibid., 414). Before the end of the *ludi Cereris*, an in-calf cow was sacrificed in each of the thirty curiae to *Tellus* (Earth) on 15 April (*Fordicidia*). When the slaughterers 'had snatched the calves from their mother's belly' (ibid., 637) and given the victims' chopped entrails to the fire of the altars, the Great Vestal burned the foetuses, whose ashes would become an ingredient in the fumigations of 21 April.

On the last day (19) of the *Cerialia*, foxes were released in the Circus Maximus, with lighted firebrands on their backs: was this a sacrificial hunt or purification? The magic of fertilising fire? At all events, the rite was concerned with the fate of future harvests.

Robigo (Rust) must also be prevented from spoiling the crops. For the *Robigalia* of 25 April, the flamen of Quirinus went to the goddess's sacred wood to offer her a ewe and a dog, before committing their entrails to the flames (Ov., F, 4, 905 ff.). Why a dog, preferably unweaned (Col., 10, 343)? Because of the Dog-star? In fact, Festus tells us (p. 358, 27–30), under the name of *sacrificium canarium*, reddish-coated dogs were sacrificed *saevitiae causa sideris Caniculae*: unless because their colour was rusty . . .?

Besides the *Palialia* celebrated in rural areas, Rome itself had its rites. On 21 April the people went to the 'altar of the Virgin' (Vesta) to purify themselves with the ashes of the calves burnt on 15 at the *Fordicidia*. They were mixed with the blood of a horse (not the *October equus*) and the 'empty straw of hard beans' (Ov., F, 4, 734).

The *Floralia*, which began on 28 April, overlapped into the next month. Becoming annual in 173 BC, the festival gathered additional days, up to 3 May. Instituted for the dedication of a temple to Flora (in 240 or 238 BC), it was the occasion for theatre shows and, on the final day, hunts in the Circus Maximus – to the cost of 'inoffensive kids and timid hares' (Ov., F, 5, 372) – with the probable intent of promoting the fertility of fields and gardens. This 'mother of flowers', as Ovid calls her (ibid., 183), had her flamen, and one of the twelve altars of T. Tatius was consecrated to her. But she was also the divine patroness of prostitutes, and the *Floralia* chiefly legitimised certain excesses. There was joyful feasting beneath the flowers, everyone trying to outdo the rest in drinking and dancing by the light of nocturnal torches. People also wore many-coloured clothing; but for the actresses in the mime shows, strip-tease on the festive boards was obligatory.

On the whole, April ritualised femininity, but with somewhat plebeian connotations (Ceres, Flora, the Erycine Venus and probably Virile Fortuna as well).

The next two months were just as contrasting as March and April, in certain respects, but on a different plane. May was the month of Maia (or Maius) who deified growth or rather, according to Ovid (F, 5, 73), the month of the *maiores*, whereas June was that of the *juniores* or *juvenes* (ibid., 6, 88). In concrete terms, things were not so simple, for the classification of the liturgical calendar bears the stamp of history, at the same time preserving evidence of older happenings.

The proof that May was the month of the *maiores* ('ancients' or 'old') lies in the fact that on the first day the Lares were honoured for the anniversary of their altar in their role of *Praestites*, 'protectors' of the city. These were the ancestors who watched over Rome. On 9, 11 and 13 May, as we have seen, the *paterfamilias* propitiated the Lemuria, spirits of the dead who were tutelary yet at the same time menacing. On the 15, the ides, pontiffs, Vestals, praetors 'and citizens with the right to attend ceremonies' (DH, *AR*, 1, 38) went to the Sublician Bridge, the oldest (wooden) bridge linking the forum Boarium with the Trastevere. The figures, or 'Argei', stored in the twenty-seven chapels visited by Jupiter's flamen on 16 and 17 March, were taken there and thrown into the Tiber. Did these wicker figures 'fashioned in human semblance' (ibid.) represent sacrificed old men, *maiores* in the proper sense of the word? They are acknowledged as substitutes for human victims, offered in atonement to the dead, like the dolls given to Mania and the Lares of the crossroads, so that the living might be spared. But the idea that once upon a time sexagenarians, or *depontani* (Fest., p. 66, 5) had been hurled from the bridge into the water obviously affronted Ovid (F, 5, 623 ff.).

The dead were linked with the earth, and on 1 May Maia was honoured, connected by the antiquarian Cornelius Labeo with *Tellus* and at the same time with the 'Good Goddess' (Macr., S, 1, 12, 20–1). In any case, the foundation of the temple of Bona Dea was commemorated on 1 May, with a prayer to her to protect Rome from earthquakes. A Vestal virgin had dedicated the sanctuary to her 'at the foot of the rock' (the Aventine); hence the nickname *Subsaxana* given to the goddess, who had a matronal cult of her own. On this day, the sacrifice to Maia was the responsibility of the flamen of Vulcan, to whom certain evidence implies a close connection with the goddess. We find Vulcan again on 23 May for a new purification of trumpets (*tubilustrium*), for the blacksmith god was their maker (Ov., F, 5, 726).

From 7 to 14 May, the Vestals ritually prepared the *mola salsa*.

On 15 May, Maia was associated with Mercury, on the day when traders celebrated the anniversary of the temple consecrated in 495 BC near the Circus Maximus to the god of business affairs. People prayed to him to let the make as much profit as possible, and it cannot be ruled out that this union of Mercury and Maia may be implicated not only in a deity of growth (*maior*) but also the land of the *maiores*, 'profound fathers' who, in the imagination of the ancients, made up the kingdom of a Pluto, frequently identified with *Plutos* ('Wealth'). Not far from the temple, near the Porta Capena, the devout *mercator*, having purified himself, went to get water from a 'Mercury's spring', using a pitcher that had been duly subjected to fumigation. He dipped a laurel branch into it and sprinkled both his goods and himself with the water, saying: 'Wash away my past broken promises, wash away yesterday's lies . . .' And Mercury would smile, as if in complicity, for he had once stolen Apollo's oxen.

We know nothing of a sacrifice offered on the 23 by the *rex* to Vejovis in his temple erected near the *Tabularium* (in Rome's town hall nowadays), or of the ceremonies that on the 29 marked the anniversary of the 'Public Fortune of the Roman people', consecrated like *Primigenia* – therefore imported from Praeneste – on the Quirinal, where the goddess had other temples.

Thanks to the written archives of the Arval Fraternity, we know more about the annual liturgy that they celebrated in Rome and in the sacred wood of La Magliana (9 kilometres from the city on the Via Campana). This was a movable feast, coinciding alternately with 17, 19–20 May and 27, 29–30 of the same month, save in exceptional instances. First and foremost, it honoured Dea Dia, but also the god Mars, the Lares and the 'Mother' (*Mater Larum*), and the *Semones* who watched over the life of seeds in the ground, where Dea Dia acted in concert with the heat and light of the sky (*Dius-Dia*). The Arvals, therefore, mobilised divine forces for the success of crops in the fields (*arva*).

On the first day, in Rome, at the house of the president of the brotherhood, wine and incense were first sacrificed before 'sampling' (for non-sacred consumption) green and dry ears of wheat, as well as loaves decorated with laurels. The idol was anointed with scented oil. Then, after a meal offered to Dea Dia, those present bathed and changed into white garments before going to table. Between the two courses, as was done in the family circle, after a new consecration of wine and incense, they sampled the first offerings which four choirboys would then place on the goddess's altar. Next they perfumed themselves, crowned themselves with roses and ate desserts.

The second day, all went to the sanctuary on the Via Campana. In front of a sacred wood (*lucus*), the president sacrificed two young sows known as 'piacular' (to expiate the pruning of trees with a knife), then a cow described as 'honorary' (thus purely in homage). If the examination of the entrails proved satisfactory, they were burned: those of the sows on the altar, those of the cow on a brazier covered with turf. After drawing up a record of the ceremony, part of the meat of the two sows was eaten. Then, wearing veils, crowned with wheat-ears tied with a white ribbon, the Arvals went to the temple where, with a flamen, they sacrificed a white ewe-lamb, and made offerings of gruel with earthenware jars (out of loyalty to the ancient tradition). But they subsequently threw them on to the slope leading up to the sanctuary, to honour the Mother of the Lares. They then sat down and shared out the fine wheaten-flour loaves decorated with laurels. Going back to the altar before the sacred wood, the president and the flamen sent two Brothers to fetch green ears of wheat which were passed from hand to hand, from right to left. Incense and honey-sweetened wine were offered. All then returned to the temple, and its doors were closed. From little books they took the text of the *carmen* which they would soon sing as they descended the slope from the sanctuary, performing a dance in triple time. This Arvalian chant, which was no longer understood, needed to be reread and memorised. In it was invoked the assistance of the Lares, Mars (called *Marmar* or *Marmor*) and of the *Semones*. Perfume was then applied to Dea Dia and the Mother of the Lares, before they were offered circlets and lighted candles. A banquet assembled the Brothers in a 'tetrastyle' (room with four columns), to which urns of must were brought in procession. The day ended with chariot races and circus acts in an area laid out for this purpose. The Arvals came back to Rome to dine at the president's.

The third day was marked by a banquet comparable with that of the first day; but after the feast torches were lit, and their light was probably related to that of the sky which ripens harvests and which Dia deified. The Arvals took home sweetmeats (*bellaria*), but also green ears of wheat in the 'Tuscan' vessel (in terracotta or bronze, of Etruscan tradition).

We see that, as it began with homage to Maia and the Lares, every second year May ended with this liturgy combining Dea Dia with the *Mater Larum*: it was the month of the ripening of cereal crops, in which ancestors played a mysterious part.

'June is the month of young people (*juvenes*)' (Ov., F, 6, 88). It sanctified the prime of life, as Juno deified the adulthood of girls. The goddess was honoured on 1 June: it was her month, as Ovid reminds us (ibid., 56), having her open canto VI of his *Fasti*. In 396 BC, some *juvenes* had been given the mission of transporting Juno Regina from Veii to Rome (Liv., 5, 22, 4). On the calends of June, the anniversary of Juno *Moneta* was celebrated, the 'warning goddess' who, thanks to her sacred geese, had saved the Capitol from the besieging Gauls (390 BC). Her nickname had been given to the 'money' being minted in the neighbouring workshop. Sta Maria in Aracoeli replaced her at the summit of the ancient citadel (*arx*).

The *juvenes* made war. On 1 June, therefore, Mars too was celebrated in his temple, dating from 388 BC and situated outside the walls near the Porta Capena on the Appian Way. The 'armed youth' of the contingent, *armati juvenes* (Liv., 7, 23, 3) gathered there on this occasion, before leaving on campaign. These calends also coincided with the anniversary of the temple dedicated to the Tempests in 259 BC (in the same district) by the conqueror of the Corsicans at Aleria, Lucius Cornelius Scipio, son of the Barbatus whose sarcophagus is preserved in the Vatican Museum.

On 3 June was the festival of the temple of Bellona on the Campus Martius; before its facade rose the column from which war was declared. On the penultimate day of the month homage was rendered to Quirinus, god of the 'gatherings of men' (*co-virio*) in his temple on the Quirinal, which was among the most ancient in Rome (Plin., *NH*, 15, 120) and was restored by Augustus in 16 BC. The ides were devoted to Jupiter the 'Invincible' for the *natalis* of a temple about which we know nothing. To Jupiter known as *Stator* (for having halted the flight of the Romans before the Sabines), Romulus had vowed a temple at the foot of the Palatine, and this was celebrated on 27.

Ritualising the vigour of armed youth, life forces were honoured in this month with Carna and Fortuna. On the calends, the first was celebrated by offering her a stew of beans: whence the expression *Kalendae fabariae*, 'because in this month the ripe beans (*adultae*) are used in the cult' (Macr., S, 1, 12, 33). We have seen that in the May *Lemuria* beans represented human lives and that Carna presided over the organs of life . . . On the day of the *Matralia* (11 June), when matrons rendered homage to Mater Matuta, there were also celebrations at the temple of Fortuna, which was the twin of hers on the forum Holitorium; the *Fortuna Virginalis* to whom girls consecrated their childhood clothes on their wedding eve. *Fortuna's* name itself contains the very idea of 'carrying' (*ferre*): pregnancy and fertility promised by the transition to adulthood. The 24 June solemnised the chapels of *Fors Fortuna*, one consecrated by Servius Tullius, the other in 293 BC by Carvilius Maximus on the right bank of the Tiber, respectively at the first and sixth 'milestone' of the *Via Portuensis*. On this day, people went down the course of the Tiber in boats adorned with flowers (*Tiberina decensio*: Cic., *Fin.*, 5, 70), offering one another many libations (Ov., F, 6, 775–80). The goddess was also important to market gardeners:

When the ripe ears turn the crop to gold (. . .) add the garlic to the onions (. . .) and when you have sold all, sing and sing again the praises of Fors Fortuna. (Col., 10, 311 ff.)

Finally, June was a month of great importance to Vesta. From 7 to 15, the secret room of her temple was open to matrons who went there barefoot to pray to the goddess. The *Vestalia* of 9 June involved millers and bakers who, on that day, gave a holiday to the donkeys that were condemned to keeping the mills turning. They were garlanded with flowers, together with their machines for grinding the grain. The garlands hung round their necks were laden with bread rolls, for Vesta was the goddess of the fire that baked them. On 15 June, her temple was thoroughly cleaned and the sweepings (ashes and various kinds of residue) were piled in a blind alley about half way up the incline ascending the Capitol (Fest., p. 466, 33 f.), perhaps before they were cast into the river:

> It is on this day, O Tiber, that by thy Etruscan waters thou carriest to the sea the filth from Vesta's temple. (Ov., *F*, 6, 713 f.)

How was Hercules 'the Guardian' (*Custos*) celebrated on 4 June near the circus of Flaminius? Ovid (*F*, 6, 209 f.) leaves us unsatisfied on this point. On 7 June, the Tiber fishermen had a high old time 'on the sward of the Campus Martius' (ibid., 237), with competitions about which we know nothing. The following day was the anniversary of Mens ('Intelligence') in her temple on the Capitol, pledged 'when thy war, perfidious Carthaginian caused a reign of terror' (ibid., 242), in 217 BC. Another corporate festivity gathered together flute-players for the ides of the 'Little Quinquatria'; they wandered the streets, drunk and masked (Cens., 12, 2), even disguised as women (Plut., *QR*, 55). As a finale, they met in front of the temple of Minerva (Varr., *LL*, 6, 17), to whom Ovid (*F*, 6, 696) ascribes the invention of their instruments. Six days later (19), the goddess was celebrated in her temple on the Aventine. As for Summanus, god of nocturnal lightning, the anniversary of his sanctuary near the Circus Maximus was celebrated the next day (20); it had been erected at the time (278 BC) when Pyrrhus had been the terror of the Romans (ibid., 732).

The month closed with the *natalis* of the temple of Hercules 'Musagetes' (for the hero of physical strength figured there as a lyre-player, in the company of the daughters of Memory). M. Fulvius Nobilior, the conqueror of the Aetolians and friend of the poet Ennius, had inaugurated it in 187 BC, on the last day of a month consecrated to Juno, the enemy of the grandson of Alcaeus.

The six months of the second half of the year bore numerical names in keeping with the Romulan calendar, and we have kept them, with the exception of *Quintilis*, which became *Julius* (July) and *sextilis*, which became *Augustus* (August).

With Juno, on the calends, the Felicity of the Capitol opened the first lunar month of the semester of summer and autumn. The *Regifugium* of 24 February seems to have been matched by the *Poplifugia* of 5 July, a holy day of Jupiter which perhaps also made sacred a time of interregnum, for it has been related to the 'scattering of the people' that followed the disappearance of Romulus (DH, *AR*, 2, 56). This explanation gives a clearer sense to the festival than the story of a rout of the Romans confronted with the people of Fidena and Ficulea, after the departure of the Gauls (Varr., *LL*, 6, 18). People readily connected it with the Caprotine Nones of 7 July (Plut., *Rom.*, 29, 2; Macr., *S*, 3, 2, 14). Between the two ferial days, the one on 6 July that marked the anniversary of the temple of *Fortuna Muliebris* was again important to women, who by their supplications had obtained the withdrawal of Coriolanus in 488 BC, when he was threatening Rome at the head of the Volsci.

On the nones the priests sacrificed to Consus on his underground altar in the Circus Maximus (Tert., *Spect.*, 5, 7). He sanctified the ensilage of the corn after the June harvests. The *vitulatio* of 8 July was a sacrifice which the Romans apparently made to a goddess called *Vitula* for the victory over the Etruscans following the *Poplifugia* (Macr., *S*, 3, 2, 11 and 14). This was again a pontifical office. Some saw her as a goddess ensuring life (*vita*), because the fruits of the earth were consecrated to her. But Macrobius (ibid., 15) refers us to the heifer (*vitula*) whose sacrifice *pro frugibus* is mentioned by Virgil (B, 3, 77).

Instituted in 212 BC after consulting the oracles of Marcius and the Sibyl, the Apollinarian Games at first took place on only one day (13 July), then three, and finally lasted from the 6 (if not the 5, in the calendar of Philocalus) to 13. With circlets on their heads, the populace attended. Matrons said prayers and, 'everywhere, with open doors, people feasted at the entrance to their houses' (Liv., 25, 12, 15). Theatrical entertainments were soon added to the chariot races in the Circus Maximus and, in Pompey's time, a wild animal hunt.

The day of the ides (15) was a festival for the knights (*Transvectio equitum*): crowned with olive wreaths and wearing the red ceremonial toga, they paraded on their white horses from the Porta Capena (the home of Mars) to the Capitol (the home of Jupiter), passing before the temple of the Dioscuri whom they honoured with a solemn sacrifice. Some of them were Luperci, as a funerary cippus in the Vatican reminds us.

Ferial days such as the *Lucaria* of 19 and 21 July, or the *Neptunalia* and the *Furrinalia* on 23 and 25 (two series of consecutive uneven days) were connected to the seasonal cycle. The *Lucaria* ritualised the work of the ground-clearing, 'letting the light' into woods and thickets, either by uprooting shrubs or cutting them down at the root to be burnt: the duplication of 19 and 21 July might well represent the two techniques. But in both instances, no assault was made on the *lucus* without showing infinite consideration towards the powers that dwelt there, woodland spirits, nymphs of the forests and glades related to Leucaria and Rhea Silvia, the mother of the founding twins. The management of water was a matter of urgency in this torrid month, and was dependent on Neptune and Furrina, who had her flamen. The first was responsible for protecting surface drainage or irrigation works, the second for drilling operations and wells. On the 25, the *Furrinalia* (Varr., *LL*, 6, 19) took place in a sacred wood where C. Gracchus had killed himself in 123 BC.

The start of the summer thus reinforced the events of spring: confirmation of the matrons (Caprotine Nones, *Fortuna Muliebris*) and the military *juventus* (*Transvectio equitum*), preservation of the crops (Consus, *vitulatio*), safeguarding the balance necessary for survival (water and plant life).

The same agricultural concerns resurfaced in August, alongside commemorations that were apparently diverse but not completely unrelated to the season, especially that of Vertumnus in his temple on the Aventine on 13 August: an Etruscan god of fruitfulness, for whom 'the first grape turns blue on its bunch, and the ear of corn swells with a milky juice' (Prop., 4, 2, 13 f.). Flora also was celebrated on this day in her temple at the Circus Maximus. To the *Portunalia* celebrated on 17, the calendar of Philocalus gives the name *Tiberinalia*, doubtless because there Portunus was worshipped, the god of gates and ports, whose temple (preserved owing to its Christianisation as the church of St Mary the Egyptian) neighboured on the river port (Varr., *LL*, 6, 19). His flamen *Portunalis* officiated there with due solemnity for the boatmen and traders of the district.

But on 9 August, the fierce heat of summer called for prayers and a sacrifice to the star that inflicted it. He was honoured under the name *Indiges* (the 'Ancestor' or 'National' god) in a temple on the Quirinal which is not otherwise know. His burning heat ripened the grapes, and on 19 August – the day of the dedication of two temples to Venus, one near the Circus Maximus, and the other in the sacred wood of Libitina (goddess of death or of the *libido*?) – Jupiter's flamen proceeded with the *auspicatio* of the grape harvests, gathering the first bunch during the sacrifice of a ewe lamb, between the cutting up and presentation of the entrails of the victim (Varr., *LL*, 6, 16), thereby sanctifying the grapes offered to the god of the sky. This was the rite of the *Vinalia rustica*. Long ago in France, on 6 August, the new season's grapes were consecrated, and a priest would squeeze the fruit so that the juice ran into the chalice for mass: a rite that was condemned by the third Council of Braga in 675.

On 21 August, the Vestals and the flamen of Quirinus took part in the festivals of Consus in the Circus Maximus, where the god enjoyed a typically 'cereal' environment, with Seia, Segeta (Segestia), Messia, goddesses of seedtime and crops, as well as Tutulina who watched over their preservation. Consus was patron of the garnering of crops, and Ops was the goddess of fertility and plenty, her day being celebrated four days later (25) at the *Opiconsivia*. As *Consiva*, this goddess of resources had in the *Regia* 'a place of worship so holy that no one entered, except Vestals and the public priest' (the Pontifex Maximus), who on this occasion wore the virgins' veil, *suffibulum* (Varr., *LL*, 6, 21).

Another kind of fire could destroy and was to be feared: Vulcan who, in dry periods, threatened to burn the harvest produce. His power had to be warded off through the *Volcanalia*, between the *Consualia* of 21 and the *Opiconsivia* of 25 (therefore on 23 August, exactly one month after the *Neptunalia*). A written fragment from the Arval Records stipulates this day for sacrificing, not only to Vulcan, but also to the Nymphs, Juturna and Ops *Opifera*. The deities of water, so necessary in case of a blaze, were thus propitiated at the same time. But the *Volcanalia* were chiefly singled out by a substitution rite. On 23 August, small live fish were thrown on to the fire *pro se* ('to redeem oneself' or 'for one's well-being') wrote Varro (*LL*, 6, 20), 'in place of human souls' says Festus more precisely (p. 276, 3), connecting the rite with the *ludi piscatori* in June. They could be bought on the *area Volcani* (at the foot of the Capitol) where perhaps the sacrifice itself took place. In this way people contented the god of fire so that they did not have to suffer from its effects.

On 24 August, *mundus patet*: a vaulted subterranean cavity was opened up, allowing the world of the dead to communicate with that of the living. This rite was repeated on 5 October and 8 November. 'It was, so to speak, the gateway of the fateful and infernal gods that was opened. That was why religion banned not only engaging in combat, but raising troops, making them set out, weighing anchor, or marrying to have children' (Varr., after Macr., *S*, 1, 16, 18). Nor was there any question, on that day, of assembling the comitia or attending to any public activity (Fest., p. 146, 1).

We return to climatic concerns with the *Volturnalia* of 27 August. Volturnus was a devastating wind, 'whirling around on the heights' (Lucr., 5, 745), which had raised clouds of dust against the Romans at the battle of Cannae (Liv., 22, 43, 10), and which seared the grapes (Col., 5, 5, 15). It was hoped to turn its ravages aside by means of a solemnity in which the 'Volturnal' flamen took part.

After the inherent anxieties in the *religiones* of a testing month, September was a corresponding time of relaxation. Its calends were consecrated, rightly and properly, to Juno, but in this instance to the *Regina* whom Camillus and his *juvenes* had brought from Veii. Like other foreign deities, this Etruscan *Uni* was installed on the Aventine (near to the present-day Sta Sabina), as well as a Jupiter of Osco-Umbrian origin whose anniversary was celebrated on the same day, 1 September: a Jupiter *Liber* or *Libertas*, god of liberty and not of wine (like the one of the *Vinalia*), thus unconnected to Liber Pater.

Above all, from 4 to 9 September, the populace enjoyed the entertainment of the Roman Games (*ludi Romani* or *Magni*) that were said to date back to Tarquin the Elder. At first held by way of an extraordinary votive offering, and lasting one day only, they did not become an annual event until the fourth century BC, and lasted up to two weeks in Cicero's time, even as much as sixteen days in homage to Caesar after his death. These games may have been the origin of the anecdote of the master who had his slave beaten on the circus track before the competitions (Cic., *Div.*, 1, 55; Liv., 2, 36; Val. Max., 1, 7, 4; Macr., *S*, 1, 11, 3–6). As this 'prelude' had displeased Jupiter, whom these games specially honoured, they were recommenced, and other religious pretexts were used to justify their extension. The festival began with a grandiose procession from the Capitol, where the dedicatee was invoked, to the Circus Maximus, via the Forum and Velabrium: a parade of cavalry and infantry, two-horse and four-horse chariots, athletes, dancers armed and ranged in age groups, flute- and cithara-players, burlesque bands clad in goatskins or rainbow-coloured cloaks (like the Silenuses and Satyrs of the Dionysiac *Pompè*), followed by urns in which incense was burnt and the gold or silver vessels brought out from the temples for the occasion (DH, *AR*, 7, 72). Gods who had statues came last, borne on litters like those which, in pious rural Italy, are still used today to carry the figures of saints. A sacrifice preceded the games, which consisted of horse races, individual or harnessed, and gymnastic competitions, followed by theatrical shows to round off the event.

On 13 September, the septemviri epulones offered a banquet to the Capitoline triad, while the Vestals prepared the *mola salsa* for the third time in the year. A fair followed the *ludi Romani* from 20 to 23, the anniversary day of several notable temples (of Mars, Neptune and Apollo on the *Campus*).

October mainly ritualised the end of the military year. To open the month, there was the festival of the 'Sister's Beam' (*Tigillum Sororium*) already mentioned in the section on gentilitial cults. Juno made the calends sacred, but in her role of *Sororia*, with Janus – the god of 'beginnings' – as *Curiatius*. The ceremony could have been deemed to release soldiers from their warlike passion, in order to turn them again into Quirites, members of the curiae. Also on 1 October, *Fides* 'Good Faith' was honoured. Numa had decreed:

> The flamens will go to his temple in a closed carriage drawn by two horses, and will cover their hands to the fingertips to celebrate the divine service (Liv., 1, 21, 4).

A 'fast of Ceres', decreed in 191 BC following prodigies, after consulting the Sibylline Books, was supposed to be repeated every five years (Liv., 36, 37, 4), but annually on 4 October in the time of Augustus, in the era and under the probable influence of the Athenian Thesmophoria, on the eve of a day when once again the *mundus* opened, sometimes known as that 'of Ceres' (Fest., p. 126, 4).

At that time, too, on the completion of the grape harvest people indulged in the fruity beverage of a must 'treated' with old wine (*Meditrinalia*), on 11 October. After the wine came the water, for on the next day but one, the 13, wells were adorned with wreaths, and springs with flowers, for the *Fonta* – or *Fontinalia*. On this day a god Fontus or Fons was celebrated (Varr., *LL*, 6, 22), 'the son-in-law of Volturnus, husband of Juturna' (Arn., 3, 29).

If the calends probably marked the return of the soldier to the civilian fold, the ides satisfied the god Mars with the 'October Horse'. This involved the right-hand courser harnessed to the winning chariot in a competition held on the Campus Martius: the poor beast was sacrificed to the god of war. The victim's head was adorned with loaves to thank Mars for having protected the harvests. When it had been cut off, the head was the stake in a tussle between the people of Subura and the Sacred Way. According to the outcome of the battle, it was hung either on the *Mamilia* tower (at the foot of the Esquiline), or on the wall of the *Regia*. The animal's tail was also severed and immediately taken to the *Regia*, so that the blood could still drip on to the altar fire. It was formerly believed that the residual blood was used in mixing the fumigations prepared by the Vestals, but there is no evidence of this. It was all as if, before the close of the war season, people were intent through this ritual on capturing the Martian spirit of victory.

On 19 October, weapons were purified (*armilustrium*) by sacrificing to Mars to the sound of trumpets (Fest., p. 17, 28 f.) on the Aventine, where tradition had it that Titus Tatius had been buried (Plut., *Rom.*, 23, 3). The shields were put away for the entire winter. On this day a Salian commanding an army had to cease operations. 'When the festival arrives, it is customary for the Salians, no matter where they may find themselves, to have to remain there for thirty days' (Pol., 21, 10).

From 26 October until 1 November, and then from 4 to 17, circus and theatre entertainments occupied the leisure time of the Roman populace; first, those that had been instituted by the dictator Sulla for his victory over the Samnite Telesinus in 82 BC, then the Plebeian games given by the aediles of the plebs, their duration, like that of the other *ludi*, having increased since the third century BC. On 13 November, the epulones invited Jupiter to a ritual feast. A three-day fair followed the games, from 18 to 20 November. Opening on 8 November, the *mundus* was concerned with both corn and the dead. After all the hard work on the land and in making war, this month combined a very necessary time of relaxation with a concern to 'ward off religious fears' (Liv., 7, 3, 1) and strengthen the assurance of divine benevolence.

In some respects, the last month of the civil year was the crowning point of all that had been gained from the agricultural season by the use to which it was put, the very means of survival.

On 3 December, at the home of the consul or the urban praetor (provided he went and slept elsewhere) women celebrated with the Vestals a liturgy that was strictly theirs alone, and it is known that in 62 BC the notorious Clodius dressed up as a matron to rendezvous with Caesar's wife in the future dictator's own house. Plutarch (*Caes.*, 9, 6) compares certain rites of this nocturnal festival 'to those of Orphism'; which would imply, in the customary acceptance of the *Orphica*, some aspects of the Dionysiac mysteries, which were similarly reserved for women, at least originally. We know only that a 'sacred snake' (ibid., 5) figured beside the Good Goddess, that vine shoots covered the tabernacles, representations of male animals were veiled (Sen., *Ep.*, 97, 2) and pictures of the generative organ were forbidden, which is not at all in keeping with the Bacchanalia. But the women danced to the sound of harps and flutes. For the antiquarian Cornelius Labeo, Bona Dea was identified with the Earth, Maia, Fauna, Fatua or Ops (Macr., S, 1, 12, 21). The celebration was performed *pro populo* – for the safety and well-being of the Roman people.

The next day but one, 5 December, the *Faunalia* were directed to the brother and husband of Fauna, but mainly affected villagers:

All the cattle frolic on the grassy plain, when the nones of December return for thee. (Hor., O, 3, 18, 9 f.)

Working oxen were given a rest-day, together with the entire hamlet making merry in the meadows, and the peasant enjoyed dancing to a triple time rhythm, trampling the earth that had made him work so hard.

Next, from 11 to 23, a series of ferial days punctuated the best part of the month; in part they matched one another, with a fairly positive social function, but almost always linked with the enjoyment of accumulated possessions.

On 11 December, the *Agonalia* were celebrated in homage to the 'Indiges' Sun (Lyd., *Mens.*, 4, 155) at the same time as the festival of the 'Seven Hills' (*Septimontium*), which consecrated the federation of the inhabitants of the Palatine, Velia, Fagutal, Subura, Germal, Caelius and Oppius (Fest., p. 459, 1–3). A sacrifice was made on each of the seven sites.

Two days later (13) Ceres and Tellus were honoured, perhaps to mark the end of the autumn sowing. Then, on the 15, the *Consualia* were fêted by games in the Circus Maximus, with carts pulled by he-mules in memory of a type of harnessed team supposed to have preceded all the others. Draught animals were given the day off, and crowned with flowers. Principally, however, the December *Consualia* complemented the August *Consualia*, both events linked with Ops, to whom prayers were offered each time four days after Consus. On 15 December, people asked the god who had looked after the harvested grain for the right to take part of it from the barns for sowing and eating. Correspondingly, on 19 December, Ops was entreated to take 'charge of the released grain' (Georges Dumézil) for subsistence or sale in the market; she was therefore invoked *ad Forum*, the business centre (*Inscr. Ital.*, 13, 2, p. 199).

But in the interval, on the 17, the Saturnalia began, when people were freed from the constraints of saving. In front of the temple of Saturn, guardian of the public treasury, as we know, there was unrestrained feasting (*convivio dissoluto*), and people shouted *Io Saturnalia* (Macr., S, 1, 10, 18). Saturn was supposed to be the husband of Ops, the 'Resource' or 'Plenty' which the Roman populace enjoyed thanks to all the hard work of the summer. In the very name of the god, it is thought the adjective *satur*, 'sated', can be recognised; an error, certainly, but etymology endeavours to justify the orgy. It is true that at that time the shortest days of the year (*angusti*) inspired the anguish (*angor*) of the solstice, deified in Angerona. For the *Angeronalia* of 21 December, also known as *Divalia*, the priests sacrificed in the *Curia Acculeia* (?) and the chapel of Volupia, at the north-west corner of the Palatine (Varr., *LL*, 6, 23; Macr., S, 1, 10, 7). The idol of Angerona, so it seems, had its mouth bound and sealed (Sol., 1, 6; Macr., S, 1, 10, 8). She had a place on the altar of Volupia to signify that by concealing one's anxieties one achieved an 'intense sensual pleasure' (ibid.). In fact, it seems that in this way the Romans personified the satisfactions of effort and work that had been accomplished, going as far as the worries inspired by the Sun who had been propitiated as *Indiges* ten days earlier.

Also on 21 December, 'a sacrifice of a pregnant sow, bread and must was offered to Hercules and Ceres' (Macr., S, 3, 11, 10). The next day but one, for the *Larentalia*, the flamen of Quirinus and the priests officiated in memory of Acca Larentia on the Velabrum, on the spot where Ancus Martius was supposed to have buried this courtesan, who had been generous enough to bequeath her wealth to the sons of the She-wolf, but had been confused with the founding twins' nurse.

Riches, voluptuousness, food: December had a decided 'third function' tone, in the sense understood by Georges Dumézil (of fruitfulness, food production and consumption).

– THE FIVE-YEAR CYCLE –

The annual rhythm based on the natural order of things remained the pivot of civic piety; other cycles, at least for the greater part, were a matter of human judgement, notably the 'lustrum' of five years.

Quinquennial, according to the Fasti of Ostia (*Inscr. Ital.*, 13, 13, p. 205), on 25 and 26 June, were the *Taurii* (or *Taurei*) games said to have been instituted by Tarquin the Proud, on the advice of oracles, following an epidemic attributed to the spoiled meat of sacrificed bulls and which afflicted pregnant women (Fest., p. 478, 25 ff.). These games consisted of horse races (Varr., *LL*, 5, 154) in the circus of Flaminius, but could originally have been kinds of 'corridas'. They involved the gods of the underworld (Fest., p. 479, 12). Livy (39, 22, 1) mentions their celebration in 186 BC 'out of religious concern' (*religionis causa*). Their purpose was expiatory, diverting misfortune on to the victims of the sacrifice (Serv. Dan., *Aen.*, 2, 140).

Similarly expiatory was the fast instituted in 191 BC for Ceres because of prodigies, and which had to be observed every five years (Liv., 36, 37, 4). A very special sacrifice was performed at five-yearly intervals 'for the college of pontiffs' (Fest., p. 50, 17 f.). We do not know the type of victim, called *cauiares*, from the name describing a part of the animal 'up to the tail', a portion that would appear to have been consecrated separately.

Was this a rite linked with the quinquennial closing of the census? At all events, the *lustrum conditum*, general and periodic purification of the Roman people at arms, assumed a singular gravity by virtue of its periodicity, even though the lapse of five years was not always strictly respected in the first century BC.

After the delicate operations of the census which socially and fiscally 'put the clock right', the civic community in its army role was assembled on the Campus Martius: horsemen and foot-soldiers organised for five years into 'centuries' (Varr., *LL*, 6, 93), with all their equipment. The censor appointed by lot to be in charge over the five-year period marched at their head, carrying the red standard which was planted on the Capitoline citadel during the days of general mobilisation. Five years earlier, Mars had been promised, if he protected Rome during that cycle, the triple sacrifice or *suovetaurilia*, which was now offered to him in fulfilment of that pledge (Fig. 11). A boar, a ram and a bull were led three times round the citizen-soldiers before being sacrificed. Then the censor pronounced prayers dictated to him by a clerk, asking the gods to improve and increase the Roman state. Scipio Aemilianus, on whom the ceremonial duty fell in 142 BC, was said to have dared to alter the formula by saying:

> Roman affairs are great and prosperous enough, so I pray the gods to ensure their safety in perpetuity. (Val. Max., 4, 1, 10)

This prayer was valid in fact for the five years to come and the extension of divine favour. Lastly, the censor led the army to the city gates, and there the soldiers dismissed.

– THE 'SECULAR' CYCLE –

'The length of the Roman century is uncertain' (Cens., 17, 7). Despite their name, the so-called 'Secular' games did not have a constant periodicity, and the Ancients themselves could not make head or tail of it. If the civil century was 100 years, they also dreamed up a biological 'century' defined by the longest duration of a human life (ibid., 2), and the number of 110 years was officially recognised in the time of Augustus for the spacing of the Secular games, which were supposed to be seen only once in a lifetime (Suet., *Claud.*, 21, 5). The first to be historically attested were in 249 BC (Liv., *Per.*, 49). But the Augustan quindecemvirs had rewritten history to support a computation that justified fixing the games in 17 BC. It seems that centuries of 100 and 110 years had been mingled, perhaps under the influence of an Apollonian tradition specific to the Delian cult. For the chronicle of Eusebius transcribed by St Jerome indicates the celebration of an initial *agon centenarius* in 453 or 454 BC, 300 years after the founding of Rome; and the emperor Claudius brought this strictly secular calculation back into favour by consecrating the eighth centenary of the *Urbs* with the games of AD 47, with the same rites as in 17 BC.

The periodicity therefore varied, and in any case the circumstances of the games' institution had nothing to do with a natural cycle. Like many other *ludi*, they were originally linked with the need to ward off the effects of an epidemic and were mainly concerned with the health (hence the role of the *Valerii*, indissociable from the verb *valere*, in the myth of their founding), the life and survival of the Roman people (hence the importance of the human biological cycle). They were held primarily in honour of the gods of the earth and the dead, with the idea that ancestors contributed from the underworld to perpetuating the family. Their ritual is unknown to us until the time of Augustus.

In May, before the harvests, heralds invited the Romans to gather for a spectacle that they had never seen before and would not see again. Then the quindecemvirs held a session at the Capitol to distribute *suffimenta* to the people: sulphur and pitch which, at the festivals of Pales, were used to cleanse cowsheds and flocks. After which, wheat, barley and beans (*fruges*) were brought to the temples of Palatine Apollo and Aventine Diana, and the populace would offer the first pickings to the gods.

The festival began overnight between 31 May and 1 June. An official sacrifice was made to the Moirai (or Parcae, Fates) at the place known as *Tarentum*, on three altars on which three goats and three ewes respectively were slaughtered. The ceremony was carried out according to the Greek rite, the officiant bareheaded and wearing not a toga but a long, embroidered, short-sleeved tunic (Fig. 12). The *Tarentum* was situated on the area of the present-day Chiesa Nuova, where there had been an altar to Dis Pater, god of the underworld. Torches were lit and 110 matrons – matching the years of the century – offered a meal to Juno and Diana seated at table. Open-air shows were given on a wooden stage, with the spectators remaining standing.

The following day, 1 June, white bulls were sacrificed to Jupiter and a white heifer to Juno, before theatrical representations offered to Apollo. On the night of 1–2 June, sacrifices were made to the Ilithyiae, goddesses of childbirth. On this occasion the offerings were not of blood; three kinds of cake (with cheese, honey and parsley), and nine of each kind, totally burnt. This time the officiant wore a toga and the rite was performed at the *Tarentum*, near the Tiber. The second day honoured especially Juno Capitolina. The emperor led the procession of the 110 matrons to the temple where, before proceeding with the sacrifice of a white heifer, he uttered a prayer, chorused by the matrons (Fig. 13) who implored the goddess to increase the empire and majesty of the Roman people, in both peace and war, and to protect the *Respublica*.

The third night was given over to Mother Earth or Tellus. The emperor went to the *Tarentum* to sacrifice a pregnant black sow, whose flesh was entirely consumed by the fire. The third day (3 June) honoured Apollo and Diana and their mother Latona, and the offerings were cakes of the same kind as those presented during the second night to the Ilithyiae. This office, performed in the temple of the Palatine Apollo, was followed by a procession: a double choir of twenty-seven youths and twenty-seven girls (3 × 3 × 3), who were *patrimi* (all having both mother and father living), intoned the secular hymn before going to the Capitol. We know that of Horace, a prayer to the 'nurturing Sun' and to Ilithyia 'so that a cycle of ten times eleven years may bring back to us the singing and games which gather the people together for three radiant days and as many pleasant nights' (1. 21 ff.), to the Parcae and Tellus, but above all to Phoebus and his sister the Moon: Apollo and Artemis, gods of Delos, where a calculation of 109 years seems to have dominated religious tradition.

Originally, the Secular games had been the answer to the urgency of an epidemic, *urgenti pestilentia* (Val. Max., 2, 4, 5), and the purificatory rites preserved that indication. As early as 433 BC a *pestilentia* had caused a temple to be dedicated to Apollo 'for the health of the people' (Liv., 4, 25, 3). 'This festival helps to cure epidemics, gangrene and illnesses' (Zos., 2, 1, 1). By celebrating it, the Romans were taking out a new 'lease' with the gods.

– RITUALS FOR SPECIAL OCCASIONS –

These could become periodic – like the inauguration of magistrates – but were not written into the calendar or prescribed at more or less regular intervals. They were not all 'extraordinary', in that they often corresponded to a traditional routine, to the *mos maiorum*, or to augural or pontifical law; but the majority were in answer to a fairly unusual sign that the gods were angry, or were imposed on the Romans by a historical situation. Their ritualism, in some respects, incorporated the unforeseeable, thanks to the Sibylline Books in particular.

– CONSULTING THE AUSPICES –

'Among our ancestors, no affair was undertaken, either in public or in private, before taking the auspices' (Val. Max., 2, 1, 1). To be more exact, whatever was undertaken or decided had to have the backing of the gods. To this end, auspices were taken in order to have the assurance of their agreement, by virtue of the signs Jupiter gave in the flight of birds or the flash of his lightning.

Romulus had founded Rome *auspicato* (Cic., *Div.*, 1, 3), after marking out the regions of the sky propitious for observation with his augural staff (*ibid.*, 30). The same would happen in army camps and Roman colonies which perpetuated its institution, like so many projections of the *Urbs* in territory foreign to the *ager Romanus*. The area inaugurated was a *templum*, a consecrated place (*effatum*). Auspices were taken to settle the siting of a temple, before setting off on campaign or engaging in battle. Every public or private action required this kind of ritual consultation. The appointment of priests or magistrates by men was not enough; the gods' consent was necessary. Like places, citizens invested with a duty of any kind had to be 'inaugurated'.

The auspices were taken after midnight and consequent action was not taken until after midday (Gell., 3, 2, 10). Once deemed worthy of ruling, Romulus rose at daybreak and went out of his hut. In a place apart – the *templum* of the augur – he proceeded with the preliminary sacrifice and prayed Jupiter to reveal a favourable sign if he approved the decision to confer sovereign power on him. Then a flash of lightning streaked across the firmament from left to right (for anyone looking east); and that was the confirmation that the Romans had chosen well (DH, *AR*, 2, 5).

Livy (1, 18, 6–10) describes for us the inauguration of his successor, Numa Pompilius:

> Conducted by the augur . . . Numa went to the citadel and sat on a stone facing south. The augur was on his left, his head veiled, holding in his right hand his smooth, crook-handled staff, called a *lituus*. From there, embracing in his gaze the town and the countryside, he invoked the gods, defined the areas of the sky from east to west, declaring that those on the right were to the south and those on the left to the north. Ahead of him, as far as his eyes could see, he fixed a reference point in his mind. Then, transferring the *lituus* to his left hand and with his right hand placed on Numa's head, he uttered this prayer: 'Great Jupiter, if religion allows Numa Pompilius whose head I touch to be king of Rome, graciously give us clear signs within the bounds that I have traced.' Then he stated the auspices he wished to obtain. As soon as they were obtained, Numa, proclaimed king, came down from the augural hill.

In other words, from the quadrangular *templum* of the Capitoline citadel: the *auguraculum* from which the augur would always take the urban auspices.

> The Romans long continued to observe this rule (of Romulus) relating to the auspices, not only during the royal period, but still . . . for the election of consuls, praetors and other magistrates provided for by the law. These days (in the time of Augustus) they have ceased to observe it, but have retained its form out of regard for its sacred nature. Those who are preparing to assume a magistracy spend the night out of doors, rise at daybreak and pronounce certain prayers in the open air. Augurs . . . then come to declare that the flashes of lightning from the left have confirmed the election, whereas nothing of the kind has actually taken place. (DH, *AR*, 2, 6)

Henceforward the form as such prevailed; the Romans clung to it to reassure themselves. They believed it all while no longer believing in it, since they did not repeat the operation in order effectively to achieve a lightning flash in the right direction, as they would doubtless have done several centuries earlier. They were fulfilling a ritual scruple, *religio*. In any case, did not Numa's augur specify the auspices that 'he wanted to obtain'? It was also important that, during the consultation, no creaking of a chair should be heard (hence the need to have a *sella solida*, in one piece, the stone on which Numa sat), or the squeak of a mouse, or some object falling, or any strange noise. It was true, however, that one could decide to take no notice.

But even when they had been inaugurated, a magistrate or priest still risked being repudiated by the gods:

> Sulpicius was making a sacrifice when he dropped his flaminical cap: he thereby lost his priesthood. The squeak of a mouse heard by Fabius Maximus and C. Flaminius was the reason for the first to abdicate his dictatorship, and the second his post as master of cavalry. (Val. Max., 1, 1, 5)

By neglecting these warnings, one laid oneself open to the worst. When Tiberius Gracchus was preparing to intensify his reforming action he took the auspices at daybreak in his own home. They were unfavourable; but he carried on regardless, and as he left the house he stubbed his foot hard enough to dislocate a toe. Then, three crows cawed when they saw him and dropped a fragment of tile in front of him. Scorning these omens, he would soon perish, battered to death with the leg of a bench (Val. Max., 1, 4, 2).

For a Roman, there was nothing fortuitous about these accidents. It was a matter of signs, and it was chiefly to avert their threats that Roman piety often had to be mobilised.

– WARNINGS FROM THE GODS –

'Expiatory' ceremonies belonged to this category of ritual. Certain signs, in fact, were not simple warnings predicting a misfortune; they sometimes were misfortunes in themselves, notably in the case of prodigies such as earthquakes, cataclysms, the damage caused by lightning, fire or flood. Where a thunderbolt had struck, it was necessary to make a kind of tomb by way of atonement. The haruspex 'buried' the scattered signs of the fire under a mound of turf (Luc., 8, 864), murmuring 'lugubrious words' (ibid., 1, 606 f.). The spot was encircled by a wall of cut stones, like a wellcurb: *puteal*, and from then on the place would be *religiosus* (Fest., p. 82, 9). This was notably the case at the *Comitium*, near the Ruminal fig-tree, under which Romulus and Remus had been suckled (Plin., *NH*, 15, 77).

Manmade fire required a more complex treatment. After the ravages of the Gaulish invasion in 390 BC, the duumvirs entrusted with the Sibylline Books decreed how the profaned temples were to be purified (Liv., 5, 50, 2). To expiate the burning of Rome in AD 64, supplications to Vulcan, Ceres and Proserpine were accompanied by a sacrifice to Juno through the intervention of the matrons, first on the Capitol, then on the sea shore at Ostia, where they collected water to sprinkle the temple and the divine idol. 'Sellisternia' (banquets offered to gods whose idols were placed on seats), and evening vigils ensured by women 'under their husband's authority' were further additions to the ceremonial (Tac., An., 15, 44, 2).

Heavily symbolic in the eyes of the Romans was the burning of a temple like that of Jupiter Capitolinus in 83 BC, then in AD 69. Tacitus (H, 4, 53), a quindecemvir *sacris faciundis*, informs us in detail of the ceremonial applied in AD 70 to the rebuilding of the sanctuary. First of all, the debris was removed and immersed in the marshes of Ostia, as after the disaster of AD 64 (Tac., An., 15, 43, 4). On 21 June, AD 70, at the summer solstice, the cleared area was consecrated and surrounded with garlands and streamers of cloth. Soldiers were brought in who bore 'a name of good omen' and were armed with branches pleasing to the gods (oak or laurel). Next the Vestals, accompanied by boys and girls whose parents were both still living, sprinkled fresh water. Then the praetor, resuming the sacramental words of the priest, purified the area by the triple sacrifice of the *suovetaurilia*. He offered the entrails on an altar of turf, invoking Jupiter, Juno, Minerva and the gods who protected the empire. He touched the strips of cloth binding the first stone, which was swathed in ropes and immediately pulled by magistrates, senators, knights and a large number of the populace to get it in position. Into the foundations people threw loose gold and silver newly-minted coins, 'together with virgin minerals untamed by any furnace, just as they were born in the soil' (Tac., H, 4, 53, 4). The expiation was followed, in this instance, by a consecration.

Among the prodigies identified with disasters, epidemics came first and foremost. Generally, the Sibylline Oracles were then consulted, and they might recommend, for example, the pledge to build a temple to the god of health, Apollo (Liv., 4, 25, 3), or the organising of a 'lectisternium'. The first of its kind took place in 399 BC:

> For eight days Apollo and Latona, Diana and Hercules, Mercury and Neptune were appeased, by putting up three beds for them, as sumptuous as could be done at that time. In the entire city, the doors of houses were open, and everyone, without exception, was allowed free use of all that one had. One conversed sweetly and benevolently even with one's enemies. There was a truce in all disputes and lawsuits. During those days, prisoners were even freed from their

chains, then people had misgivings about putting them back on men to whom the gods had thus given aid. (Liv., 5, 13, 6–8)

A fine example of peace with the gods through peace among men . . .

Goddesses were offered 'sellisternia', where they were seated, while the gods remained reclining (Val. Max., 2, 1, 2), in keeping with early Roman custom at family meals.

In 364 BC, however, a lectisternium was not enough to call a halt to the ravages of illness. Scenic games were thus instituted, 'a novelty for a warlike people who until then had enjoyed no other show than the circus' (Liv., 7, 2, 3). Nevertheless, the sickness persisted, being aggravated, as often happened, by mental disorders and by prodigies that solved nothing. Then people recalled a custom that had fallen into disuse; it consisted of hammering in a nail each year on the ides of September, and Livy (7, 3, 7) quotes the annalist Cincius Alimentus, speaking of Volsinii, an Etruscan town where, in the temple of Nortia, nails indicated the number of the years. Inaugurating the temple of Jupiter Capitolinus, the consul M. Horatius was said to have applied this ritual. But the nail knocked in by a dictator appointed for this purpose (clavi figendi causa) seemed to hark back to another magico-religious tradition reported by Pliny (NH, 28, 63). It was a matter of 'transfixing' the sickness to cancel out its effects: a piaculum applied not only to illnesses (Liv., 9, 28, 6), but also to social disturbances like the secession of the plebs (Liv., 8, 18, 12) and a poisoning affair involving the deranged minds (captis mentibus) of matrons (ibid., 11). On each occasion, it was the physical or mental health of the state that was at stake.

Frequently, after consulting the Sibylline Books, an obsecratio was organised (an earnest prayer with rites involving action on the part of the gods), or more generally a supplicatio. On such occasions the people did the rounds of the temples to implore the gods reclining on their cushions (pulvinaria). Holding a laurel branch, men crowned with foliage offered wine and incense; the women knelt, sweeping the altars with their loosened hair (Liv., 3, 7, 8; 26, 9, 7–8). Boys and girls with both parents living had to sing hymns. In 190 BC, lightning struck the temple of Juno Lucina; it rained soil at Tusculum, while at Reate a she-mule gave birth. Then the supplication was provided by ten boys and ten girls meeting the same conditions.

As early as 249 BC, a prodigy had been warded off by 'Tarentine' games lasting three nights on the Campus Martius, and a 'secular' chant intoned by choristers. In 207 BC, the evil sign was a gigantic hermaphrodite, who was crated up while still alive to be cast into the sea. Livius Andronicus composed a *carmen* which was to be sung by three groups of nine young girls (and which Livy judged to be unworthy of the taste of his contemporaries!) But while they were learning the words in the temple of Jupiter *Stator*, lightning struck the temple of Juno Regina on the Aventine. To expiate this prodigy, twenty-five matrons gave money from their dowries to provide a gold bowl to offer to the goddess. Two white heifers left Apollo's temple, going towards the Forum by the Carmental Gate. Behind them were carried two cypresswood statues of Juno, and these were followed by the twenty-seven maidens, dressed in garments with trains, singing the hymn composed by Livius Andronicus. After them walked the decemvirs, wearing the toga praetexta and crowned with laurel. Once arrived at the Forum, the girls, all holding the same note, stamped their feet to the rhythm of the chant. After which, all returned to the Aventine to set up the two idols, when the two heifers had been sacrificed (Liv., 27, 37, 715).

But divine warnings were not always heeded. For want of noticing, or at least understanding, a voice that came from the sacred wood which descended from the Palatine towards the Via Nova, Rome suffered the invasion of the Gauls. It redeemed itself by deifying Aius Locutius or Loquens, who would have his altar in a sacred enclosure (Cic., *Div.*, 1, 101). On the other hand, the voice of Juno issuing from her Capitoline temple, after an earthquake which she ordered to be expiated by the sacrifice of a pregnant sow, was obeyed. She became *Moneta*, 'the Warner' and a temple on the citadel was pledged to her. But lo and behold, another prodigy immediately followed its dedication: a rain of stones and black night at the height of day. A dictator was appointed to arrange ferial days and supplications (Liv., 7, 28, 4 and 7).

Certain procedures were more precisely suitable for this or that kind of prodigy. In 191 BC, two oxen were burnt alive on the roof of a building, and their ashes thrown into the Tiber (Liv., 36, 37, 2). After showers of stones falling from the sky, the decemvirs declared a fast in homage to Ceres and, most often, a novena of sacrifices (*sacrum* or *sacrificium novemdiale*). But if, during this nine-day period, a dog ate the meal served to Juno, such a worrying sign called for reparation or, rather, 'lustration' (Obseq., 52).

It was often important to purify the city. In 102 BC, for nine days after the purification, once the ashes of the victims were scattered in the sea, the magistrates had to lead processions of supplicants round all the temples (ibid., 44). The *amburbium* was a purification, and Lucan (1, 592 ff.) describes its liturgy, when gloomy presages foretold civil war. At the head walked the priests, the Vestals, followed by the quindecemvirs, augurs, epulones, Salians and flamines. Citizens wearing the toga, a fold of it over their head (*ritu Gabino*), took part in the procession which went all round the city, escorting the victims that were to be offered to the gods. It happened that this solemn lustration was undertaken because of a bird known as 'incendiary', an owl or an eagle-owl, another 'bird of ill omen' (Plin., *NH*, 10, 36; Obseq., 40 and 51).

In 226 BC, the threat of a Gaulish invasion inspired the Romans to a disconcerting interpretation of the Sibylline Oracles: they buried alive two Greek and Gaulish couples in the forum Boarium, a sacrifice that was repeated in 216 BC after the disaster at Cannae, on the same spot enclosed with stones 'already in the recent past sprinkled with the blood of human victims: a ceremony that is far from Roman' (Liv., 22, 57, 6). The breaking of a Vestal's vow was a prodigy expiated by the live burial of the culprit; but as that terrible act itself called for an expiation, in 114 BC two more Greeks and Gauls were buried. According to Plutarch (*Marc.*, 3, 7), in November certain secret rites were performed in memory of the victims. The question has been raised whether (notably in 216 BC) the Romans were resuming an Etruscan tradition, as if to demonstrate to the gods that they were not afraid of competition from Punic piety on this matter.

Nevertheless, besides the various methods of atonement, vows were made promising the gods festivals, supplications, sacrifices, games, temples or a 'sacred spring'. Originally, a pledge had been made to sacrifice all creatures – human or animal – born in the springtime; but later, this was replaced by leading outside the boundaries of the city the boys and girls who had been pledged at their birth and would now depart to survive elsewhere; they were veiled (like the victims of a *devotio* or the dead) (Fest., p. 519, 31 ff.). Then livestock was pledged under this name *ver sacrum*, animals that had been born between the calends of March and the eve of the calends of May (Liv., 34, 44, 3). The promise often fell due at five-year intervals, but sometimes there was a delay in fulfilling it. In 217 BC, to safeguard the Roman people during the five years that lay ahead, the populace was persuaded to vote for a *ver sacrum* (Liv., 22, 10, 2–6):

> Whatever spring produced in the flock or herd of pigs, sheep, goats and calves, and is not pledged elsewhere, will be sacrificed to Jupiter on the day ordained by the Senate and the people. If the animal to be killed happens to die, let it be deemed to be not consecrated, and there is no fault; if anyone wounds or kills it unintentionally, let this not be considered fraud . . .

and other precautions characteristic of the religious legalism of the Romans. However, the pledge would not be fulfilled until 195 BC, thus over twenty years later (Liv., 33, 44, 1–2). Talk about the patience of the gods!

But they revealed their wrath by other ordeals than the prodigies recorded in the priests' annals; for example, drought:

> When the sky is leaden, and the year is barren, *nudipedalia* (barefoot processions) are ordered, magistrates strip themselves of their purple, the fasces are turned upside down, litanies are recited, and victim upon victim is sacrificed. (Tert., *Ieiun.*, 16, 5)

Petronius (44, 18) evokes the time when 'barefoot women in long robes, their hair unbound and their heart pure, went to the Capitol to beg Jupiter for water'. A cylindrical stone (usually placed in the temple of Mars at the Porta Capena) was dragged and rolled by priests as far as the Capitol (?). According to Festus (p. 2, 24 ff; 115, 7–12), it was the *lapis manalis*, and this *aquaelicium*, reminiscent of the Rogations, might have had some connection with Jupiter *Elicius*, he whose lightning was 'attracted' (*elicere*): 'You search the sky on the Capitol, you await the rain from the roofs of your temples!' (Tert., *Apol.*, 40, 14).

Lastly, there are some unique instances. In 362 BC, an earth tremor caused a vast chasm beside the Forum. In vain attempts were made to fill in this abyss, and they had no success until soothsayers, advised by the gods, declared that whatever, above all else, constituted the power of the Roman people must be consecrated on this spot. Then a soldier in the prime of life, Marcus Curtius, solved the riddle by his own example:

> His gaze fixed on the temples of the gods that dominated the Forum and the Capitol, his hands outstretched now to the heavens now to the yawning chasm in the earth and the Manes gods, he sacrificed himself: mounted on a horse as magnificently adorned as possible, he leaped fully armed into the gulf. A crowd of men and women spread offerings and fruits over him. (Liv., 7, 6, 4–5)

This place of expiation would become the 'Lake of Curtius' which, in Ovid's time (F, 6, 403), 'bore an altar on its dry soil', with a sacred enclosure also explained as a 'site struck by lightning' (Varr., *LL*, 5, 150).

The variety of ritual 'medicaments' applied to the scourges, prodigies and unprecedented accidents as such, demonstrates yet again how well, in religious matters, Roman empiricism was able to manage the unpredictable.

– KEEPING THE GODS ON-SIDE –

Both the *aquaelicium* and M. Curtius's *devotio* warded off the results of celestial anger with the sole aim of becoming reconciled with the power of the gods. Expiatory supplications were matched by '*propitiatory*' supplications, which had the same intent and the same methods. Imminent danger that was the equivalent of a warning in fact demanded recourse to similar procedures: the pledge of games, temples and sacrifices, lectisternia and sellisternia, supplications lasting one or several days.

Livy has passed on to us the formulas of vows uttered at the height of a decisive battle, or before departure on campaign. In the firing line of a confrontation with the Samnites in 296 BC, Appius Claudius, using archaic wording, solemnly declared:

> Bellona, if thou givest us victory today, I will pledge thee a temple. (Liv., 10, 19, 17)

A century later, in 197 BC, on the point of attacking the Cenomani and Insubres, the consul Cornelius Cethegus promised a temple to Juno Sospita, if the enemy that day was beaten and put to flight. Then the soldiers cried out that they would fulfil the consul's vow (Liv., 32, 30, 10): a typically Roman example of voluntarism reinforcing piety. The temple was dedicated three years later on the forum Holitorium, and is now the church of San Nicola in Carcere.

Before reaching Greece in 192 BC, the consul Manius Acilius declared, at the dictation of the chief priest:

> If the war ordained by the people against King Antiochus is ended as the Senate and Roman people desire, then for thee, Jupiter, the Roman people will hold great games for ten consecutive days, and sums of money whose amount will be set by the Senate will be offered at every funeral bed. (Liv., 36, 2, 3)

It was promised that all would be carried out correctly (recte), no matter who the magistrates were, and no matter when or where the games, when the Roman people fulfilled the vows. After which, the consuls decided on two days of supplications (ibid., 4–5).

When making war, it was necessary to be within one's rights and therefore to have the gods on one's side. The Romans knew only war that was 'just and in keeping with piety' (bellum justum piumque), made legitimate by the preliminary steps taken by the fetiales. If not, it would be a sacrilege, nefas. Civil war was a bellum nefandum, as was any offensive in foreign territory without a declaration of intent (indictio belli) and statutory complaint, as in a lawsuit. A war could not be engaged in without the gods' approval:

> The worst has happened! Flying in the face of presages and oracles, scorning the divine will, they all want the execrable war, infandum bellum. (Virg., Aen., 7, 583 f.)

The ritual followed by the Romans for an *indictio belli* was attributed to Numa, but he was said to have borrowed it from the tribe of the Aequicoli, although they were reputedly wild and rapacious (Virg., *Aen.*, 7, 747 ff.). In the case of a complaint against a neighbouring country, a fetial wearing sacred robes and ornaments was dispatched and, having reached the frontiers of the incriminated people, this 'officiating father' (*pater patratus*) veiled himself with wool (which isolated him from the profane) and said:

> Hear me, Jupiter, hear me, frontiers (he specified which), and may righteousness (*fas*) hear me! I am the accredited spokesman of the Roman people. I come charged with a just and holy mission: let my words be given credence!

The appeal to the *fas* was enough by itself to justify the name and function of the fetial. He therefore stated his demands, and then called Jupiter to be his witness:

> If I fail in what is just and holy in asking for the restitution of these men and these objects to the Roman people, may I cease to be a citizen of my country. (Liv., 1, 32, 6–7)

He repeated these words as he crossed the frontier, and said them again to the first man he met when he opened the gate and entered the forum, altering few words in the invocation and the oath. If he was not granted what he demanded, when thirty-three days (a holy number) had expired he declared war in these terms:

> Hear, O Jupiter, and you, Janus Quirinus; all of you, gods of the sky and you, gods of war, and you, gods of the earth, and you gods of the underworld, hear me! I call on you to witness that this people (naming them) is unjust and refuses reparation.

He brought back this information to Rome so that it could be debated, and the Senate was then consulted. When the majority had declared themselves for a 'just and holy' war (*puro pioque bello*), the fetial returned to the enemy frontier with a spear tipped with iron or wood hardened in the fire, and there, in the presence of at least three adult males, he declared for instance:

> Whereas the peoples of the Ancient Latins (those whose confederation would be dissolved in 338 BC) have committed actions and offences prejudicial to the Roman people of the Quirites, and whereas the Roman people of the Quirites have decided to enter into war against the Ancient Latins (. . .); for these

reasons, I and the Roman people hereby declare and make war on the peoples of the Ancient Latins. (ibid., 13)

With these words the fetial hurled his spear towards their territory. When, with the expansion of the Roman world, enemy frontiers were too far away for the weapon to reach its target, one of Pyrrhus's captured soldiers was made to buy a plot of land to represent the opposing country, in order to hurl the symbolic spear into it over a 'war column' (*columna bellica*), near the temple of Bellona. By this procedure, the Romans engaged the gods on their side, even before having to give pledges.

At that point the 'temple' of Janus was opened, although strictly speaking it was not actually a temple, rather, a passage (the real meaning of the word *janus*) open to the east and the west on the Argiletum; hence the name Janus *Geminus* (Suet., *Ner.*, 13, 4) or 'double doored' (Plut., *Num.*, 20, 1); *Fort. Rom.*, 9, 322 *a*):

> There are two gates of war (as they are called), consecrated by religion and fear of Mars the Cruel. One hundred bronze nails and the eternal strength of his iron bars keep them closed, and their guardian Janus never leaves the threshold. When the Senate's decision has been for war, the consul in person – distinguished by the trabea (robe of state) of Quirinus and his toga draped in the Gabine fashion – opens these strident gates; he gives the summons to war. The young men follow him, and bronze bugles in unison shrill their harsh sounds. (Virg., *Aen.*, 7, 607–15)

When peace returned, the Janus was closed; this happened only ten times in more than a thousand years.

It would be an empty victory, however, if the treaty consecrating it did not ensure what had been gained by reassuring the victors that they had the backing of the gods. Two fetials intervened here. The *verbenarius* went to the Capitol (on the citadel from where the auspices were taken) to gather a 'pure herb'. With his holy branch he touched the head and hair of the man who then became 'pater patratus', and whose task was to 'accomplish' or solemnise the oath of the agreement (Liv., 1, 24, 6). Thus consecrated, this spokesman addressed the enemy's pater patratus or whoever stood in for him. Calling on Jupiter as his witness, he promised that Rome would not violate the clauses of the agreement, for if this occurred,

> on that day, O Jupiter, strike the Roman people as I am about to strike this pig, here and now, and may the blow be all the greater as thy power and might are greater than mine!

Whereupon, he slaughtered a pig with his flint knife (ibid., 7–9).

According to Polybius (3, 25, 6–9), recording the terms of the two treaties with Carthage, Romans called upon Jupiter *Lithos* or 'Stone' to be their witness, invoking Mars and Quirinus. The fetial picked up a pebble and, in the name of public good faith, declared:

> If I keep my promise, may heaven be kind to me; but if I think or act otherwise, while all other men shall be safeguarded in their own country, with their own laws, their possessions, their cults and their tombs, may I be cast out and fall like this stone.

And upon these words, he threw the stone.

But the blow killing the pig explains the expression *foedus ferire*, 'to strike a treaty', with the god's stone as the guarantor of the oaths taken. *Pax* was a noun of action that concerned peace with the gods just as much as with men; it would be unthinkable to be at peace with the second without being solidly and sacramentally at peace with the first. There was no *de facto* peace without a treaty linking a sacrifice with the oath. The Senate in 321 BC was therefore able to repudiate the *pax Caudina*, the peace agreement of the Caudine Forks (Liv., 8, 5, 2–3).

The hardwood used to make the spear declaring war magically took possession of the territory to be subdued, as the one that Romulus had once hurled from the Aventine to the Palatine had taken root: it had become a much revered tree that was tended like a precious fetish until the day when, in Caligula's reign, a workman's pick made it wither (Plut., Rom., 20, 6–8). But the wood of the red dogwood, especially in the fetials' rite, probably also possessed the mysterious power to make the horrors of war rebound on to the enemy. There was thus a parallel religious procedure threatening the belligerent opponent with a kind of curse: the *devotio*. That of M. Curtius was expiatory; but there was another kind which, in desperate circumstances, could force the gods' hand, so to speak.

In 340 BC, the consuls P. Decius Mus and T. Manlius Torquatus confronted the coalition army of the Latins. As was right and proper, a sacrifice was offered, but the 'head' of the liver was split on the side that concerned Decius; in fact, the Romans' left wing which he commanded gave way before the enemy thrust. Then Decius cried to the priest M. Valerius, 'Tell me the right words to sacrifice myself for the legions.' The priest made him don the purple-edged toga and, with his head veiled, one hand protruding from the toga to touch his chin, his feet on a spear laid on the ground, Decius uttered the ritual formula:

Janus, Jupiter, Father Mars, Quirinus, Bellona, Lares, New gods, Native gods, deities who have power over us and our enemy, and you, gods of the underworld, I pray, supplicate and beseech you to grant strength and victory to the Roman people, the Quirites, afflicting the enemy with terror, dread and death. By virtue of the words I have uttered, on behalf of the state of the Quirites, the army, the legions, the auxiliaries of the Roman people, I devote the legions and auxiliaries of our enemies with my own person to the gods of the underworld and the Earth.

Immediately binding his toga around him in the Gabine fashion (with a fold over his head, as if for a sacrifice), Decius leaped fully armed on to his horse and plunged into the main bulk of the enemy troops (Liv., 8, 9, 4–8). By pledging or 'devoting' himself to the infernal gods, he pledged the enemy to death by contaminating them. Noteworthy is the invocation to the Lares and the Manes embracing the 'Native' gods whom the Ancients also regarded as the deified dead (Serv., G, 1, 498; *Aen.*, 12, 794) and those enigmatic *divi Novemsiles* (or *Novemsides*), new gods, who, like the former were concerned with the subterranean world where the ancestors were sleeping (Arn., 3, 39). If the enemy managed to capture the spear, Mars had to be offered the triple sacrifice of the *suovetaurilia* (Liv., 8, 10, 14). Half a century before Decius Mus, old men wearing the insignia of their former dignities had ritually 'devoted' themselves (vowed to offer themselves as sacrifices) to ensure the rout of the Gaulish invaders (Liv., 5, 41, 1–3 and 9). In 295 BC, Decius's own son 'devoted' himself to posthumous victory over the Samnites (ibid., 10, 28, 13, 18).

A general could also pledge 'in his place, any citizen he wished in a Roman legion. If this pledged man dies, the sacrifice is deemed to be perfect; if he does not die, a seven-foot (2.07 metres) statue is buried and a victim sacrified in expiation. Religion prohibits a magistrate from standing on the mound where the statue is buried' (ibid., 8, 10, 11–12).

Typical of Roman opportunism and triumphant realism was the ritual of the *evocatio*. In good polytheistic logic, the tutelary deities of an enemy people could not be conquered, so it was necessary to get them on the Roman side before the final assault, because in any case the pillaging of temples would expose the Romans to sacrilege, and they 'thought it impious to take gods captive' (Macr., S, 3, 9, 2). The solution lay in making them emerge, calling them out from their sanctuary (*e-vocare*) in order to install them in Rome. In 396 BC, Camillus thus 'evoked' Juno Regina from Veii:

After our victory, deign to follow us to our city which will become thine: there, may thy majesty find a temple worthy of her! (Liv., 5, 21, 3)

After taking Veii, 'it was their duty to carry off the gods' treasure and the gods themselves, but as worshippers rather than abductors' (ibid., 22, 3). A delegation of young soldiers, purified by ablutions and dressed in white, was entrusted with the mission of carrying the goddess to Rome, but they were held back by religious scruples because, according to Etruscan tradition, 'the idol had never been touched except by a priest of a certain family.' Then one of the *juvenes* said to Juno, 'Do you want to go to Rome?' 'The goddess indicated "yes"' (*adnuisse*, a verb containing the root of *numen*) cried the others. Juno had therefore consented and the removal of the idol went ahead effortlessly. She would have her temple on the Aventine (ibid., 4–7).

Two and a half centuries later, Scipio Aemilianus brought Tanit from Carthage, and the Romans revered her under the title *Caelestis*:

> If there is a god, a goddess who watches over the people and city of Carthage, you above all who have been entrusted with the protection of this town and its people, I pray, implore and beseech you to leave the people and city of Carthage, to quit all its places, temples, cults and the town, to go far away from them (. . .) and come to Rome, to me and my people (. . .) so that we may know and understand that henceforward we, myself, the Roman people and my soldiers, are under your protection. If you do so, I make a vow to offer you a temple and games. (Macr., S, 3, 9, 7–8)

After he had spoken, a sacrifice was made so that the approval of the gods might be verified from an examination of the victims' entrails.

All in all, it was a betrayal and if, in any case, the town could do nothing but fall, one must not believe in gods incapable of saving it. But the Romans knew, too, that discontented gods sometimes put unfaithful people to the test, and it was in that spirit that the *evocatio* seemed to them to consecrate an irrefutable fact. They were so convinced of the effectiveness of the rite that they feared its power should it be used against them. They therefore kept secret the sacred name of their city and the deity who protected it (Serv. Dan., *Aen.*, 2, 351; Macr., S, 3, 9, 3). Some identified her with Angerona, who puts her finger on her lips; others with Ops Consivia (ibid., 4).

After this ritual capture of the enemy's last trump, towns and armies were consigned to the gods. Macrobius (ibid., 10–11) has preserved the formula for us. Dis Pater was invoked, together with Vejovis and the Manes, to throw the enemy into flight, panic and terror. They were implored to ward off those who bore both offensive and defensive weapons, the inhabitants of towns and countryside, to remove the light of the sky from them and to consider 'cursed' and vowed to destruction those soldiers, towns and fields, their heads and people of every age:

> If you let me know, feel and understand that you will act in this way, whoever has promised to sacrifice three black ewes to you, wherever he has done so, let it be understood that he has acted within the rules! I call on you to witness, Mother Earth, and you, O Jupiter.

When Earth was named, the ground was to be touched with the hands; when Jupiter was named, the hands must be raised to the heavens; when the vow was made, it was done with both hands touching the breast.

In the eyes of the Ancients, every religious act was intended to obtain divine favour; but propitiatory supplications, vows, the *devotio* and the *evocatio* were intended to put the gods in the right mood, so to speak, with a voluntarism that was very characteristic of the Roman mind. Roman prayer never had any aura of the mystical; it was a request made in the right and proper form, as strictly regulated as a petition in court.

— OFFERINGS, PLEDGES AND TRIUMPHS —

After the Gaulish invasion, Jupiter was offered the Capitoline games, for he had saved the citadel. To this end a college was created, recruited from the inhabitants of the hill (Liv., 5, 50, 4).

But sometimes people forgot to thank the gods, and fulfilment of pledges had a tendency to be delayed when all was going well. In 203 BC, Rome felt a sense of ease; Hannibal had returned to Africa after fifteen years of war. The old senators at the time commented that men were less sensitive to fortune than misfortune: there was no one to propose giving thanks to the gods! Five days of prayers were therefore decreed around all the gods' cushions (a lectisternium), plus the sacrifice of 120 fully grown victims (Liv., 30, 22, 6–10). The senate sometimes had to order the consuls not to leave Rome before they had fulfilled the vows which had not been carried out by the due date (Liv., 30, 2, 8; 27, 11). Even Camillus, that incarnation of the exemplary Roman, in the opinion of Fustel De Coulanges, did not live up to his promise to consecrate to Apollo a tithe of the booty from the capture of Veii; hence the anger of the gods, demanding 'ceremonies of atonement and gratitude' (Plut., *Cam.*, 7, 7). The holders of the booty had to hand over a tenth to the Treasury to pay for a gold crater, or wine bowl, which would be sent to the temple at Delphi, thanks once again to the jewellery of the matrons who thus earned their right to funerary eulogies.

The general who won a battle sent his messengers to the Senate, bearing the victory notice adorned with laurel leaves. In announcing the news, he asked that 'honour should be rendered to the gods', and a 'gratulatory' or thanksgiving supplication would then be decided upon. This could last from one to five days, depending on the magnitude of the success or the gravity of the situation. In 191 BC, after the defeat of Antiochus at Thermopylae, the Senate decreed a three day supplication: 'The praetor was to offer forty fully grown victims to the deities of his choice' (Liv., 36, 21, 9). As always in such cases, the matrons and magistrates went in procession from one temporary altar to the next to render thanks to the gods on their cushioned seats (*pulvinaria*). Sacrifices were organised, accompanied by public prayers. Women (dressed in their best finery) played an important role in these demonstrations; in 396 BC, they even took the initiative after the fall of Veii.

The offerings, games and temples pledged to the gods in the heat of battle consecrated the gratitude of the Roman people. Responsible for the vow (*voti reus*) that he had pronounced, the victorious general was then *voti damnatus*, 'sentenced' to fulfil it. The siting of a temple had to be confirmed by auspices, which were followed by a solemn declaration. On the *locus effatus*, the laying of the first stone called for special rites (as we saw in the case of the rebuilt sanctuary for Jupiter Capitolinus). Once built, the temple was 'dedicated' (we would say 'inaugurated', using a verb which the Romans applied to the space defined by the augurs). The priests issued a notice before officially authorising the dedication/inauguration. They drew up a deed of foundation (*lex templi*) setting out the extent of the hallowed site, the income necessary for its functioning and the appropriate rites.

The dedicant was either (generally) a magistrate in office, or whoever had pledged the temple or had had its construction commenced. The chief priest or, if he was unable, a member of the pontifical college would veil his head before pronouncing the sacred formula while holding one of the door jambs, and the dedicant in his turn would repeat it, making the same gesture. From then on this dedication would be commemorated annually as the 'birth day' (*natalis*) of the temple. The religious furnishings, such as the altar and the table 'where meat, libations and money offerings were placed' were consecrated at the same time as the temple (Macr., S, 3, 11, 6).

The games in which people delighted were first offered to the gods, omnipresent in places where shows were given, notably in the circus where Consus had his subterranean altar and where 'every ornament is a temple' (Tert., *Spect.*, 8, 3). Before the chariot races, a procession (*pompa circensis*) went from the Capitol to the Circus Maximus by way of the Forum, the *vicus Tuscus*, the Velabrum, the forum Boarium and then covering the full length of the track. Dancers, musicians, bearers of perfume burners or incense vessels preceded the images of the Immortals, which were carried on stretchers, and the gods' symbols transported on special cars (*tensae*) which were usually stored in premises on the Capitol. It was a solemn ceremony. Should a dancer stop, or a flute-player break off, or one of the children required to lead the *tensa* drop the reins, it was an offence that must be expiated: everything had to begin again (Cic., *Har.*, 23). The consul Varro lost the battle of Cannae (216 BC) because he had irritated Juno: he had let a young actor 'of rare beauty' (Val. Max., 1, 1, 16) ride on the *tensa* of the Most Good and Great Jupiter. Besides the defeat he suffered, that provocation had to be atoned for with sacrifices.

The fulfilment of pledges was crowned by the triumph, when the glory of the victor in some sort bordered on the honour of the gods. Often made on the Capitol by the general before his departure on campaign, vows were concluded by the triumphant victor's solemn homage to Jupiter Capitolinus (see Liv., 45, 39, 11).

Originally, it had been a purificatory rite (Liv., 1, 28, 1), connected with the *Tigillum Sororium* and the lustration of weapons at the close of the war-making season. Festus (p. 104, 23 ff.) indeed reminds us that the soldiers followed the chariot of their triumphant leader, crowned with laurel so that they could enter the town 'purified, so to speak, of the human blood that had been shed'. Laurel, which we regard as a symbol of victory, was at first used as a plant to be burnt for fumigation.

The honours of a triumph were granted on certain conditions by the people and Senate; so generals sometimes had to wait at the gates of Rome (outside the pomoerium, on the Campus Martius), unless they celebrated their triumph at the sanctuary of Mount Albanus, like the leaders of the Latin Confederation in former days. Lucullus had to be patient for three years before he obtained satisfaction in 63 BC.

At all events, a triumph never rewarded anything but a ritually declared war involving neither an enemy unworthy of the Roman people (slaves or pirates) nor fellow citizens (Val. Max., 2, 8, 7; Gell., 5, 6, 21). People put on white clothing to attend the festival. The procession entered Rome through a Triumphal Gate which might have been no more than a temporary opening (if not a breach) that was stopped up again afterwards. It crossed the entire length of the Flaminian Circus and the Circus Maximus, passing through the Velabrum and the forum Boarium, before regaining the Sacred Way on the east and climbing the Capitoline slope. Temples, public and private buildings were adorned with garlands of flowers, and incense fumes wafted everywhere.

The triumphal pomp sometimes lasted three days; for that of Aemilius Paullus (167 BC), first of all the statues, idols and paintings seized from the enemy went by on 250 cars. The next day, there were chariots laden with glittering weapons: helmets, quivers, cuirasses, swords and shields piled up as they can be seen on Roman arches. Behind came 3,000 men bearing wine bowls, goblets, rhytons, vessels filled with silver coins. Two days later, at dawn, the war trumpets were sounded before 120 fat oxen, adorned for sacrifice with the ritual sash (*dorsuale*), garlands of flowers and with their horns gilded. Gold coins followed, in huge urns, then the sacred goblet which Aemilius Paullus had had fashioned in solid gold, and the royal dishes of the defeated enemy. Perseus walked behind his children and their tutors, then came those bearing 400 crowns sent by the Greek towns to the victor who, standing in his chariot, brought up the rear of the procession with his army (Plut., *Aem.*, 32–4).

The triumphant leader, whose face was coloured with vermilion (Serv., *B*, 10, 27), personified Jupiter. He wore the *tunica Jovis* (Juv., 10, 38) – embroidered with palm leaves – under his purple toga scattered with golden stars (App., *Pun.*, 66). In one hand he held a laurel branch, in the other an ivory staff crowned by an eagle. A laurel wreath was on his head; round his neck hung a gold ball enclosing talismans against envy (Macr., *S*, 1, 6, 9). Behind him, a slave held the golden crown said to be of Etruscan origin (Tert., *Cor.*, 13, 1) borrowed for the occasion from Jupiter. Four white horses were harnessed to his chariot, making it worthy 'of the king and father of the gods' (Plut., *Cam.*, 7, 2). But the slave would say to him, 'Look behind you; remember that you are a man' (Tert., *Apol.*, 33, 4); and with the acclamations (*Io triumpe* the soldiers mingled gibes that were supposed to exorcise him of immoderate conceit. A phallic amulet attached beneath the chariot also protected him from the evil eye (Plin., *NH*, 28, 39).

Prisoners, too, took part in the *pompa*, and people carrying placards listing the towns or peoples who had been defeated, or pictures recalling battles, sieges, rivers crossed, or mountains and sites that had been conquered. When they arrived at the foot of the Capitoline slope, captives were dragged from the procession to be executed in the Mamertine prison: perhaps a bloody ritual of Etruscan tradition? Once at the Capitol, the hero of the triumph offered Jupiter the laurels from the fasces and his own, before sacrificing the victims that were due to him. For the occasion, the colouring of the wooden or terracotta head of the sovereign god was also enhanced with red lead paint (Plin., *NH*, 33, 111; 35, 157). In 46 bc, Caesar gave thanks to Jupiter by going up the Capitol steps on his knees (DC, 43, 21, 2), something which the emperor Claudius would also do after conquering the Britons, but he was supported on the arm of his two sons-in-law (DC, 60, 23, 1). The victor offered his victory as homage to the one who had granted it to him. Such reciprocity was at the very heart of Roman piety.

The Ancients linked the origins of the triumph with the ritual of *opima spolia* (arms taken by one general from another) inaugurated by Romulus.

Confronting Acron, king of the Caeninenses, in single combat, he vowed to consecrate to Jupiter the vanquished man's weapons. After killing him and putting his army to flight, Romulus ascended the Capitol with the enemy leader's *spolia* which he carried on a stretcher (*ferculum*) before hanging them on the trunk of an oak. Clad in purple and crowned with laurel, he intoned a triumphal paean taking the trophy on to his shoulders, and consecrating it to Jupiter Feretrius in a temple pledged for this purpose, the oldest in Rome (Liv., 1, 10, 5–7; DH, AR, 2, 34; Plut., *Rom.*, 16, 3–5). After Romulus, only Cossus, who killed the Etruscan Tolumnius with his own hand (437 BC), and Claudius Marcellus, victor over the Gaul Britomartus (222 BC), would have the glory of the *opima spolia*.

When neither the war nor the enemy was 'just' or worthy, the victorious general had the right to an *ovatio*: he went on foot or on horseback in procession, in the toga praetexta and crowned with myrtle, the attribute of the Etruscan Turan or of Venus *Victrix*, consecrating a success without bloodshed (Plin., *NH*, 15, 125; Gell., 5, 6, 21 f.). The name is explained by the victims sacrificed on the Capitol: sheep (ovine) instead of oxen (bovine) (Serv., *Aen.*, 4, 543). But the verb *ovare* applies to the cries of joy emitted at the festival (Fest., p. 213, 6 f.). Some ovations, like that of Marcellus after the fall of Syracuse (Liv., 26, 21, 6–9), had almost as much splendour as a triumph.

At all events, every action of any importance in Rome began and ended with a sacrifice.

However, the religions of the state suffered the repercussions from crises that affected it. Greek philosophy wrought havoc in Romans' consciences, whether by way of epicurism which, by denying the gods' actions in this world here below, rendered acts of civic piety superfluous, or the euhemerism which, by identifying the gods with illustrious dead, gave advance legitimacy to the cult of leaders. In the first century BC, the auspices were no longer used except in electoral manipulations, and signs from the gods were neither invoked nor rejected except for political ends. Like a bandit invoking the Virgin before striking a blow, Milo made a vow in order to succeed in killing Clodius and, after the murder, a woman presented herself on his behalf to the Vestals of Alba Longa in fulfilment of this pious obligation (Asc., *Mil.*, 28). Prodigies were hardly recorded or interpreted any more; many rites fell into disuse and temples into ruin. Moreover, people felt no reluctance at destroying a chapel of Diana on the Caelius or other sites that had formerly been consecrated (Cic., *Har.*, 32), and Clodius set fire to the temple of the Nymphs which housed the archives of the census, in order to falsify the registers as he pleased (Cic., *Mil.*, 73).

Roman men and women were upset by all this. Atticus's grandmother, for example, died heartbroken not only because she would not see her grandson again, but also because she had learned that the Feriae Latinae were no longer being celebrated following the rules of traditional devotion (Cic., *Att.*, 1, 3, 1). Cicero indecently mocked the bigotry of an old lady; but Rome had always had those with a nostalgia for the ancestral religion.

1. *Funerary relief. Rome. Palazzo Albani del Drago. Photo: German Archae-ological Institute, Rome.*

2. *Marcus Aurelius sacrificing before the temple of Jupiter Capitolinus. Rome, Palazzo dei Conservatori. Photo: Alinari.*

3. Sacrifice of a bull. Paris, Louvre Museum. Photo: Giraudon.

4. Immolatio of the victim. Rome, Capitoline Museum.

5. *Haruspex. Tübingen, University Archaeological Institute.*

6. *Domestic lararium. Herculanum. Ins. V. 31.*

7. *Lupercus. Vatican Museum.*

8. *Augustus as an augur. Florence. Uffizi Museum. Photo: Alinari.*

9. *Quindecemvir* sacris faciundis. *Paris, Louvre Museum.*

10. *Banquet of the Vestals. Rome, Museo Nuovo.*

11. Suovetaurilia. *Paris, Louvre Museum.*

12. *Sacrifice to the Moirai. Coin of Domitian, private collection. Photo: 'Monnaies et Médailles', Basle.*

13. *The emperor dictating a prayer to the matrons. Coin of Domitian. London, British Museum.*

14. *Priest of Bellona. Rome, Capitoline Museum.*

15. Egyptian festival. Rome, National Museum.

16. Jupiter Dolichenus and his companion. Rome, Capitoline Museum.

17. *Sacrifice to the Augustan Lares. Rome, Museo Nuovo.*

18. *Sacrifice to Nemesis. Rome, Museo Nuovo. Photo: German Archaeological Institute, Rome.*

CHAPTER 4

Religions of the Empire

A city with universal authority could not become immovably set in its own national pantheon – which in any case incorporated its share of already longstanding Greek influences, together with the Etruscan heritage. As the family had opened out into the city, so Rome opened out to a world it had conquered or had yet to conquer.

Through the river port, on the forum Boarium, trade had in very early days imported representations of eastern origin, and the Hercules Olivarius (or of the oil traders), worshipped in the round temple formerly mistakenly attributed to Vesta, could well convey the powers of a Phoenician Melqart. The failures as well as the successes of the *Urbs* helped to extend the range of its piety. As we have seen, by calling for consultation of the Sibylline Books, times of ordeal or fear imposed a need to resort to hitherto untried cults and new gods. As we read in Livy, rarely does a *pestilentia* fail to cause a great upset, and physical contagion was inevitably accompanied by moral contagion, opening the way to foreign 'superstitions'. Such crises thus strengthened the Hellenisation of Roman religion. In fact, its fundamental pragmatism caused it to try other practices when its own rituals appeared ineffectual. The gods themselves, by signalling their anger, encouraged entreaty to rival gods. In Roman or Graeco-oriental polytheism, there was no jealous or exclusive God, but a pantheon that tended to diversify almost indefinitely.

In order to obtain victory, new temples were always promised to deities already revered in the *Urbs,*, but henceforward hallowed under other identities, connected with the circumstances of the pledge: for example the Fortuna 'of this day' (*huiusce diei*) invoked in 101 BC at Vercellae by Lutatius Catullus (Plut., *Mar.*, 26, 3). But victory also transported new gods to Rome by way of the *evocatio* and the influx of slaves who brought their various forms of worship with them. Contact with Greek life and oriental luxury, the inevitable price of conquest, had a corresponding effect on the outlook of the conquerors; hence the xenophobic reactions of Livy and, later, Juvenal (3, 62), for whom 'the Syrian Orontes overflowing into the Tiber' is the image of an apocalyptic cataclysm. But conquest also brought political results whose religious repercussions were no less decisive. Success then rather intoxicated generals or *imperatores*, to the point of inspiring them with divine pretensions or, at least, making them claim a special relationship with the gods: something that did not fit in with the collectivism of civic piety.

Already the triumph of Camillus over Veii, in a chariot drawn by four white horses, which put him on a par with Jupiter or the Sun, had caused the comment, 'this is not the act of a citizen, or even of a mortal' (Liv., 5, 23, 5). Such a comparison bordered on sacrilege (ibid., 6). Later, Scipio Africanus made out that he held private conversations with Jupiter Capitolinus, and let the rumour spread that he, like Alexander, was the son of a divine serpent . . . (Liv., 26, 19, 7), as Augustus would be supposed to be the issue of Apollo (Suet., *Aug.*, 94, 4). Sulla, who claimed links with the Anatolian Bellona, was also the darling of Venus Felix, the fertile goddess of love and luck. Marius was accompanied by Martha, a Syrian prophetess who, when he sacrificed, alighted from her litter with a garlanded spear, and not before fastening her purple double cloak (Plut., *Mar.*, 17, 4). The descendant of Venus, Caesar invoked her and, with the name *Genitrix*, dedicated a temple to her which he consecrated in 46 BC, preceded by elephants bearing torches, like Dionysus triumphing over the Indians. In the last century BC, coins struck in the name of the *imperatores* emphasised their priestly insignia. By having himself elected Chief Priest, it was as if Caesar foresaw the future importance of this title, which would be assumed by Augustus in 12 BC and by all the emperors who succeeded him.

The existence and management of an empire were incompatible with the regime of a city-state. Functionally, universal monarchy tended to place on a superhuman level the holder of a power that went beyond the laws of the Republic or, more precisely, one who henceforward embodied absolute law at the same time as the unity of the empire.

All these factors, contained in embryo from the time when Rome expanded outside its own bounds, transformed its religious landscape even inside the city itself where, on the Capitol, the Sanctuary of Romulus symbolically foreshadowed its cosmopolitan future.

– FOREIGN CULTS –

The population of the *Urbs* changed during the course of the centuries and in the time of Augustus no longer had much in common with the people of

Cincinnatus's period. Rome's vocation to annex foreign nations by absorbing them went hand in hand with the incorporation of their deities. The process had started with the plebeian population who had at first lived on the fringes of patrician families, with their gods and *religiones*.

– Gods of Greece and Great Greece –

In 493 BC, at the foot of the Aventine, that extra-pomoerial hill where mostly non-native inhabitants settled, a temple was founded to Ceres, Liber and Libera, a plebeian triad who from then on matched the Capitoline trio. This cult, imported from Great Greece, was usually served by Greek priestesses (from Naples or Velia) 'and all the language used there is Greek' (Cic., *Balb.*, 55). People prayed to the gods 'following exotic rites . . . but with a national and civic spirit' (ibid.), in other words, Roman. However, the decor of the temple was the work of Greek artists (Plin., *NH*, 35, 154), and the Aventine triad was quickly likened to the one at Eleusis, which honoured Demeter, Core and Iacchos (or Plutos). Besides the *Cerealia* or Games of Ceres which were celebrated between 12 and 19 April, from the third century (Liv., 22, 56, 4) a *sacrum anniversarium Cereris*, lasting nine days (Ov., M, 10, 434) fêted the discovery of Core-Proserpine (Fest., p. 86, 8). Obliged to fasting and continence, Roman women clad in white offered the first-fruits of the harvests. Cicero speaks of initiations, and nocturnal mysteries that were performed *Graeco mori* (Leg., 2, 21 and 37), but involved only women or priestesses. It is noteworthy that the plebeian triad was dominated by a goddess, unlike the patrician triad in which Jupiter Capitolinus had precedence.

Sixty years later (in 431 BC), an appeal was made to the healing god Apollo to confront a 'pestilence'; but he was installed outside the pomoerium in the 'Flaminian fields' (Liv., 3, 63, 7). In 293 BC, his son Aesculapius arrived in the form of a snake to bring yet another contagious outbreak to an end. He chose to reside on the Tiberine island – thus still outside the sacred enclosure – but in company with Vejovis, the underworld Jupiter who had another temple on the Capitol. On each occasion, those whose duty was to interpret the Sibylline Books had naturalised the foreign gods.

In the sanctuary of Aesculapius, its site now occupied by the church of San Bartolomeo, opposite a hospital that is still faithful to the medical tradition of the island, people would come to sleep in order to receive the god's instructions in their dreams – a typically Greek procedure. This 'incubation' was performed under porticoes set up near the temple to receive the sick. Aesculapius was thanked with ex-voto offerings, found in their hundreds near the Fabrician bridge during the construction of new wharves along the Tiber between 1885 and 1887. They were of terracotta, marble, bronze, silver or even gold, depending on the means of the faithful whose prayers had been granted, but chiefly of clay, the majority of the clientele of the island in the Tiber being of humble estate. There were feet, hands, breasts, intestines, viscera in an open torso, genital organs, eyes, ears, mouths . . . Above all, it was necessary to demonstrate gratitude by way of an inscribed tablet bearing the account of the miraculous treatment. Sometimes several edifying cures were grouped into one detailed report:

> At that time, the god gave an oracle to a blind man named Caius: he was to go to the sacred altar, prostrate himself before it, next go from right to left and place his five fingers on the altar; he must then take his hand away and put it on his eyes. And he saw, in the presence of the crowd, who congratulated him . . .

> Lucius suffered from a pain in his side; everyone despaired for him. The god gave him an oracle: he was to come and take some ash from the altar, mix it with wine and apply it to his side. And he was cured, and publicly gave thanks to the god, and the crowd congratulated him.

> Julianus was losing blood; everyone despaired for him. The god gave him an oracle: he was to come and take some pine cones from the altar, and eat them mixed with honey for a period of three days. And he was cured, and publicly gave thanks to the god before the crowd. (*IGUR*, 148)

This personal relationship between the devout person and his god, the conviction of being the object of exceptional solicitude, were certainly in contrast with the strict legalism of traditional piety. The ancient goddess Health (*Salus*) on the Quirinal did not have such a 'rewarding' ceremonial for the psychology of the ordinary sick person. At that time, the spiritual sickness accompanying a physical one almost always worked to the advantage of religious exoticism. In 428 BC, after the ravages of a testing drought,

> new rites for sacrifices were introduced into private homes by those soothsayers who exploit souls who are the victims of credulity. (Liv., 4, 30, 9)

When 'foreign and unusual sacrifices were seen in every street and chapel' the aediles were given 'the task of tolerating no other than the worship of Roman gods, in keeping with the only national rite' (ibid., 10–11). In vain! Sooner or later, an answer would have to be deciphered from the Sibylline Books to cope with the popular unrest. When the situation demanded it, a bold initiative could be taken. After the disaster of Trasimene (217 BC), Fabius Maximus pledged a temple to the Venus of Mount Eryx, who was the patroness in Sicily of a sacred prostitution of Phoenician tradition. But she was installed on the Capitol, because she was, so to speak, 'one of the family'. Courtesans would attend another temple (pledged in 184 BC), at the Porta Collina.

It was mainly women who upset liturgical order. When an epidemic raged, they were involved in a poisoning affair (Liv., 8, 18, 10), or indulged in scarcely orthodox practices from the viewpoint of the *mos maiorum*. In 213 BC, when the war with Carthage was dragging on, discouraged spirits deteriorated at the same time as loyalty to ancestral rules:

> It suddenly seemed as if men or gods had changed. It was not only in secret, within the walls of houses, that Roman rites were done away with. In public, in the Forum, on the Capitol, a crowd of women were to be seen failing to observe the customs of their fathers, either by sacrificing or praying to the gods. (Liv., 25, 1, 6–7)

In vain did the urban praetor order clandestine books of 'prophetic' texts, incantatory or sacrificial formulas, to be handed over to him, the trend was irrepressible. Less than ten years later (204 BC), the black stone of Pessinus would have to be imported, and women would play a sufficiently spectacular role in its final journey to imply that they were by no means indifferent. Some time afterwards (186 BC), they were once more to be found in the foreground in the affair of the Bacchanalia, then in the entourage of Marius supporting the prophetess Martha, and above all in the popularisation of the Isiac cult.

– THE MOTHER GODS OF ANATOLIA –

The first eastern religion was imported into Rome very officially, with the agreement of the Senate, after consultation of the Sibylline Books. In 205 BC, after a new and more serious outbreak of showers of stones (hail?), customarily expiated by a sacrificial novena, the Books were believed to indicate that the interminable war with Carthage would end in victory if the 'Idaean Mother' was transferred from Pessinus to Rome (Liv., 29, 11, 4–5). It appeared that ambassadors who had taken an offering to Delphi had brought back an oracle also announcing that victory was close. But why go and look for a baetyl in Phrygia? Because that sacred stone was supposed to have fallen from the skies (like the showers of stones)? or because Cybele was the compatriot of Rome's Trojan ancestors? In fact, Livy reports a religious psychosis (*repens religio*) which, as nearly always, must first have afflicted the women. It was not mere chance if, this time, a 'Mother' was enthroned. Jupiter Capitolinus, father of gods and mankind, had not constantly responded to the entreaties of the Romans; so why not rather invoke the mother of all the gods, whose sovereign dignity should be more decisive?

According to Ovid (F, 4, 259 f.), the Sibyl said:

> The Mother is far off: I command you, Roman, to go and seek the Mother. When she arrives, let a chaste hand receive her.

Indeed, a delegation of fifty former magistrates, with five quinqueremes, went to Asia, and the Delphic oracle told them, in passing, that the best man in the world (*vir optimus*) should do the honours of making her welcome. P.Scipio Nasica, therefore, went to Ostia in anticipation of Cybele, with senators and knights, but above all in the company of Vestals and matrons to whom the 'best' of all Romans had to entrust the divine burden. The women passed the goddess from hand to hand to transport her to the temple of Victory, until such time as her own sanctuary was built on the Palatine. The Romans lit perfume-burners and burned incense in front of their house doors, entreating the Great Mother to enter the city and look kindly upon it (Liv., 29, 14, 10–13).

Livy, who tends to play down the women's role in this affair, mentions nothing of a miracle in the form of a test related to us by Ovid (F, 4, 295 ff.). At the mouth of the Tiber, men tugged in vain on the hawsers to haul the boat bearing the black stone upstream, and eventually gave up, stricken with fear. Then Claudia Quinta, a matron who was too beautiful and elegant for her virtue to be above suspicion, drew some water from the river and poured it three times over her head, before raising her hands to the sky and kneeling to pray to the goddess:

> People deny my chastity . . . But if I am innocent, thou who art chaste will obey my chaste hands.

And, unfastening her girdle, she freed the vessel. This miracle would be staged (ibid., 326), like a medieval mystery play, perhaps at the Megalesian Games. A votive altar and a medallion of Faustina Senior illustrate its popularity.

Men therefore cut their losses, at the same time taking restrictive and protective measures. The cult was supervised (like that of Ceres) by foreign priests (a Phrygian man and woman), as well as by *galli* (priests of Cybele) castrated like Attis, the companion who was both lover and son to the goddess. They emerged from the sanctuary only on procession days, notably when they went to bathe the idol in the waters of the Almo, on 27 March. At that time they had the right to make a collection, to the sounds of cymbals and tambourines. Lucretius (2, 617 ff.) is a witness to the great impression still made on his contemporaries by these festivals which were so contrary to the Latin temperament:

> . . . Trumpets offer the menace of their raucous sound, and the Phrygian rhythm of the flutes drives the senses wild. They brandish weapons as a sign of frenzy to throw terror into the ungrateful souls and impious hearts of the mob, who are frightened of the goddess' power . . .

Bronze and silver scattered the road, and roses rained down on the sacred idol. Lucretius evokes the 'Phrygian Curetes' who 'leaped rhythmically, rejoicing in the blood that drenched them' (ibid., 631).

But no Roman could make a collection for the goddess, dressed in many-coloured garments according to the Anatolian rite, as the law prohibited the castration of citizens. Senators celebrated the Great Mother by giving mutual banquets or *mutitationes*, and in order to do this organised themselves into fraternities. The decemvirs, then quindecemvirs *sacris faciundis*, would keep control of the cult and its clergy to the very end of paganism.

The aerolith was enclosed in the silver head of the idol. Placed in the temple of Victory on 4 April 204 BC, she had a temple to herself alone on 10 April 191 BC on the Palatine, not far from Romulus's hut, thus within the pomoerium, because of her links with the Aeneads (Ov., F, 4, 272). That is why each year, from 4 to 10 April, games were celebrated (*Megalesia*): theatrical shows in front of the temple and chariot races in the Circus Maximus on the last day. Several of Terence's comedies were performed at the Megalesian Games. Traces of the tiers intended for spectators have been discovered around the square opposite the sanctuary.

Officially, only the Mother existed, and her naturalisation earned the Romans an exceptional harvest in 204 BC (Plin., *NH*, 18, 16), as if she were trying to outdo Ceres. But numerous clay ex-votos depicting Attis, (many of which are datable to the second century BC), unearthed during excavations in the temple *cella*, prove that the god had already reached the ordinary populace. Also discovered were rounded objects representing the bulging tip of a penis (*glans penis*) which might refer to the pretended consecration of the organ.

Noteworthy variations distinguish the versions of the legend, but from the time of Claudius (AD 41–54), Romans took part in March in a kind of 'holy week' whose rites conveyed the myth of Attis, a god who died and came to life again each year; it was the first of its kind in the liturgy of the *Urbs*. The methods may have evolved before becoming fixed in the

Antonine period, but its highlights were celebrated as early as the first century.

The 'passion' of Attis began on the 15 with the procession of the 'cannophori' or 'bearers of reeds' who, having (apparently) come from the banks of the Almo, made their entry into the city to go to the Palatine sanctuary. The ceremony probably recalled the exposure of Attis on the banks of the Gallos, a tributary of the Sangarios (the Sakarya, north of Mount Dindymus). Rescued by Cybele, the child blossomed 'like a flower' (Jul., Or., 5, 165 b), and the Mother of the gods 'fell in love with him' (Sal., 4, 7). A week later, 22 March, the procession of the 'dendrophori' or 'bearers of the tree' entered Rome. They carried to the Palatine a pine tree felled in a wood consecrated to Cybele (Prud., Perist., 10, 196), after sacrificing a ram on the rooted stump (Firm, Err., 27, 4). This funereal procession evoked the death of Attis, who emasculated himself at the foot of a pine. The tree was wrapped in wool, as the corpse of the Phrygian shepherd had been by the daughter of King Midas, and garlands of violets recalled the blood that had flowed from the fatal mutilation (Arn., 5, 7). This was also the day – dies violae – when tombs were decked with flowers. The next day, 23, was given over to mourning and fasting, while the Salians blessed their trumpets (tubilustrium). In fact, abstinence had begun earlier for true believers, and they had gone without bread since the day before. Hence Christian taunts – quite worthy of Voltaire – about those faithful who ate pheasant 'in order not to sully the gifts of Ceres' (Jer., Ep., 107, 10)!

The 24 March is marked on the calendar under the name Sanguis – the 'day of Blood'. The galli beat their breasts, shrieking, flagellated themselves with whips made of small bones, and slashed themselves with blades to make the blood spurt, which they offered to the goddess. In their wake, to the piercing sound of curved flutes and the strident rhythm of the tambourines, came the candidates for priestly eunuchism who, in the dizzying excitement of this frenzied dance, used a flint to sacrifice their manhood. It was the 'sacrament of the order' (H. Graillot). They became 'Attises', and their testicles were the object of a consecration in the Palatine temple, whose pediment – renovated under Augustus – shows the Mother's throne flanked by eunuchs, just a few yards from the imperial palace: the religious universe of the Romans had decidedly changed! These new 'Attises' had themselves tattooed with red-hot needles to bear the mark of the Mother's seals (sphragitides). After their death, gold leaf was applied to the scarred parts (Prud., Perist., 10, 1076 ff.)

The emperor Julian (Or., 5, 168 d) wrote that on the third day 'the ineffable and sacred harvest of the god Gallos was cut': the phallic symbolism of the cornear which the Earth Mother causes to sprout, but demanding part of the grain for the future crop. The metaphor legitimised a ritual that embarrassed the Romans, before arousing the indignation of Christians. Seneca (see Aug., *CG*, 6, 10) deplored this blood-soaked obscenity:

> One amputates his manhood, another slashes his arms. Can one fear the gods when one seeks their favour in this manner?

Prudentius (*Perist.*, 10, 1061 ff.) would later portray

> a fanatic who propitiates the Mother of the gods by slashing his arms . . . Another dedicates his genitals which he has cut off to appease the divine power by mutilating his sexual organs. A eunuch, he offers the goddess 'an infamous gift' and 'feasts her on the blood that runs from them.'

At all events, it was better not to undertake anything on 24 March, and Suetonius (*Oth.*, 8, 5) remarks, disapprovingly, that Otho left Rome to march against Vitellius 'on the very day when the faithful of the Mother of the gods began to groan and feel sorry for themselves': it was a bad omen.

But after a night of doleful lamentation, on 25 March the joy of the Hilaria erupted, celebrating the revived Attis. In the imperial period it became the great springtime festival enlivened by a kind of carnival:

> As one then enjoys total freedom, one can give oneself up to every imaginable kind of amusement and assume any appearance one desires: there is no dignity so great or so considerable that it is not permissible for anyone who likes to assume it: reality is disguised in fun, and well enough to make it hard to distinguish the imitation from the original. (Hdn., 1, 10, 5)

Under cover of these unbridled rejoicings, in AD 187 the conspirator Maternus, disguised as a praetorian, hoped to assassinate the emperor Commodus, but word of the plot got out, and Commodus did not fail to ascribe his safety to Cybele, who was honoured in the coinage of that time.

A rest day (*requietio*) followed the carnival, before the grand procession of 27 March that bore the goddess to the Almo. At the head of the cortège walked the quindecemvirs *sacris faciundis* (Luc., 1, 599 f.), together with other important persons, wearing the toga but barefoot before the carriage of the Idaean Mother:

> You place on a float a blackish stone set in a silver head of a woman, in order to transport it. You take it to be bathed at the head of a procession, over a road that hurts your shoeless feet. (Prud., *Perist.*, 10, 154 ff.)

The idol was washed with ashes (perhaps those of the pine from the preceding year), together with the instruments of the cult. This *lavatio* had its origins in an old Anatolian rite intended to bring rain. The return to Rome by the Via Appia and Porta Capena, under a shower of fresh flowers (Ov., *F*, 4, 346), again gave rise to popular jubilation.

In the fourth century AD, the calendar of Philocalus (*CIL*, 1², p. 260) notes on 28 April: *Initium Caiani*, which may mean 'initiation to the Caianum', in the sector of Gaius Caligula's circus, on the area extending opposite the present St Peter's basilica. In 1609 a series of altars hallowing the memory of 'taurobolia' was unearthed. The taurobolium was a ritual that has been compared to a baptism of blood, and was first attested in AD 160 (*CIL.*, 13, 1751). It involved a sacrifice performed in the *Phrygianum* of the Vatican, set up in the time of Antoninus Pius, and certain contorniate medallions with the effigy of Faustina the Elder probably show us what it looked like. The initiation on 28 March could therefore have been of those who underwent the taurobolium.

But why did this ritual in some way duplicate that of the emasculation which every year, on 24 March – the Day of Blood – created new Attises? As the law ruled out castration, a procedure had to be provided that would confer an equivalent 'sacrament' on those who wished to remain Roman citizens. It was a special problem for the archgallus, who was officially in charge of the galli but, as a Roman priest, could not be castrated. His office was bound up with the taurobolium, at first celebrated in the port of Ostia (so it seems) before it was performed in the Vatican and the rest of the empire 'to safeguard' the emperor. This substitution sacrifice, in fact, spared the devout follower of the Mother the incon-veniences of emasculation. Prudentius (*Perist.*, 10, 1011–50) gives us a very detailed description:

> A trench is dug, and the high priest to be consecrated (*summus sacerdos . . . consecrandus*) climbs into it, magnificently adorned with streamers of cloth, with festive ribbons around his temples beneath a golden crown that holds his hair back. His silk toga is draped in the Gabine fashion, with one of its free ends forming a belt. Above him, a lattice grating is constructed by assembling the planks without binding them. Many slits and holes are pierced, using a gimlet . . . Here a fierce and shaggy bull is brought. Garlands of flowers are hung about its shoulders or entwined in its horns. Gold shines from the victim's forehead: a gilded plaque gleams on its hide.

The bull was thus adorned as for a traditional Roman sacrifice, and the way the priest was attired *cinctu Gabino* proves that he was involved in public worship. But the animal's breast was pierced 'with blows from a holy spear', and a rush of hot blood spurted from the wound on to the floor where the victim lay:

> Then through innumerable channels from a thousand holes, this filtered rain falls like a foul dew. Enclosed in the trench, the priest receives it, exposing his hideous head to every drop. His garments and his whole body are impregnated with its stench. Even worse: he throws his head back, offers his cheeks, ears, lips and nostrils to it, even moistens his eyes with the running gore; and not sparing his palate, he drenches his tongue, until he is completely saturated in the dark blood.

When the 'flamines' had removed the bull's rigid and drained cadaver, the trench was opened. The 'taurobolised' man emerged 'repulsive to look at', revealing his dripping face, clogged beard, soaked bands and blood-saturated clothing. He was hailed and worshipped from a distance 'in the belief that vile blood and a dead ox have purified him, hidden in that sordid pit.'

By impregnating himself in this way with the victim's blood, he was identified with it by way of a ritual pretence. Epigraphy informs us also that the bull's testicles were removed to be consecrated in the temple, as happened to those severed by the galli. The taurobolium was usually coupled with a 'criobolium', the sacrifice of a ram whose testicles played a mysterious role in the myth of Deo recorded by Clement of Alexandria (*Protr.*, 2, 15, 2). The apologist immediately goes on to speak of the formulary or 'symbol' of initiation to the Mother-worship cult; the candidate had to say:

> I have eaten from the tambourine; I have drunk from the cymbal; I have penetrated behind the curtain of the nuptial bed. (ibid., 3)

In the fourth century in Rome, Firmicus Maternus (*Err.*, 18, 1) knew a variation of the same symbol:

> I have eaten from the tambourine, I have drunk from the cymbal, and I have thoroughly learned the mysteries of the cult.

But in the Greek version quoted immediately afterwards, the last statement is different: 'I have become an initiate of Attis.'

The initiation apparently comprised a rite of communion (with food and drink taken from the instruments of the Metroac orgy), and a hierogamy, union with the goddess 'behind the curtain' which turned the initiate into a new Attis. African inscriptions associate the rite of 'sacred vessels' with the taurobolium, possible receptacles for the victim's blood. There was no question of it in Rome itself. Firmicus distinguishes the mystic 'symbol' of the taurobolium, which had to be repeated after twenty years, although in AD 376 one who had taken part declared himself to be 'reborn for eternity' (*CIL*, 6, 510), perhaps to challenge those who, through baptism, claimed to be 'reborn in Christ'. It was, in fact, a time of extreme tension between the converts and the last of the pagans. Easter happened to coincide with the Mother-cult liturgies in March, and the Fathers of the Church could not find harsh enough words to denounce the horrors of the Anatolian cult.

Nevertheless, it had undergone some 'modernising'. Sallustius (4, 10), the friend of Julian, allegorically justifies (just like the 'Apostate') all the ritual phases of the 'passion' of Attis, with whom his faithful 'ascend' to the gods. After a time of fasting, 'milky food represents our rebirth'. Like the silver dish of Parabiago, contorniate medallions show us Attis in Cybele's chariot, a celestial triumph in which his faithful followers hope one day to have their part. The holy week of the Phrygian cult is also related to the solar cycle. With the attributes of the Sun and the Moon (as he was likened to the Mên of the Pisidians), in other words the guarantors of cyclic eternity, Attis acquired the cosmic dimension of a sovereign god; but that did not mean the exclusion of all other gods. The Romans admitted that different gods enjoyed full powers in order to be sure of having all the luck on their side.

Even more gory than the dance of the galli was the armed dance of the 'fanatics' devoted to another Anatolian Mother: Mâ-Bellona, whom legionaries had brought back from Cappadocia at the time of the first campaigns against Mithridates. In a dream Sulla saw the goddess handing him the thunderbolt capable of wiping out his enemies (Plut., *Sull.*, 9, 8) and, a little later, a man prophesied in the name of Bellona to predict his victory over Marius (ibid., 27, 12). But any unhappy lover could also invoke her menacing oracles against the seducer or the unfaithful woman. Tibullus, a Roman so attached to ancestral cults (as we have seen), appealed to the august priestess of Mâ in order to hear her inspired voice:

> Once set in motion by the transports of Bellona, in her frenzy she fears neither the heat of the fire nor blows of the whip. With a double-edged hatchet, she violently wounds her arms, sprinkling the goddess with her blood, yet feeling no pain. Standing, her side pierced by a dart, her breast torn, she prophesies events which the powerful goddess makes known to her: 'Beware of profaning the young woman who is watched over by Love, so that you do not later rue the lessons of a terrible punishment! Touch her, and your wealth will be dispersed like the blood from my wounds, or as this ash is scattered by the wind.' (Tib., 1, 6, 45–54)

In the time of Martial (12, 57, 11), a century later, the demonstrations of Bellona's priests contributed to the sounds of the urban throng, and their dismal garments (Tert., *Pall.*, 4, 10) were a part of the motley picture of imperial Roman life (Fig. 14).

The mendicant eunuchs of Atargatis, who called upon both Bellona and the Idaean Mother (Ap., M, 8, 25, 3), with their gaudy shirts, saffron yellow robes or red-banded tunics, were also a part of it. They, too, slashed their arms with hatchets or swords before uttering prophecies (ibid., 27, 1–6). But literary tradition takes no account of their presence in Rome itself, although their goddess had had worshippers there since the first century AD, and an epitaph bears witness to one of her galli (*CIL*, 6, 32462).

– DIONYSUS AND SABAZIUS –

Euripides likened the Bacchanalia (*Bacc.*, 78 ff.) to the orgies of Cybele. In the time of Augustus, Dionysius of Halicarnassus (*AR*, 2, 19) admired the loyalty of the Romans to their ancestral liturgies:

> What I admired above all else was that in spite of the influx of innumerable nations into Rome, each one imperiously demanding to worship its gods according to its native traditions, never did the city show a desire to adopt these exotic customs officially, as a number of towns have done to their cost.

There follows the example of the Great Mother, incorporated into Roman worship with all the 'precautions taken by the city towards foreign religious practices.' And the historian hails the repugnance felt by Romans for the 'woolly-minded' or indecent pomp of the galli, gesticulating in their multi-coloured robes to the sound of flutes.

Nevertheless, not all Romans, even in the golden era (in the century of the Scipios), felt this fundamental repugnance, as is evidenced by the success of the Bacchanalia, in the wake of the Second Punic War. Livy speaks of it as an evil that had already been hatching for several years in 186 BC. At that time a horde of foreigners had settled in the *Urbs* (Liv., 39, 3, 6), and from then on their numbers outstripped any means of controlling their flow and component elements. Near the river port, on the forum Boarium, on the sides and at the foot of the Aventine where the plebeian triad had their temple, were Italians from the north and south, Greeks and various groups who were living on the fringes of the city. It was in this sector that the Bacchantes gathered, both men and women, to get drunk, dance and rave 'to the rattle of timbrels and cymbals' (ibid., 8, 8). Uttering frenzied cries and swaying their bodies, they prophesied, and the matrons, their hair blowing about as if they were Maenads, rushed down the slope to the Tiber, where they plunged their torches into the water without extinguishing them, thanks to a mixture of lime and sulphur (ibid., 13, 12).

But this 'hotbed of every corruption' (ibid., 10, 6) eventually aroused concern. The 'to-ing and fro-ing, the shouts and cries which resounded throughout the city at night' (ibid., 15, 6) raised questions, until the day when a nice young man, whose mother wanted to initiate him into the mysteries, was put on his guard by his girl friend. For ten days of sexual abstinence were imposed on the candidate and, when he informed her of this, she let loose a stream of imprecations: whoever was introduced into the 'sanctuary' or *Bacchanal* 'was handed over to the priests like a victim' (ibid., 10, 7), which implied an obviously fictitious death, the initiate having to die to be reborn into a new life. But chiefly it was a place of ill fame where the noise of cymbals and timbrels smothered the cries of those being assaulted. Very probably the ritual comprised a sexual initiation (ibid., 13, 10) akin to tribal initiations. As for the reluctant, they were sacrificed 'like victims' (ibid. 11), or they were made to disappear, 'chained to some kind of machinery, in secret caverns' (ibid., 13): a rite of 'catabasis' or descent into hell, Dionysus having supposedly snatched his mother Semele from the abode of the dead, and would thus one day bring back his initiates from it.

At first reserved for women, as originally in Greece, the initiation was performed on three set days in the year, before being available five times a month for men (ibid., 13, 8–9), preferably the under-twenties (ibid., 10, 16). From being diurnal, the Bacchanalia became nocturnal. This adaptation – typical of the mobility and flexibility of the Dionysiac mysteries – was due to a Campanian priestess, Paculla Annia, who initiated her sons, the two *Cerrinii*. Their name contains that of Kerri, the Osco-campanian Ceres, and it was no accident that their religious activities took shape in the shadow of the Aventine triad that associated the goddess with Liber, identified with Bacchus.

The initiates committed themselves by a fearsome oath, violation of which condemned the culprit to the fate of Dionysus Zagreus, who was torn to pieces by the Titans (ibid., 13, 5). This *sacramentum* isolated the Bacchant from the Roman community:

> In your opinion, citizens, should young initiates who have been enrolled by such an oath be turned into soldiers? Should weapons be given to this troop that has emerged from a sanctuary of obscenity? (ibid., 15, 13)

The *Respublica* could not tolerate such a deviation, which chiefly involved women and young men. But this society on the fringes of family and civic worship now constituted 'another people' (ibid., 13, 14), and their numbers worried the authorities: over 7,000 Bacchants, so it was said (ibid., 17, 6). The religious notion of a 'people' unconnected with the city-state was simply revolutionary! The 'conspirators' were accused of every kind of crime, besides debauchery: murder, bearing false witness, forging wills, falsifying seals and various types of fraud. In order not to incur the wrath of the god, the cult of Bacchus was not formally banned, but its exercise was restricted. No more than five people could take part in a ceremony, and there could be no communal funds or clergy (ibid., 18, 9). Only those places hallowed by an idol or an ancient altar were tolerated; all other *Bacchanalia* were destroyed.

As for the Bacchants, some left Rome, others killed themselves. Those who, 'sworn by an impious oath to undertake every criminal and perverse act' (ibid., 18, 3) had not actually committed any, were thrown into prison. Capital punishment was inflicted on the rest. One of the officials, the Campanian Minius Cerrinius, was interned at Ardea: his priestly status (perhaps in connection with Ceres-Cerrus) required some compromises. Women were handed back to their relatives or those on whom they were legally dependent (husbands or brothers), to suffer their punishment in private (ibid., 6). The affair would have consequences within families, where the patriarchal religion was inexorably called into question.

Even when repressed, Dionysism continued to haunt imaginations through the theatre and Greek art, whose representations supplanted the terracotta gods (Liv., 34, 4, 4). Paintings in the Villa Item in Caesar's time – and he was supposed to have authorised the transfer of the Bacchic mysteries to Rome (Serv., B, 5, 29) – testify to the incorporation of their myth and rites into the closed environment of wealthy houses: a phenomenon illustrated half a century later by the stucco decoration of two little rooms discovered in the Villa Farnese, probably arranged for Julia, Augustus's rebellious daughter, who was well worthy of those who in 186 BC had already shaken off the yoke of family worship. The initiation of the infant Dionysus into his own mysteries can be seen, and certain references to secret liturgies.

At all events, Bacchanalia remained the affair of private societies or 'thiasi', sometimes organised within the *familia* in the Latin sense of the word (including the domestic staff): for example, the thiasus of Torre Nova which around AD 160–6, comprised some 500 members (*IGUR*, 160). The iconography of the Dionysiac mysteries and literary tradition relating to them place them in rural circles or, at least, on the fringes of urban life. The candidates became 'Herdsmen', *boukoloi*. They were draped in a nebris, or skin of a fawn which, originally, the Maenads had torn to pieces live to eat its raw meat (omophagia). At Torre Nova, the 'guardians of the grotto' ἀντροφύλακες imply a performance evoking either the childhood of Bacchus, or his return from the underworld. Ordeals probably made the initiates, the new Dionysuses, relive the acts of their dead and revived god. Their consecration was completed by the rite of the winnowing-basket being passed over their head, which was covered with a veil like the basket in which, amid various kinds of fruits, a pastry phallus arose, the symbol of the generative and regenerative power that was a guarantee against death.

Another Thraco-Phrygian god, Sabazius, known for his nocturnal orgies and the role played in them by a snake (as in the Bacchic cult), made news in 139 BC. At that time his followers were expelled from Rome by the praetor peregrinus; Valerius Maximus (1, 3, 3) confused them with the Jews who worshipped Sabaoth. Cicero (*Leg.*, 2, 36) approved of the comedy writer Aristophanes driving out from the city 'Sabazius and other foreign gods, after making them stand trial.' The Sabaziasts (traces of whom have been found in Teos, Rhodes and Piraeus) must have landed at the river port and created an uproar in the area where the Bacchants had formerly held sway. When the rebellion of the Thracian Spartacus erupted in 73 BC, making Rome tremble, perhaps people wondered if the snake seen by the slave in a dream, twining about his face, when he had been brought to the *Urbs* to be sold, might have some connection with the sacred orgies of his companion, a prophetess of the same race as himself, who had predicted that he would have 'a great and formidable power' (Plut., *Crass.*, 8, 4).

– GODS OF THE NILE AND AFRICA –

The Roman conquest of the Mediterranean basin encouraged the movement of men from all kinds of different cultures, at the same time as the influx of captives brought back by triumphant victors altered the city's ethnic and religious aspects. These foreigners brought with them their native deities who, uprooted, would soon cohabit with the gods of the Roman people, sometimes eventually supplanting them. For the victors themselves were not slow to succumb to the appeal of exoticism or the charms of 'Greek life'. Soldiers fighting in distant lands sometimes returned from them with certain cults to which they believed they owed their life or health. And 'who can say how much influence ladies' maids from Antioch or Alexandria may have obtained over the mind of their mistress?' (F. Cumont)

Like Dionysus, the Egyptian gods reached Rome by way of Campania. In the second century BC, traders on Delos made the acquaintance of Isis and Serapis, whom a priest from Memphis had imported at the beginning of the preceding century. Many of these *negotiatores* were originally from southern

Italy where, with Alexandrian sailors, they spread Nilotic representations. Very soon Pompeii had its Iseum and Pozzuoli its Serapeum. The faithful formed themselves into 'colleges'. Rome had one of 'pastophori' (bearers of the curtain that opened the sanctuary) which traced its institution to the time of Sulla. As we have seen, the dictator was not indifferent to the charisma of eastern deities.

But the enthusiasm of the urban plebs for the gods of the Delta caused some disturbances. In 59 BC, when the Senate ordered the destruction of the altars of Serapis, Harpocrates and Anubis, they were very soon reinstated 'owing to the violence of the people's intervention' (Varr. from Tert., *Nat.*, 1, 10, 17). On the calends of January 58 BC, a turbulent mob upset the sacrifice to Jupiter Capitolinus, and while the consul was examining the victim's entrails, he was heckled 'because he made no decision about Isis and Serapis' (ibid., 18): in other words, because he had not satisfied their followers. This was the time when the clubs (*collegia*) were growing restless, at the instigation of the notorious Clodius. Politics and religion were then a dangerous threat to public order. With his gangs, Clodius invaded the scene of the sacred theatre at the time of the Megalesian games of 56 BC. The ground groaned and shook at Potenza: Cybele, whose games had been profaned, 'shuddered as she ran through fields and woods' (Cic., *Har.*, 24).

Far from being disheartened, Isiac militants had chapels privately built, but the Senate ordered their destruction in 53 BC (DC, 40, 47, 4). Three years later, the Senate again ordered the demolition of the temples of Isis and Serapis, but no workman dared put his hand to the task. Removing his toga praetexta, the consul seized an axe and struck the sanctuary doors (Val. Max., 1, 3, 4). Two years on (48 BC), as prodigies had affected the Capitol, the augurs recommended razing the sacred enclosures of the Egyptian gods that had been built on the hill, where a 'priest of Isis Capitolina' perhaps officiated (*CIL*, 6, 2247). The fact that an exile managed to escape his would-be-killers thanks to Isiac costume and the mask of Anubis is evidence of the respect shown to the Nilotic gods (Val. Max., 7, 3, 8; App., *bc*, 4, 47). Significantly, too, the triumvirs Octavian, Antony and Lepidus, promised to build a temple to Isis and Serapis to win favour with the populace (DC, 47, 15, 4). But the promise was not kept, and the war setting Octavian against Cleopatra's lover would become a war of the gods, between Apollo and 'barking Anubis' (Virg., *Aen.*, 8, 698; Prop., 3, 11, 41). In 28 BC Octavian prohibited Egyptian cults within the pomoerium (DC, 53, 2, 4) and in 21 BC Agrippa forbade anyone to practise them, 'even in the suburbs, this side of an eighth half-stade' (ibid., 54, 6, 6), that is, less than a kilometre.

Such coercive measures reveal the progress and success of Alexandrian worship, which worried a government that was anxious to restore the values of Romans' most traditional qualities. Isis had the bewitching charm, beauty and goodness of a Madonna who would above all listen to women and the unfortunate. She had undergone the ordeals of widowhood before restoring Osiris to life, after he had been the victim of Seth, the spirit of evil. Anubis, the jackal- or dog-headed god, had helped her to discover the traces of her dismembered husband. In commemoration, the Isiac liturgy repeated the sufferings of god and goddess. As for Serapis, he was a Graeco-Alexandrian reinterpretation of Osiris in his role of sovereign and protector of the dead. In Hellenistic and Roman worship, he had acquired the attributes of a healer-god, helpful to anyone who invoked him. When they were delocalised, these gods tended to become universal, or at least available to all and sundry, anywhere people had need of them. For this universality did not conflict with their quality of very personal gods, constantly close to their faithful followers, which rendered them all the more demanding:

> I myself have seen someone sit down before the Isiac altars, confessing to having offended the linen-clad goddess. Another, deprived of his sight for a similar fault, cried out in the middle of the street that he had deserved it. The gods like people to make this kind of confession, which proves and bears witness to their holy power. (Ov., *Pont.*, 1, 1, 51–6)

This attitude, so fundamentally alien to the religion of the old Romans, was akin to that of the devout followers of the Syrian Goddess, who linked the confession of their sins to the sufferings of a real penance (Ap., M, 8, 28, 1–3).

The Isiacs, who wounded their chests with blows from a pine cone to lament the suffering and death of Osiris (Minuc., 22, 1; Firm., *Err.*, 2, 3), drew attention to themselves because of their lacerations. In the streets of imperial Rome, one could meet shrieking women crawling on their knees; and men who, with a lamp in their hand in broad daylight, shouted that a god was angry, and the crowd of gawking onlookers let themselves be impressed (Sen., *VB*, 26, 8):

> At daybreak, in winter, our devout woman will break the ice on the Tiber to plunge into it three times and will dip her shivering head into the eddies; then, naked and shuddering, she will drag herself on her bloodied knees the length of the Field of the Proud king. (Juv., 6, 522 ff.)

This Field of the last Tarquin was the Campus Martius, where there was a great temple to Isis, the *Iseum Campense*.

The goddess obliged the women she protected to observe periods of sexual abstinence which were not at all to the liking of their lovers (Tib., 1, 3, 23 ff.; Ov., *Am.*, 3, 9, 34). But they were the first to call upon her should their beloved risk death after an abortion (ibid., 2, 12, 7 ff.): Saving her, you will restore life to two victims?' If a wife fell short of the strict observance of the holy days, there could always be some sort of arrangement with the priest of Osiris: 'A fat goose, a little cake, and the god lets himself be corrupted!' (Juv., 6, 540 f.).

Whatever the unbelievers might say, and even though Tibullus submitted with an ill grace to the sexual restrictions of Isiasm, it did not prevent him from appealing to her once he had fallen ill:

> Now, help me. For many pictures in your temples prove it: you can cure! My Delia, fulfilling the vows I utter, will sit, clad in linen, before the sacred portals and, twice a day, with her hair loosened, she will sing hymns to your glory, beautiful to behold in the crowd of the faithful of Pharos. (1, 3, 27–32)

The ex-votos Tibullus mentions gave equal honour to the healing deity and the queen of heaven 'Our Lady of the Waves', to whom sailors prayed.

The favour of the Egyptian gods in the circles of the demi-monde sometimes involved them in shady schemes. Decius Mundus despaired of seducing Paulina, a lady of illustrious blood and uncompromising virtue, when he learned that she was devoted to the cult of Isis, 'the procuress' (Juv., 6, 489). He arranged with the priests to set up a rendezvous with Anubis, whose place he would take. With the consent of her husband, Paulina went by night to the temple and satisfied the 'god'. The lovely lady bragged about it, but so did her seducer, and the scandal came out into the open. Tiberius had the priests crucified, the temple razed and the idol of Isis thrown into the Tiber (Jos., *AJ*, 18, 65–80). This repression linked Judaic rites with the Alexandrian ceremonies, and 4,000 individuals 'infected with these superstitions' (Tac., *An.*, 2, 85, 5) were deported to Sardinia. All the cultic instruments and Isiac vestments were burnt (Suet., *Tib.*, 36, 1).

Like the phoenix, however, Isiasm was once again reborn from its ashes; and it was Caligula, Tiberius's successor, who not only rebuilt the *Iseum Campense*, but also made the inclusion of the festivals of Osiris in the Roman calendar official.

In AD 70, Vespasian and Titus spent the night in this temple before celebrating their triumph over the Jews, and the coins minted then show us its facade. But a fire destroyed it in AD 80, and Domitian who, in Isiac costume, escaped from the Vitellians while leaving the burning Capitol (Suet., *Dom.*, 1, 4), restored the Iseum magnificently. The obelisk in Piazza Navona glorifies the emperor 'beloved of Isis and Ptah', who rebuilt and embellished the sanctuary. To the south it was repeated in a semi-circular Serapeum extending as far as the present-day church of Sto Stefano del Cacco, whose name is a reminder of the granite monkey dug up from the foundations. This Iseum, where an enclosure isolated the sacred area from the secular environment, formed a kind of enclave in the urban fabric. According to an Egyptian priest who had come to see the philosopher Plotinus around AD 260, it was the 'only pure place to be found in Rome' (Porph. *V. Pl.*, 10). With its avenue lined with statues of Apis, lions, sphinxes and dog-headed gods, its campaniform capitals and shafts of pink granite bearing liturgical scenes, for the Romans it was like finding a little bit of Egypt in the heart of the town. Moreover, it was Nile water that was displayed every morning for their adoration, when the gates of the sanctuary were solemnly opened. They were shut once again around two in the afternoon, and this closing service was punctuated with chants, like the opening ceremony in the morning.

Besides this daily ritual, the Isiacs had their annual festivals, which became those of the Roman people from the time of Caligula. From 28 October to 3 November, the death and rediscovery of Osiris were staged in the sanctuary, and his 'reassembly' and resurrection, which were celebrated in the streets with Hilaria comparable to the great Metroac festival of 25 March.

Seneca 'derides the tears shed for the lost Osiris and the great joy that is shown when he is found again, when his loss and rediscovery are mere fiction' (Aug., CG, 6, 10, 2). Followers played the part of Anubis, uncovering for Isis the traces of the dead god. Juvenal denounces someone 'who, escorted by his linen-clad and shaven-headed troop, goes through the town wearing the mask of Anubis, laughing up his sleeve at the contrition of the populace' (6, 532 ff.). But the indignation of the philosopher and the satirist was to no avail; the Isiac contagion spread to aristocratic circles and even to men. Otho, the future emperor, assiduously participated in the ceremonies, wearing a linen robe (Suet., *Oth.*, 12, 2). In the fourth century, sober senators wore the face of the dog-headed god (*Ad sen.*, 32), *latrator Anubis* (*Carm. c. pag.*, 95). But the emperor Commodus took advantage of it to mortify his co-religionists and used the canine mask to hit them (SHA, C, 9, 4). Caracalla revealed a doubtless more sincere fervour for Serapis.

Another very popular annual ceremony was the *navigium Isidis* which, on 5 March, reopened shipping trade in all the big sea ports like Ostia, but probably also in Rome itself, in the river port that had developed at the foot of the Aventine. A kind of carnival preceded the procession of stolists miming the idol's toilette, sacred musicians and choristers, shaven initiates in white linen robes and priests carrying the symbols of the gods. A new boat was moored, and purified with a torch, an egg and some sulphur, before being laden with 'presents and votive objects of happy omen' (Ap., M, 11, 16, 9). It was then set adrift and, on returning to the temple, a hierogrammat said prayers for the emperor, the Senate, the equestrian order and the Roman people (ibid., 17, 3). This just shows how Egyptian ritual was incorporated into public worship; but in certain sanctuaries, exoticism remained indomitable (Fig. 15).

Up to the end of the fourth century, coins with Isiac themes were minted and circulated in Rome for the *Vota Publica*, but perhaps for those made at the beginning of the civil year, on 3 January. After Theodosius's victory over the pagan coalition (6 September AD 394) and the death of Nicomachus Flavian, 'the last of the Romans' (A. Stein), Egyptian gods no longer enjoyed the 'freedom of the city'. But in November AD 417, at Falerii, the Gaul Rutilius Namatianus (1, 375) could still see peasants rejoicing because 'Osiris at last revived is making the seed grow for the new crops.'

Besides the *Iseum Campense*, where the foreigner in transit could feel spiritually at home, *religionis autem indigena* (Ap., M, 11, 26, 3), Rome had several Egyptian sanctuaries. 'Beloved of Serapis' (*Philosarapis*), Caracalla, who revered the sovereign healer in this Alexandrian god, dedicated a colossal temple to him on the Quirinal (within the pomoerium), and some enormous fragments of its architecture can still be seen in the gardens of the Villa Colonna. Two monumental staircases allowed access to it from the Campus Martius. The Dioscuri who today adorn the Piazza Cavallo, opposite the presidential palace, possibly framed the entrance to the Serapeum which, in its height and proportions, almost rivalled the temple of Jupiter Capitolinus.

On the Aventine, excavations of the Sta Sabina church revealed the existence of curious premises which, in the reign of Marcus Aurelius (161–80) were a meeting-place for 'mystes' of lowly status and questionable morals, as the graffiti deciphered on the walls testify. These poor people had special friendships that were not at all impeded by an intense faith. 'Believe and do not weaken: take heart!'

The paintings decorating this vaulted room evoke the piety of the faithful followers, their offerings, the ibis and the sacred water of the Nile, the roses dear to Isis (as they would be later to the Virgin). A fragment of fresco opens like a window on to the dream of a happy life by the sea, far from the urban crush, but without any apparent connection with the *navigium Isidis*.

Other deities from the African continent gained a foothold in Rome: Jupiter Ammon, a god from Cyrene, was there chiefly through iconography, in the forum of Augustus (in memory of Alexander, the haunting model of universal monarchy), but also on funerary altars where his head with ram's horns safeguarded the tomb. Septimius Severus consecrated a 'gigantic' temple (DC, 77, 16, 3) to the gods of his homeland, Leptis Magna 'the Great': Hercules and Liber who represented the Punic Melqart and Eschmoun. The *Virgo Caelestis*, 'evoked' in 146 BC by Scipio Aemilianus, also enjoyed the favour of Septimius Severus, whose coinage shows the goddess on a lion's back, like Cybele in the Circus Maximus. On the Capitol she was to be found associated with Sabazius, her neighbour, unless she had offered him hospitality – a small courtesy that was known among foreign gods. A votive monument shows two pairs of bare feet pointing in opposite directions: perhaps the departure and return of a traveller who had arrived safe and sound? Another dedication (*CIL*, 6, 77) bears two sculpted ears: those of a deity who, like Isis, knows how to listen to her worshippers.

– CULTS OF THE LEVANT –

Numerous Syrians played an active part in imperial Rome. Deploring the fact that 'the Syrian Orontes has long overflowed into the Tiber', Juvenal (3, 63 ff.) at once plunges us into the non-native population carried along by this influx, with

> its language, its customs, the flute-players, the cross-strung harps, the native drums, the prostitutes of the Circus Maximus . . . these barbarian she-wolves with their gaudy headdresses!

There were also astrologers (Cic., *Div.*, 1, 132) and other charlatans (Hor., *S*, 1, 6, 113; Juv., 6, 588) or traders in shoddy goods (Tac., *An.*, 15, 38, 2). The man in search of a passing affair took care not to forget the zone where, in July, women bewailed the death of Adonis (Ov., *AA*, 1, 75), the Phoenician god of vegetation; perhaps in the *Adonaea* on the Palatine where Heliogabalus would mime Salambô 'with all the lamentations and gesticulations of the Syrian cult' (SHA, *Hel.*, 7, 3). The Syrian *ambubaiae* (Hor., *S*, 1, 2, 1) who played a flute accompaniment to the funereal chants also offered their charms for sale.

The worship of the Levantine gods chiefly involved their compatriots and was concentrated in the Trastevere area, which has provided the great majority of evidence. The fact that certain followers had their commercial interests on the other bank of the Tiber, in the warehouse zone, is no proof that they also practised their cults there.

Unfortunately, we know nothing, or next to nothing, about those practices. Setting aside the very singular instance of the 'Syrian sanctuary of the Janiculum', we must remember first that the imported worship of a Phenico-Cypriot Zeus 'who descends in a flash of lightning' (*Keraunios*) and of Jupiter Heliopolitanus (from Baalbek) was grafted in the second century AD on to the cult of the Nymphs *Furrinae*, in a wood sanctifying well-water, the kind that had to be sought and piped. The inscription (*IGUR*, 109) of a certain Gaionas, carved on a slab on either side of a large perforation, reminds us that this person 'has effected this powerful link to make sacrifice to the gods possible'. The document belongs in the same context and, very obviously, the 'powerful link' in question means the piping of water that has successfully been harnessed.

The same Gaionas, whose epigraphy (*IGUR*, 166) informs us of his connection with Marcus Aurelius and Commodus, was a flamen of the imperial cult, and calls himself *cistiber Augustorum* (traditionally in charge of nocturnal security on the near side of the Tiber). According to the first dedication, he was also 'the organiser of feasts' (*deipnokrites*). The religious importance of banquets in the Syrian east is well known. Followers of Jupiter Heliopolitanus had to meet in a sanctuary in the Trastevere district where water had a role to play, as in the temples of Atargatis which were complemented by a pool containing sacred fish. This Syrian goddess was part of a triad worshipped in Baalbek, with a divine son likened to Mercury: he is shown in a small relief found on the Palatine which may have been used in the devotions of Syrians belonging to the imperial household staff.

On the slope of the Janiculum, Hadad (with the titles *Libaneotes* and *Acroreites*) was worshipped, as well as a Jupiter *Maleciabrudus*, 'king of Yabruda', an area of the Anti-Lebanon. Elsewhere, in Rome itself, the Jupiter of Damascus, Jupiter *Bellefarus* ('Baal of Efara', a Syrian place-name), *Balmarcodes* ('Baal of dances'), *Turmasgades* ('Mountain of Adoration') similarly had their devout followers, but nothing at all is known about the rituals applied to them.

We have hardly more factual knowledge of the cult of the Palmyranians for Aglibol (lunar god) and Malakbel (solar god) in their Porta Portese district. An altar found in this sector associates with the 'very holy Sun', carried on an eagle (and whose chariot drawn by gryphons occupies the left side), the bust of Saturn, the night-time sun in Babylonian astrology. 'Among the Assyrians, Bel is called both Saturn and Sun for a reason connected with the ceremonies' (Serv., *Aen.*, 1, 729): what 'ceremonies'?

We are slightly better informed, although very summarily, about the ritual for Jupiter Dolichenus, identified in numerous dedications (like Jupiter Heliopolitanus) with the 'Most Good Most Great' god of the Capitol. True, it is always a matter of a celestial sovereign, god of the storm and lightning. Originating in the country 'where iron is born' (*CCID*, 427), this Dolichenian Baal brandishes a thunderbolt and an axe, standing on a bull, while one of the deer family bears his partner 'Juno', carrying a sceptre and a mirror. On certain religious reliefs, their images are shown paired with Isis and Serapis (*CCID*, 365, 386).

In Rome, this Commagenian couple had at least two temples (on the Aventine and Esquiline), besides a possible place of worship in the barracks of foreign cavalry forming part of the imperial guard, near San Giovanni Laterano. The Esquiline sanctuary was also attended by soldiers, the one on the Aventine drawing its worshippers more from civilian circles. In any case, they were people who were firmly attached to the traditions of their place of origin.

Liturgical banquets assembled them in a *triclinium* recorded by epigraphy (*CCID*, 415) and recognised on the Dolichenian site on the Aventine (*CCID*, 355). Two Egyptian-style statuettes were found there, each holding an offerings table on which the symbols of bread and water can be deciphered (*CCID*, 396), which suggests that, as in the Mithraic cult, the two elements were consecrated. On a relief from the same source (*CCID*, 371), we see a priest in eastern costume (long robe and ornamental headdress) leading a bull destined for sacrifice, for the person holds a libation patera, just like the sacrificer in the Roman rite (Fig. 16). Before the sacrifice and the ritual feast, ablutions were performed. The discovery and written evidence of large bowls or basins are clear indications of purification rites, to say nothing of the 'tetrastyle nymphaeum' on the Esquiline (*CCID*, 408) and premises arranged for this purpose in the Aventine sanctuary (*CCID*, 355).

Dolichenian epigraphy records *lecticari dei* (*CCID*, 375, 381), or 'bearers of the divine litter': which implies processions transporting the sacred idol, as were known in the Semitic east, but also (as we have seen) in the Mother-worship cult. Did they take place in the area around the temple or in the streets of the district? Literary tradition, so long-winded regarding the demonstrations of Isiasm or Phrygianism, breathes not a word about them, not even mentioning so much as the name of the god of Doliche.

His followers were organised in communities. In the one on the Aventine they called one another 'Brothers' (*CCID*, 373, 381). Those who aspired to priestly ministry, or *candidati*, were intitiated under the guidance of a 'father', *pater candidatorum* (*CCID*, 373, 375, 381), who held a priesthood. However, a *notarius* (*CCID*, 380/1) had precedence over him: possibly a kind of 'chancellor' of the holy writings? Alongside the clergy, *patroni* formed a kind of parochial church council, looking after the material management of the premises. This cult must have had to be discreet in imperial Rome.

We have a better understanding of the cult of Baal of Emesa, mainly because of the scandal that its Chief Priest turned emperor provoked in the *Urbs* between AD 219 and AD 222.

Before the accession of Heliogabalus, his god had had sporadic worshippers in the Antonine era, but mostly around AD 201–2 (*CIL*, 6, 708, 1603, 2269), under Septimius Severus, whose wife Julia Domna was the daughter of a priest of Elagabal at Emesa (Homs). As it was a fringe cult at the time, the worship of *Sol Invictus Alagabalus* aroused no noticeable reaction in historiography.

In Emesa, it was all about a baetyl supposed to be an image of the Sun, which had fallen from the skies. In AD 217, Bassianus, Julia Domna's great-nephew, danced 'around the altars to the sound of hautboys, flutes and other instruments of all kinds' (Hdn., 5, 3, 8). The future emperor was wearing a 'barbarian' outfit, of purple shot with gold (a long-sleeved tunic) over thigh-high multi-coloured hose (ibid., 6). His grandmother, Julia Maesa, put it about that he was the natural son of Caracalla, whom Macrinus had had killed and who was greatly missed by the army. The legion stationed near Emesa proclaimed Bassianus under the name of his alleged father: *Antoninus*. Macrinus was defeated and killed.

The pseudo-Antoninus then set out for Rome, but with his god: a long journey in procession, marked by sacred halts along the way. For these liturgies, wearing a jewel-encrusted headdress, the emperor donned the apparel of Levantine priests 'in which gold mingled with purple' (ibid., 5, 3). He had a portrait of himself painted in this costume and sent the picture to Rome, with the command to place it above the famous statue of Victory before which the senators burnt incense and made libations of wine. Certainly, an *imperator* had never been seen in such an outfit. But the Romans had become accustomed to this image when Heliogabalus made his entry into the *Urbs* in AD 219, with his baetyl on a chariot. They told themselves that after all, if his god had given him victory, it would be better to win his favours and allow his chief priest to serve him according to his native tradition.

However, after the painting, the shock of the realities of sight and sound tended to antagonise the city's opinion. For his solar stone, Heliogabalus set up a grandiose sanctuary next to the imperial palace, on the site of the future church of San Sebastiano. In a vast sacred area, where he had several altars erected, the emperor was able to display all the pomp of his eastern cult:

> Every morning, he appeared at dawn and sacrificed huge numbers of bulls and a large quantity of smaller livestock, laid them on the altars, covered them with all kinds of aromatics, then poured over them many amphorae of the oldest and choicest wines, so that mingled streams of blood and wine flowed. Then he danced around the altars to the sound of various instruments, accompanied in his

movements by women of his country who, with cymbals and tambourines, ran around the same altars. The entire Senate and the equestrian order surrounded him, seated in a circle as at the theatre. As for the victims' entrails and the aromatics, placed in gold vessels, they were not carried on the heads of servants or any riff-raff, but by prefects of the praetorium and dignitaries of the highest rank, wearing wide-sleeved, ankle-length Phoenician-style robes with a purple band round the middle, and shod in linen like the prophets of those countries. (Hdn., 5, 5, 8–10)

With his mother and grandmother, Heliogabalus intoned 'barbaric chants' (DC, 80, 11, 3). He also had the bizarre idea of shutting in a lion, a monkey and a snake with his god (ibid.).

He associated Elagabal with two goddesses: Pallas-Allat and the 'Caelestis' of Carthage, whom the Romans identified with Juno but who was not unrelated to Venus-Astarte. A capital found on the Forum provides indisputable evidence. The *Augustan History* imputes to the emperor an ambition to centralise in his *Elagabalium* all the fetishes of the Roman cult (the idol of Cybele, the shields of Mars, the *Palladium* and Vestal fire) but this is the result of the distortions of a polemic perhaps targeting Christian monotheism, in the very period when the biography was written.

In the gardens of the Vecchia Speranza, where Constantine's mother would have a basilica built to house the relics of the 'holy cross of Jerusalem' that she had unearthed on Calvary, Heliogabalus consecrated a secondary temple to which, every year in July, the baetyl was carried in procession, in a chariot drawn by six white horses adorned with gold and gleaming trappings. In front of Elagabal, the emperor ran backwards holding the bridles and looking at the god, who was supposed to guide his priest along the entire road. Beneath his feet, the soil was strewn with gold dust, the metal and colour of the sun:

> The populace accompanied him running on either side, with all sorts of torches, and threw flowers and circlets over him. The statues of all the gods, all the costly and precious offerings, all the insignia of imperial dignity and luxury items, then the knights and the whole army solemnly opened the procession of the god. (Hdn., 5, 6, 8)

After conducting him to his summer residence and offering him sumptuous sacrifices, the emperor mounted one of the towers that frame the monumental entrance of Syrian temples, and with which he had endowed this periurban sanctuary. From the top of the building he threw down to the crowd gold and silver goblets, clothes and materials of every kind that all and sundry could appropriate, as well as all sorts of domestic animals, with the exception of pigs, because he abstained from this meat in accordance with the Phoenician custom. (ibid.)

The stampede to obtain these presents caused injury and death. At Hieropolis-Bambyke (Syria), living victims were also hurled from the top of the propylaea (Luc. Sam., *Syr.*, 58).

Such noisy, violent and even bloody exoticism (the chief priest was reputed to sacrifice children), but above all the unheard-of claim to give the Sun of Emesa more importance than Jupiter Capitolinus (DC, 80, 11, 1) alienated the Romans from Heliogabalus; they deplored the fact that this 'Antoninus' bore so little resemblance to those whose prestigious name he had usurped. Furthermore, Isis showed her discontent by turning her head towards the interior of her sanctuary on the Campus Martius (ibid., 10, 1). Grandmother Maesa, who sensed the way the wind was blowing, made the emperor adopt his cousin – the future Alexander Severus – so that power could remain within the family and under its control. Heliogabalus was killed by the praetorians, his cousin proclaimed emperor and the god of Emesa sent home. He would have his revenge half a century later, by helping Aurelian to vanquish Zenobia.

– MITHRAS –

Another *Sol Invictus* had been discreetly winning over officers of the army and administration since the end of the first century AD. He was the Iranian god of light whom Cilician pirates propitiated by 'strange sacrifices' and a clandestine cult in the mountains of Lycia around 70 BC (Plut., *Pomp.*, 24, 7). After defeating them, Pompey seems to have settled a good number of them in Calabria (Serv., G, 4, 127). Plutarch (*loc. cit.*) ascribes the celebration of the mysteries of Mithras to them, 'who were the first to make him known, and whose tradition is maintained to this day', that is to say, around AD 100.

Twenty years earlier, in Statius's *Thebaid*, at the end of canto I (719 f.), there appears for the first time in literature the figure of a Mithras overcoming the bull 'beneath the rocks of the Persian cavern'. It was also the era when the first Mithraists emerged epigraphically in the circles of the imperial household (CIL, 6, 732). The oldest known statuary group representing the bull-slaying god belongs to the same generation: its base in fact bears the dedication of a slave farmer of T. Claudius Livianus (CIL, 6, 718), praetorian prefect in AD 101. Keeping just to the *Urbs*, this religion made sufficient progress there to arouse the Christian indignation of Justin

(I *Apol.*, 66, 4), who reproached the 'evil demons' for imitating the eucharist in the mysteries of Mithras. He informs us, indeed, that 'bread and a cup of water were presented, while certain formulas were uttered'.

It must be said that the Mithraic liturgy consisted basically of a meal shared by the faithful, who reclined Roman-style on two parallel benches or *podia*, their heads towards the 'chancel' where the image of the god slaying a bull gleamed as a painting, a relief or an in-the-round sculpture. The victim's blood was deemed to nourish animal and plant life: a dog, a snake and a lion took immediate advantage of the invigorating liquor running from the wound; but trees appeared or blossomed round about, while ears of corn radiated from the wound and the tail. A scorpion pinched the animal's testicles. On either side of the scene, whose cosmic significance was underlined by the Sun and the Moon, the planets or the zodiac, two dadophori torch-bearers held torches, one (Cautes) held his aloft and the other (Cautopates) held his lowered. They corresponded respectively to the rising and setting sun, alternately ascending and descending in relation to the equator.

The slaying of the bull thus saved the whole of creation menaced by the evil powers of drought and shadows.

'And thou hast saved us by shedding the eternal blood,' says a line painted in the *Mithraeum* of Sta Prisca on the Aventine, the 'eternal' blood being the divine flow which animates living creatures. That was what was explained to the mystae in a form of instruction commentating on the sacred iconography, before the banquet re-enacting that of the Sun and Mithras on the carcase of the bull.

This banquet brought together the members of the community in premises that were often half underground and vaulted, like the cavern where once Mithras had struck the still resistant animal in the hollow beneath its shoulder. This imitation grotto, the ceiling of which was often painted to resemble a starry firmament or encrusted with pumice stone, could be found installed in the shadow of private or public establishments: under Caracalla's baths, adjoining the Circus Maximus or in the 'Foreigners'' barracks (on the Caelius). The richest and most spacious, under the church of Sta Prisca, had been installed in the Severian period in a *domus* that had belonged to the emperor Trajan. The nave walls show us a procession of mystae presenting the victims (bull, ram, pig and cock) and offerings intended for the banquet, presided over by the images of the Sun and Mithras. The niche of the 'chancel' housed a stucco group of Mithras slaying the bull, behind the majestically outstretched god Oceanus, draped in celestial blue. On the external side of the chancel a graffito can be deciphered, giving the date of its consecration: 20 November AD 202. To the north of the nave, and with access to it, rooms must have been used for intitation ceremonies.

Besides the religious relief reminding the mystae of the very act of salvation, in the caverns or *spelaea* there were statues of Cautes and Cautopates, a 'Petrogeneous' Mithras emerging from the rock with his torch and knife, a lion-headed monster entwined by a snake, deifying the cosmic fire, and other divinities such as Hecate or Serapis. Votive altars, shelves or sideboard tables for use at banquets, braziers, and wine or water containers variously furnished the *Mithraea*, which generally had kinds of offices or changing-rooms.

The priestly hierarchy ran to seven grades or stages of initiation. One became successively Raven, Bridegroom or Newly-wed (*Nymphus*), Soldier, Lion, Persian, Heliodromus or 'Messenger of the Sun' and finally Father. Each of the mystae attaining these titles wore the costume appropriate to his office, and the frescoes of Sta Prisca give us some idea of them. They were respectively under the protection of Mercury, Venus, Mars, Jupiter, the Moon, the Sun and Saturn. The Raven served the guests, the Nymphus gave them light. Marked on his forehead (perhaps branded), the Soldier who had been consecrated by the rite of a crown proffered on a sword-point (Tert., *Cor.*, 15, 3), in his turn put candidates for initiation to the test. The Lion, who was purified by having honey instead of water poured on his hands, looked after the fire. The Persian was the 'guardian of the fruit' (Porph., *Antr.*, 16). In the sacramental meal, the Heliodromus represented the Sun beside the Father representing Mithras. The Raven and the Lion wore masks suitable to their name.

This was a religion of small groups, certain caverns being incapable of holding more than ten or twelve participants. Bound by an oath which repeated the handshake (*dextrarum junctio*) uniting the god of light with the Daystar, the Mithraists knew and helped one another like the brothers of a Masonic lodge. As soon as one community expanded, another was organised rather than exceed the right measure of intimacy. How many *Mithraea* did Rome have? The probably exaggerated number of 700 has been suggested, but in any case there were around a hundred.

They met perhaps every evening at dinner time, or at least every Sunday (day of the Sun), for the planetary week had been in operation since the first century. Certain days in the year were more specially celebrated: the solstices of summer and winter (our 'Christmas', *natalis solis invicti*), the equinoxes (especially spring, the season when the world was born and Mithras saved it). Besides the consecrated water and bread (Just., I *Apol.*, 66, 4; Tert., *Praescr.*, 40, 4), wine, as a substitute for blood, and various kinds of meat were consumed, often the flesh of victims sacrificed to the gods of the city, which was sold in the markets. Verses were chanted, perhaps like those to be read on the walls of the cavern excavated under Sta Prisca:

> Chicken livers taste good, but concern governs the man piously born to a new life . . .

> You must all live together through dark days in ritual action.

Although Mithras recruited many followers in the imperial household, it is not evident that the Caesars – at least up to the Tetrarchy – honoured him openly. Marguerite Yourcenar's enchanting prose must not make us forget that Hadrian had been initiated (and in a taurobolic trench, to boot!). The *Augustan History* (C, 9, 6) reproaches Commodus for having sullied the Mithraic mysteries by a real murder where the ritual tested candidates 'for a shadow of fear', *ad speciem timoris*; but that evidence remains unconfirmed. A freedman of Septimius Severus is known, who called himself 'Father and priest of Mithras the Invincible *domus Augustanae*' (CIL, 6, 2271); but all the same, could we, like F. Cumont, speak of a 'chaplain in the palace of the Augusti'?

In fact, if Mithras, like Jupiter Dolichenus, was invoked 'for the well-being' of the emperor or the empire, neither of these two gods had public cults in the *Urbs*, unlike Isis and Cybele. Their faithful followers organised themselves outside the official rites, but would reinforce their effects, should the need arise. The development of the associative phenomenon in religious matters is also characteristic of a fairly mobile population, where the individual was no longer part of a fixed family or a city in the traditional sense of the word. These cultist clubs housed in the Mithraic caverns, the dolichenian temples or even some Bacchic thiasi gave the rootless immigrants to Rome, of every race and class, the feeling that they had found the comfort of a piety closer to gods and men. Nevertheless, the fervour of the private cenacle was not incompatible with the omnipotence of a universal god, nor with an ardent loyalism towards the sovereign.

– THE IMPERIAL CULT –

The emperor 'was a god because he was the emperor' (Fustel de Coulanges). The sanctifying of power, inherent and necessary to the very exercise of authority, was in this respect rooted in republican tradition. If the *imperium* was consecrated by the auspices (thus by Jupiter), the *tribunicia potestas* rendered the tribunes 'sacrosanct'. Anyone who made an attempt on their person was consigned to Jupiter (Liv., 3, 55, 7). The ruler combined *imperium* and *potestas* with the office of chief priest which made him, so to speak, a 'pope' of the Roman religion. As *imperator* he was always victorious and very quickly tended to monopolise the personal qualities that almost turned the triumphant victor into a Jupiter for the day. Lastly, the posthumous deification of Julius Caesar made his heir the son of a god, destined for the same apotheosis. The emperor belonged to a family of *divi*. But the Roman family, too, had its heroised ancestors. Whatever may have been said, the apparent innovations of the imperial cult – at least in part – descended directly from the *mos maiorum*.

After crushing the Cimbri and Teutones (102/101 BC), Marius was offered libations in private lararia, alongside the family gods (Val. Max., 8, 15, 7; Plut., *Mar.*, 27, 9), as Augustus was later. At Rome's crossroads, Marius Gratidianus had his statue, to which wine and incense were offered (Sen., *Ir.*, 3, 18, 1). In his lifetime Caesar had the right to sacrifices, a fraternity of Luperci, a flamen, games, a lying-in-state bed, and 'supplications' in company with the gods. His picture was carried on a chariot in processions preluding the races in the Circus Maximus and in lectisternia. His birthday was celebrated by public religious services, and his name given to the month of his birth (*Julius*), as the following one would bear the name of Augustus. On the Capitol and in the temple of Quirinus – the name of his deified ancestor Romulus – a statue was erected to the dictator dedicated to the 'invincible god': for he was *invictus* (Cic., *Marc.*, 12), as Alexander had been in the past. Cicero himself compares Caesar to a god, *simillimum deo* (ibid., 8). The Senate named the new god *Iuppiter Iulius*, and Antony would be his *flamen Dialis* (DC, 44, 6, 4).

Caesar's apotheosis initiated the series of imperial 'consecrations' that turned the dead ruler into a *divus*. On an ivory bed draped in purple and gold, the dictator's body, at first placed on view in a chapel recalling the temple of Venus *Genitrix*, was burnt in the middle of the Forum on a pyre on to which matrons threw their jewellery, their children's togae praetextae and gold bullae, and veterans their weapons, flute-players and actors the triumphal robes worn for the ceremony (Suet., *Caes.*, 84), at the place where the altar and temple of *Divus Julius* would be built. Soon afterwards, a comet – *sidus Julium* – shone in the sky, seeming 'to signify to the people that Caesar's soul had been received into the company of the immortal gods' (Plin., *NH*, 2, 94). His likeness would crown the statue erected by Augustus in the temple of Venus, the ancestress of the Julii. This birth into immortality in no way negated the earthly *natalis*, and the Senate ordered the Romans to celebrate it annually 'on pain of being consigned to the wrath of Jupiter and of the deceased himself' (DC, 47, 18, 5). Human sacrifices bloodied the new cult. Octavian is said to have had 300 of those who had surrendered after the siege of Perugia in 40 BC executed 'as victims for the ides of March, before an altar set up in honour of the divine Julius' (Suet., *Aug.*, 15, 2).

While Mark Antony paraded as Dionysus, and Sextus Pompey claimed Neptune as his father, Octavian officially called himself *Divi filius*, at the same time invoking the patronage of Apollo. He put an end to the civil wars that had avenged his father and brought peace to the Roman world. The cult of Mars *Ultor* (to whom Augustus dedicated a temple on the first of the month that bears his name, in the very year when, like Caesar before him, he received the title 'Father of the Country'), matched the cult of the Augustan Peace, of which the emperor was the guarantor, together with universal happiness. The altar of Peace consecrated the 'peace' or favour of the gods, which was ensured by the piety of the descendant of Aeneas, *Pius Aeneas*. For he had eighty-two temples rebuilt, and restored certain forgotten rites, such as the 'augury of well-being', celebrated every year on condition that no army was engaged in war at the time. The son of a god, he became 'August' in January 27 BC, meaning 'consecrated' by the gods. He was the head or *paterfamilias* of the great Roman house. On the Palatine, his residence had a chapel to Vesta, the goddess of the hearth: 'On its own, the palace has three eternal gods' (Apollo, Vesta and the emperor), Ovid felt able to write (*F*, 4, 954).

This paternalism conveys the actual situation, in which the head of state had the prerogatives of a *patronus* towards all his fellow-citizens (and not only his subjects in the Roman people). From the cultic point of view, the consequences were not fundamentally alien to tradition. Oaths were sworn by the *genius* of the master, and just as that of the *paterfamilias* was honoured in domestic lararia, henceforward Augustus's 'Genius' had his place in private chapels. But the veiled *genius*, who exemplified piety with his patera for libations and promised happiness with his horn of plenty, was often replaced by the sovereign's picture. Statuettes or miniature heads of emperors found in excavations away from public sites bear witness to quite a wide popular use:

> You know how, on all the money-changers' tables, in all the shops and taverns, under all the awnings, in hallways, on windows, your portraits are to be seen everywhere commonly on display, badly painted for the most part, it is true, and even crudely fashioned or sculpted in clay. (Front., *Ep. M. Caes.*, 4, 12, 4)

That was how the ploughman ritually shared his meal with the emperor 'in image', prayed to him as he poured his wine and combined his name with that of the Lares (Hor., *O*, 4, 5, 30 ff.).

As early as 30 BC (after the victory at Actium), the Senate decreed that libations should be offered to the 'Genius' of Octavian at all public or private banquets. This practice was institutionalised in 7 BC by the reorganisation of the colleges known as *compitalicia* ('of the crossroads') in the 265 districts of Rome. From then on their Lares rubbed shoulders with the *Genius Augusti*, and those in charge of the cult (or *vicomagistri*), who were mostly of modest status, strengthened its base among the populace. In May and in summer the altars were decked with flowers.

> See how Rome has a thousand Lares and the Genius of the Leader who has restored them. Each district honours three divinities. (Ov., F, 5, 145 f.)

Pigs were sacrificed to the imperial Lares, bull – calves to the *Genius Augusti* (Fig. 17). Inherent in domestic and local life, this devotion to the one on whom the survival of all depended was smoothly incorporated into ancestral religion, but went beyond its former perspective.

Naturally, the ruler's birthday was celebrated, as the master's always had been but also his mother's, and that of the empress and their children. Birth, assuming the toga of manhood, marriage – all the important religious occasions in the imperial family caused a great public stir. The anniversary of the accession (*dies imperii*) was again an opportunity to give thanks to the gods, to hold celebrations. The doors of houses were adorned with laurel, lamps were lit, people drank and ate; the city 'was transformed into a tavern', and houses into 'lupanars' (Tert., Apol., 35, 2–4). For his 'decennium' in AD 263, Gallienus offered the Romans the spectacle of a real triumphal *pompa* to the Capitol, with 100 white oxen girded with silk, 200 sheep, ten elephants, 1200 gladiators, 200 tamed wild animals and several hundred barbarian prisoners. At their head marched the people and the army, all wearing white, behind bearers of torches or candelabra. The emperor, surrounded by senators and knights, paid homage to the guarantor of his power, who on the reverse of coins is shown handing him the globe of the world. With their banners, the corporations (*collegia*) took part in the procession in company with the idols (SHA, Gall., 8).

Appointed and upheld by divine providence, the emperor had an almost superhuman authority, and not only from his *genius* but also from his *numen* direct effectiveness was expected, as from all the Roman gods. When the exiled Ovid received silver statuettes of Augustus, Livia and Tiberius, he pronounced himself happy that he could now have them 'present', in other words, able to help him:

It is something to be able to speak with a true divinity! *cum vero numine..* (*Pont.*, 2, 8, 10 and 52)

Such adulation profited and inaugurated a real ceremonial at the court of the Caesars. The father of the future emperor Vitellius no longer dared to come before Caligula unless 'he had his head veiled and walked backwards before prostrating himself' (Suet., *Vit.*, 2, 9). In the late Empire, this ritual of the *adoratio* would become official.

Worship of the imperial *numen* theoretically anticipated the apotheosis properly speaking. 'To be a god is, for a mortal, to help a mortal, and that is the road to eternal glory' (Plin., *NH*, 2, 18), for the emperor was deified after his death for having acted like a god during his lifetime. Pliny also quotes the example of Vespasian 'who succours the exhausted empire'. The author of a guide to phytotherapy dedicated it to 'the divine Augustus', with the wish that 'the emperor's majesty might always remedy all humanity's ills' (ibid., 25, 4). He was therefore invoked as a saviour and healing god. Rome, moreover, had its thaumaturge emperors, such as Vespasian (Tac., *H*, 4, 81; Suet., *Vesp.*, 7, 5–6) and Hadrian (SHA, *H*, 25, 2).

But in exchange, the man who safeguarded peace among men at the same time as peace with the gods, needed the former to pray to the latter for his 'well-being', which was identical with that of the empire. There was no contradiction in renewing annually, or every five, ten, or even twenty years, prayers for the ruler's health. In this regard, too, the religion of the sovereign remained faithful to the Roman notion that sacrifices were made (*mactare*) to the gods to increase their strength. Hence Varro's fear that they would perish for want of liturgical service. In AD 22, the Roman knights pledged an offering to Equestrian Fortune for Livia to be cured. But since the goddess had no temple in Rome, it was suddenly realised that she had one at Antium, and that in Italy all gods were under the authority of the Roman people (Tac., *An.*, 3, 71, 2). The gods needed men, as men needed the gods.

The emperor was a god who died, but only to become more of a god than ever. After a senatorial decree conferring the apotheosis or *consecratio* on him, the funeral pomp turned the *funus imperatorium* into a kind of ultimate triumph in which the great bodies of the state, the people and the army, took part. Around the pyre, a parade of cavalry (*decursio*) gave the deceased military honours. This liturgy brings to mind the one Varro ascribed to the ancient Romans: they circled the tomb, which was looked upon as a temple, declaring that the dead man was a god from then on, after the incineration (Plut., *QR*, 14). At the funeral ceremony of Augustus, centurions set fire to the pyre (*rogus consecrationis*), from the summit of which an eagle flew off as if carrying away the soul of the new *divus*. A praetor even swore that he had seen his phantom rising to the skies (Suet., *Aug.*, 100, 7; DC, 56, 46, 2), just as Julius Proculus, 730 years earlier, was supposed to have seen that of Romulus (Liv., 1, 16, 5–7).

But the ceremonial had grown more complicated during the two following centuries, owing to the elaboration of funerary rites and the change from cremation to interment. The pyre, in the shape of a four-level truncated pyramid that we see on coins, was derived from the same model as that of Hephaestion, Alexander's companion (DS, 17, 115). Filled with combustible materials, the edifice was draped with gold-embroidered fabrics and adorned with ivory statues or various paintings. In the time of the historian Herodian (4, 2, 8), a wax model of the deceased was displayed for a week on a great ivory bed at the entrance to the palace, where the simulation of imminent death took place. After this, the bed was carried to the second level of the pyre, laden with herbs, fruit and fragrant essences. The heir or heirs then set light to the *rogus*, which would henceforward serve as a mock incineration, when the corpse was actually interred. But the flight of the eagle, released from its cage on the last level continued to enact symbolically the astral apotheosis of the deified emperor. The wife (or *Augusta*) of the emperor, reigning or dead, had a right to the same honours. But, according to the coins, it was Juno's peacock which ensured the dead empress' heavenward ascent. However, on the pedestal of the Antonine column, two eagles are transporting Antoninus and Faustina.

After the death of Augustus, a college of *sodales Augustales*, which numbered members of the imperial family in its ranks, gave homage to the *divus* in the name of the *gens Julia*. This fraternity therefore officially carried on the domestic tradition of the heroised ancestor. The *Augustales* would also become *Claudiales* after the apotheosis of Claudius. Other sodalities would be instituted for the cult of Vespasian, Titus, Hadrian and Antoninus. Each *divus* had his flamen, and each *diva* her flaminica.

They also had their own temple, at least up to and including Marcus Aurelius. Celebrated there were the anniversaries of their birth, death and consecration, and even of the temple itself, with the sacrifice of a bull, as for the *Genius Augusti*. Perhaps a daily service took place at Augustus's mausoleum (Sen., *Tranq.*, 14, 9). Chariot races and shows were also given. The 'Palatine Games' specially honoured Augustus, but it was private celebration, to which only relatives and friends of the emperor were invited. On 17 January, the four major colleges (pontiffs, augurs, quindecemvirs *sacris faciundis* and epulones) sacrificed in a chapel of the *domus Augusta*. Then, from 21 to 23, shows were put on in a theatre set up for the occasion in front of the palace.

There is epigraphic evidence of a temple of the *divi* on the Palatine in the second century AD. Even though the reigning emperors had no kinship with the Julio-Claudians or the Flavians, their deified predecessors formed a kind of great ancestral family protecting the imperial house, soon qualified as 'divine'. A sort of heaven-sent and cultic solidarity united the living and the dead, as in the ancient religion of hearth and home. In the middle of the third century, Decius Trajan issued a series of double denarii with the effigies of the *divi*, from Augustus to Alexander Severus: an inheritance of charismas useful to the well-being of the empire. Later, the emperor Tacitus is said to have had a *templum divorum* built where libations would sanctify their respective anniversaries (SHA, *Tac.*, 9, 5). Even in the fourth century (in the heart of the Christian Empire), the *natales* of the eighteen deified emperors were celebrated; the list of them up to Alexander Severus partially matched that of the *divi* glorified in the coinage of Decius Trajan.

The apotheosis of the pathetic Claudius and the farcical account Seneca gives of it in his *Apocolocyntosis* ridiculed the institution. Nero himself deconsecrated the site of the *templum divi Claudii* to turn it into the nymphaeum of his Golden House. But when he had a daughter by Poppaea, he had her put in the heavens as *diva Virgo*. Poppaea herself, whom he kicked to death when she was pregnant, had divine honours: which cost the incredulous Thrasea a lawsuit (Tac., *An*, 16, 22, 6). For Lucan (7, 455 ff.), the gods had abandoned Rome and liberty when they gave victory to Caesar. But history avenged Rome by making the imperial Manes the rivals of Olympus. In other words, that cult of the dead was a prelude to the death of the gods, and furthermore, the persecuted Christians' refusal to worship the Caesars contributed to the official decline of paganism. However, the *Augustan History* may be believed when the biographer of Marcus Aurelius wrote:

> People of every age, sex, status and dignity rendered him divine honours. Anyone who did not keep a portrait of him in the house was considered impious. And in our day, still, in many families statues of Marcus Aurelius have their place among the Penates gods.

Marcus Aurelius had an unworthy son; but the existence of an heir reinforced the feeling of dynastic security in public opinion, and the empress who gave a Caesar to the reigning Augustus was likened to the Mother of the gods, the successor having, like his father, a vocation for apotheosis.

Images of the *divi* went in procession in the *pompa* of the circus, in company with gods from a traditional background, sometimes on chariots drawn by elephants (which reflected triumphal and, more precisely, Dionysiac symbolism). In the lararia or in public life, as we have seen, deceased or living emperors entered the daily devotions of the Romans. The first, like the Indigetes or Novemsiles – such as Aeneas, Romulus or the mythical kings of Latium – were 'men become gods' (Serv., *Aen.*, 12, 794) who 'merited' it (Arn., 3, 39). The second were the incarnation of 'the breath, the life that so many thousands of beings breathe', as Seneca says (*Clem.*, 1, 4, 1), quoting Virgil (G, 4, 212 f.), and comparing the empire to an immense beehive whose unity depends on the well-being of its queen. For the Latin philosopher, the emperor resembled the Stoics' *pneuma* which, born of the fire of Zeus or the divine Word, gave life to the universe: *spiritus vitalis*. This cosmic dimension found its historical logic in a regime where 'for a long time Caesar had been confused with the republic' (ibid., 3): he was its soul (ibid., 5, 1) whose well-being was identified with that of the empire.

Now, the Stoics, from which notably Cicero (*Rep.*, 6, 17) and Pliny the Elder (*NH*, 2, 13) drew their inspiration, made the sun the soul or spirit of the world, 'who governs not only the seasons and the lands, but the very stars and the sky' (ibid.). So the imperial cult appropriated some solar theology. 'Restore the light to your country,' says Horace to Augustus:

> When your face, like spring, has dazzled the people with its brilliance, the day becomes more joyful and suns shine more brightly. (O, 4, 5, 5 ff.) 7

Later, addressing Nero, who gladly identified himself with Helios-Apollo and whose Golden House had the colour of a solar palace, Seneca does not hesitate to proclaim:

> When one faces you, there is a profusion of light. It polarises the gaze of all. Do you think of going out of the palace? You are a rising sun. (*Clem.*, 1, 8, 4)

In the *Apocolocyntosis* (4, 1, 1, 22 ss.), he makes Phoebus say:

> This prince who resembles me in looks and beauty . . . will bring happy times to exhausted men . . . As the radiant sun contemplates the universe . . . so appears Caesar.

The mystique of a new age of gold inaugurated by the accession of an emperor (*oriens Augusti*) went hand in hand with that of a heliac epiphany, in part inherited from Hellenistic monarchies.

From the time of Nero, the imperial effigy wore a crown with radiating points on the double asses (*dupondii*), minted in an alloy – orichalc – that had the golden appearance of the sun. Later, the rayed crown distinguished the double denarii (*Antoniniani*) in Caracalla's time, and then the double sesterces and gold smaller denominations. Thus the expression of an inherent idea of imperial sovereignty passed from hand to hand up to the fourth century. As in Plato (*Rep.*, 6, 508 c) the sun was the visible image of the invisible Good, the emperor the actual and personal incarnation of the life-imparting Daystar who, by handing the globe of the world to him on the reverse of coins, made him his vicar and a kind of co-regent. Their images side by side in the third century, and still on the obverse of Constantinian coins, even conveyed a kind of 'consubstantiality' (F. Cumont). The rayed crown of the emperors was matched for the empresses by a crescent moon, the curve of which contained their likeness. The two luminaries, indeed, symbolised cyclical eternity; and this iconography capitalised a veritable cosmic theology of the reigning couple.

People readily ascribed the attributes of the gods to both emperors and empresses. Augustus and Septimius Severus were represented as Jupiter, Livia as Venus *Genitrix* or Cybele, Hadrian and Sabina as Mars and Venus, Julia Domna as Juno, Isis or Demeter. But in the third century the solar epiphany of the emperor became almost official. Caracalla displayed himself in a chariot 'like the Sun' (DC, 77, 10, 3), laying claim to that likeness. Gallienus had his hair dusted with gold and often appeared *radiatus* (SHA, Gall., 16, 4). He is said to have considered having a statue of himself erected on the Esquiline as the Sun in his quadriga, in an idol twice the size of Nero's colossus (ibid.): the testimony is unreliable, but one gets the feeling that conditions at the time were favourable for institutionalising a universal solar cult consecrating the religious unity of the Roman world.

That is what Aurelian attempted. A Sun god – the one from Emesa – had given him victory. The *imperator* returned from the east after defeating Zenobia, queen of Palmyra, like a rising sun (*oriens*), in the splendour of a triumph as luxuriant as Bacchus's after his Indian campaign, with unprecedented exotic animals (SHA, A, 33, 4). Aurelian consecrated the cult of the 'Invincible Sun' (*Sol Invictus*) in a gigantic temple, embellished with the spoils of Palmyra. He gave it a special college of pontiffs, and instituted four-yearly games. We know nothing of the special rituals applied to this *Sol Invictus*. The new sanctuary followed an eastern tradition, with its tholos, or dome, in the centre of a closed courtyard isolating the sacred area from the profane world. This rotunda brings to mind what Macrobius (S, 1, 18, 11) wrote about the temple of Sebadius or Sabazius in Thrace, lit by an *oculus* (like the Pantheon) at the top of its vault 'to show that the sun lights everything with its rays from the height of the sky': a symbolism appropriate to the theocosmology of the *Sol Invictus Imperator*.

But at that time, so it seems, in both Rome and the provinces, the imperial cult lost a great deal of its popularity. In ever-growing numbers, Christians refused to burn incense before the images of rulers claiming the absoluteness of their sacred person. Aurelian called himself *deus et dominus*, like Carus whose profile faces that of the Sun (as those of the emperor and empress or his son had formerly) with the legend: DEO ET DOMINO CARO AUG (*usto*). Aurelian had himself described as DEO ET DOMINO NATO, with a dative of homage as to a true predestined god (*nato*). The Daystar is hailed as the 'companion' (*comes*) of the reigning Augustus. At the end of the third century, one had to behave towards the sovereign as if before the idol of a god, falling at his feet and lifting a fold of the imperial purple to one's lips. But was this still real 'religion'?

Inevitably a mystique of the Empire interacted with the cult of the emperor, underlying or even sublimating it in the collective consciousness. It was not a *religio* in the old sense of the Latin word, but a piety that was necessary to the cohesion of that great 'city' which the Roman world had become, chiefly after the edict of Caracalla, whose motives purported to be religious:

> To render to the majesty of the most sacred gods the duties that are owed to them, with all the necessary magnificence and piety, I believe that I must unite all the foreigners who have become my subjects in the worship of these gods.

Urbem fecisti quod prius orbis erat, the Gaul Rutilius Namatianus would proclaim (1, 66): 'In giving the vanquished the same rights as in Rome, you turned the entire universe into a town.'

In the provinces, Rome was twinned with the living emperor as immortal power temporarily personified by its *imperator*. Architecturally, this mystique of the city-empire was materialised in Hadrian's Pantheon. Augustus's son-in-law, Agrippa, had consecrated what was not a temple properly speaking to the glory of the *gens Julia*, founder of a new regime. It held statues of Mars and Venus, the divine ancestors of this heaven-sent family. Hadrian turned it into a vast rotunda, its vault evoking the firmament from which light fell through an *oculus*: a representation of the universe lit by the Sun and the *pax Romana* ensured by the emperor. There is nothing to show that the building was used for special liturgies about which we are ignorant. The cultic articles or priestly attributes sculpted above the garlands of fruit that decorate the vestibule imply nothing other than Roman piety in solidarity with imperial greatness: 'Thy submission to the gods gives thee the right to command' (Hor., O, 3, 6, 5).

Similarly, Hadrian glorified the cult of Rome together with Venus in a double temple where the two goddesses housed back to back brought to mind the palindrome *Roma-Amor*. It is known that pontifical law forbade the dedication of the same sanctuary to two deities (Liv., 27, 25, 8); therefore at least a double *cella* was required. Here again, we know nothing of the ritual practices applied in this temple, which sanctified the eternity of the *Urbs* promised to Venus by Jupiter in the *Aeneid* (1, 278 f.) together with the rise of the Caesarian dynasty. We know only that from AD 176 young married couples sacrificed there, before the statues of Marcus Aurelius and Faustina (DC, 72, 31, 1–2).

Another deity was able to unite people's hearts around the heirs of the prestigious line: the Genius of the Roman people. In the republican period, he was spared a thought only occasionally, in fairly grave situations. Thus in 218 BC, in expiation of some sinister prodigies, the city was purified, a lectisternium was carried out and the Genius was offered five large victims (Liv., 21, 62, 9). A branch of the *Cornelii* perhaps devoted special worship to him, to judge by the denarii of Cn. Lentulus struck in 75 BC, with the bust of the god together with a sceptre, which can be found on the reverse with a globe and a tiller: obvious symbols of the universal vocation of the master-race. But, as the *Genius Urbis Romae*, whose gender was unknown (*sive mas sive femina* – a phrase incribed on a shield preserved on the Capitol), the Genius of the Roman people had scarcely any devotees. He had fewer than the *Genius Augusti*, with whom he could be confused, the emperor having been delegated with all the powers of the *populus Romanus*. In fact, on a series of bronze coins the GENIUS P(*opuli*) R(*omani*) has the features of Gallienus (AD 253–68).

It was the tradition to sacrifice to the *Genius publicus* on 9 October, at the same time as to *Fausta Felicitas* and 'Victorious' Venus, two deities who had a vital and historic link with Rome. Significantly, too, the Genius of the Roman people was coupled with the Most Good, Most Great Jupiter, and an inscription invokes his anger, as well as that of the deified emperors (*numina divorum*), against possible violators of an altar (*CIL*, 6, 29944). The *Chronographer of 354* (p. 279, 1 f., R. Valentini-G. Zuchetti) attributes to Aurelian the erection of a gold statue of the Genius near the Rostra, and his image is on the reverse of the large silvered bronzes (*folles*) which Diocletian's monetary reform inaugurated in AD 296. The *Genius populi Romani* holds the patera for libations (sometimes in front of a lit altar) and the horn of plenty; these were attributes of the piety and felicity that symbolised Rome's vocation embodied by the emperor *Pius Felix*, two titles that had been added to his description since the time of Commodus.

It was again the *Genius Publicus* who appeared in a dream to Julian, on the eve of his proclamation as emperor in Paris in AD 360, and whom he saw passing sadly into his tent a few days before his death (Amm., 20, 5, 10; 25,

2, 3). This relationship of the *Genius* with the emperor's reign perhaps still inspired the pious loyalty of a few pagans.

But the Christian emperor inherited a share of the devotion to the sovereign, and incense was burnt before his holy image (Philost., 2, 17), lamps were lit at the foot of his statues, and he was invoked on equal terms with a tutelary god to divert the ills that threatened people (C. Th., 15, 4, 1) just as in the heyday of official polytheism.

_ THE OCCULT, NECROMANCY AND STRANGE _ DEVOTIONS

In matters of religion, the family and the city-state had subjected the individual to as strict a way of life as possible. Almost daily, auspices and prodigies conditioned citizens' activities. Now, there were no longer active citizens, and the city had become an empire whose members were, to varying degrees, all subjects of the sovereign. Even though, in people's homes or among the Palatine household staff, the imperial cult might assume the appearance of a personal devotion, it could not fill the immense void left in the Romans' conscience, simultaneously subjugated and liberated, by the ruins of a collective piety which for several centuries had dominated their everyday existence.

True, the festivals in the calendar continued to be celebrated and, in regard to out-of-the-ordinary liturgies, the Secular Games or the ceremony of a triumph could still rouse the fervour of the *Urbs*. But the emperor monopolised that grandiose procession, which in any case was becoming more infrequent. The question of *devotio* or *evocatio* no longer arose. Above all, prodigies were apparently not important any more, although Tacitus sometimes reports them, but almost always as signs of an inevitable future; such fatalism was alien to the genuine Roman religion which had treated them as warnings or threats to be averted by the *procuratio prodigiorum*. Propitiatory and expiatory supplications no longer had occasion to spangle the warp and woof of the religious calendar. Livy (43, 13, 1) was already lamenting the fact in the reign of Augustus:

> Because of the offhandedness which is commonly casting doubt on divine warnings, prodigies are hardly ever officially announced, and are no longer recorded in the annals . . .

With even greater cause in the fourth century, Ammianus Marcellinus (19, 12, 19) deplored that henceforward they would no longer be expiated, and even passed unnoticed.

In any case, the emperor set the example of incredulity. The chief priest, and thereby a member of the four major sacerdotal colleges, Tiberius did not think it necessary to consult the Sibylline Books after the Tiber overflowed (Tac., *An.*, 1, 76, 3). The sky's bad omens failed to bother Galba who 'scorned these details as mere chance happenings' (Tac., *H*, 1, 18, 1).

But Tiberius believed in astrology and Galba devoted a personal cult to a statuette of Fortune found at his door after a premonitory dream (Suet., *Galb.*, 4, 6–7). This double phenomenon – the influence of occult sciences and devotion to a particular deity – affected many Romans during the imperial era.

Instead of taking auspices or observing signs from the gods, people consulted detachable tablets bearing the figures and names of the signs of the zodiac, in the best Egyptian tradition, like those of Grand (Vosges): see Juv., 6, 573 f. At great expense a diviner was brought from Phrygia (ibid., 585). But the Etruscan haruspex 'who buries the thunderbolt in the name of the state' (ibid., 587) retained all his prestige, and the Tuscan sciences of hepatoscopy or brontoscopy would always haunt the minds of the last pagans. Besides Tiberius, Nero, Otho and Vespasian all had their astrologer. Titus, Domitian and Hadrian were sufficiently expert themselves to draw up a horoscope, and Septimius Severus (who married Julia Domna after making enquiries about marriageable daughters of royal blood) dispensed justice in a hall of the palace where his own astral horoscope was painted on the ceiling (DC, 77, 11, 1).

Magic similarly encroached upon religion, while making use of it, for it was deemed to constrain the gods and counter fatalism. Even the philosopher-emperor Marcus Aurelius is said to have succumbed to the temptation, notably in the fierce Danubian wars illustrated on his column, with the Egyptian hierogrammat Arnouphis and the magus Julian 'the Chaldaean' or his son Julian 'the theurge', whose verse oracles would enchant the Neoplatonists a century later.

We have seen that some traditional practices were concerned with magic, although Roman law condemned its exercise; but other forms and procedures gained popularity whether or not connected with religions foreign to the *mos maiorum*. Necromancers exploited the bitterness caused by victims of a violent or premature death, to divert it on to those whom one illwished. The remains of a corpse were stolen, funeral pyres were pillaged. Lucan's sorceress (6, 533–43)

> robbed the smoking ashes, the burning bones of dead young people, the very
> torch held by their parents, bits of the funeral bed still emitting black smoke; she

collected garments that were falling to dust, embers that retained the odour of limbs . . .

If it had been a burial,

she greedily tore at the joints, plunged her fingers into the eyes, enjoying extracting the ice-cold orbs, and picked at the pale excrescences with an emaciated hand.

A small lead plate bearing a carved imprecation was placed in the tomb, to bring the force of the avenging and baleful Manes to bear. If necessary, a child was put to death, as in the example of the sinister female magicians cursed by Horace (*Epo.*, 5) and their innocent victim (ibid., 89 ff.), buried alive on waste ground in the ill-famed Subura district. Cicero (*Vat.*, 14) accuses Vatinius of 'the habit of calling up souls from hell, and appeasing the Manes gods with the entrails of children', which in Juvenal's time (6, 552) were inspected on request by 'a haruspex from Armenia or the Commagene'.

This outburst of civic or family piety also benefited the cult of personal deities. In a Rome where so many religions were in competition and cohabited in anarchic confusion, with none debarred (except by Jews and Christians), polytheism did not prevent individuals favouring a certain god or goddess who could be said to prevail over the others – not necessarily in the hierarchy of the traditional pantheon – but in daily life, for the reasons and purposes of circumstance, maybe sometimes only temporarily. Like many Romans, certain emperors thus had their 'patron saint': Apollo for Augustus, Minerva for Domitian, Hercules for Commodus, Serapis for Caracalla. After adoring only the Syrian Goddess, Nero fell ardently in love with the figurine of a young girl which a man of the people had given him as a talisman against conspiracies (Suet., *Ner.*, 56). Sulla in combat wore over his heart a gold statuette of Apollo, seized at Delphi (Plut., *Sull.*, 29, 11). Apuleius was never separated from his little Mercury (*Apol.*, 63, 3). But the favourite deity naturally had its place also in the lararium, among the Penates gods.

It could be a god connected with the trade or craft practised, or the 'Genius' who protected it. The praetorian cohorts and the watchmen had their *genius* (*CIL*, 6, 233–8), as did the corporations, schools, depots, even the thermal baths and every place where human activity went on. At all events, tradesmen honoured Mercury, wine merchants Bacchus, oil sellers Hercules *Olivarius*, artisans and teachers Minerva, sailors Castor and Pollux or Isis *Pelagia* ('Our-Lady-of-the-Waves'), soldiers Mars and courtesans Venus or Flora.

'Everything to do with shows is concerned with idolatry' (Tert., *Spect.*, 4, 3). Theatrical performers had Liber Pater as their patron, whose altar at the theatre was the neighbour of that belonging to the divinity celebrated by the games (Don., *Com.*, 8, 3). Gladiators, who earned their living by confronting death, certainly prayed to Mars, Hercules or Diana, but devoted special worship to Nemesis, the goddess of destiny (Fig. 18).

> Why do we combat spells by a special supplication, some invoking the Greek Nemesis, who to this end has a statue on the Capitol, although she does not possess a Latin name? (Plin., *NH*, 28, 22)

These 'spells', indeed, threatened those involved in the spectacles. The circus charioteers were exposed to curses inscribed on small lead plaques (a metal dear to Saturn, whose planet was unlucky). A nail, fixing the plaque firmly, served to 'immobilise' hated competitors: this is the proper meaning of *defixio*. On these defixion tablets, together with their identity, there was a picture of the drivers who were to have a spell put on them, showing them with their arms and legs tied, under a representation of Typhon-Seth, the same donkey-headed god carved on so many magic intaglios. One tablet even shows us demons chaining the chariot-driver involved. The gods solicited were those of the dead and the underworld (Aidoneus, Osiris), Apis, Ares or *Anangke* ('Necessity'). Typical is the image of Osiris entwined in the coils of a snake, also to be found on the Graeco-Egyptian stones formerly called 'gnostics'. In the fourth century, the astrologer Firmicus Maternus advised against attending shows, in order to avoid the accusation of favouring this or that faction (*Math.*, 2, 30, 12). Magic and astrology were hand in glove at that time, sometimes in connection with devotions of eastern origin.

We have seen that the trials or sorrows of life led the Roman to invoke the relevant *numen*, as the Christian resorted to saints. Pagan Rome had at least as many (if not more) sanctuaries or chapels and gods as Christian Rome had churches and saints. Ovid makes the Great Mother say: 'Rome is a place worthy of the presence of all the gods (*F*, 4, 270).'

In this *Urbs* which had become *orbis* (ibid., 2, 684), the cosmopolitan density of the population reflected the world that Rome had conquered or, rather, to use the words of Athenaeus (1, 36, 20 *b-c*), it was a 'summary of the world', a 'universe-city' (*ouranopolis*). This meeting-point of humankind was consequently also that of men's many idols. The 'sacrosanct city' (Ap.,

M, 11, 26, 2) well deserved the title bestowed upon it by Arnobius (6, 7) of worshipper of all the gods, *numinum cunctorum cultrix*; for, besides those I have spoken of, there were numerous others whose names we do not know, or whose composite and disconcerting iconography we can find on the amulets mentioned earlier, among others. All those gods and demons mingle their names or attributes in bizarre conglomerations. There are even surprising contagions of Graeco-Roman or orientalising paganism with Judaism and Christianity. Alongside the Romans who were fond of a single deity, others 'collected' them, so to speak:

> Concern for the gods is lacking in some people and in others takes a shameful form. They belong to foreign cults and wear the gods on their fingers (an allusion to rings bearing the effigy of Harpocrates or Serapis); they go so far as to worship monsters (this is aimed at the animals of the Egyptian pantheon). (Plin., NH, 2, 21)

To his friend Amelius, who never failed to sacrifice at each new moon, Plotinus dares to say: 'It is for the gods to come to me, not for me to go to them (Porph., *V.Pl.*, 10).' But he agrees to take part in the summoning of an Egyptian priest's demon in the *Iseum Campense*. The philosopher's presence provokes the intervention

> of a god who was not of the race of demons. And the Egyptian said to Plotinus: 'Thou art fortunate to have a god for a demon and art not attended by a being of an inferior kind!' They were unable to question the demon, or observe his presence any longer, for a friend who was there as a spectator, looking after the birds, smothered them out of jealousy, or perhaps fear. (ibid.)

In this instance, the birds must have been used in a service of theurgic kind: alive, they were supposed to favour the demon's appearance.

Not content with their personal devotions, individuals gathered on the fringes of official or public rites. Already in Cicero's time (*Mil.*, 65), when traditional piety was suffering from the competition of Isiac and other non-native cults, a tavern-keeper on the Circus Maximus went ahead with 'mysterious sacrifices' in order to 'purify' the slaves who gathered in his premises (Asc., *Mil.*, 45). These societies proliferated in the second and third centuries, in a Rome that was verging on a million inhabitants, and where the concentration of anonymous masses generated a need for a religious or, at least, convivial intimacy (as we have seen in the instances of Mithraic and Dolichenian communities).

Certain great households, where several hundred (if not more) slaves could live and work without knowing one another, under one master who did not know them all and was even unaware of their number (Sen., *VB*, 17, 2), constituted by themselves some large heterogeneous groups:

> We have nations in our household staff, with their diverse customs, foreign forms of worship, unless they have no religion at all. (Tac., *An.*, 14, 44, 5)

This last negative observation may have been aimed at Christians (who were deemed to be atheists), at the time when the historian was writing his *Annals*, around the end of Trajan's reign.

Slaves therefore got together, within their *familia* or away from the house, to make their devotions among their co-religionists, like the freedmen or with the freemen and other elements of the urban plebs. Splinter groups swarmed in Rome, thanks to legislation on colleges which was fairly liberal in practice, except towards Christians in periods of persecution; but often they were persecuted only when people became aware of the long-tolerated results of their increase in numbers. In the reigns of the worst emperors, they prospered in the shadow of the palace, and the Christian Marcia, concubine of Commodus, had a hand in the successful plot to murder him (Hdn., 1, 17, 4–11). Among the servants of the imperial court, or *caesariani*, there were many followers of the new faith in the time of the Severi, alongside Isiacs or Mithraists. The Christian slaves of private households held their meetings in a part of the house, sometimes together with their masters, to celebrate the *agape*, just as the faithful of the Persian god set up their *Mithraeum* in a secluded part of the *domus*.

Similarly, in the religious ferment of the Antonine and Severian periods, there occurred a strange profusion of sects or somewhat aberrant variations of Roman and foreign cults. On this matter, the testimonies of Juvenal in the second century AD and Hippolytus a century later merely lift a fold of the veil shrouding the mysteries of the *Urbs*:

> Gradually, you will manage to be received among those who, between four walls, put long ribbons round their foreheads, and necklaces round their necks and win the Good Goddess's favour with the belly of a young sow and a large vessel of wine. But, turning the rite upside down, they drive away women, barring them from the threshold: 'Go away,' they shout, 'non-believers! No flute-player will make her instrument wail here.' Such were the orgies celebrated by the Bapts by the flickering light of the torch used in their mysteries (an allusion to the Thracian cult of Cotytto). (Juv., 2, 83–91)

This bacchanalia of homosexuals no longer had anything to do with the former festival of 3 December, although the example of Clodius disguised as a woman in order to woo Caesar's wife may have put ideas in the minds of the sect's instigators. But elsewhere it was women who, in their own fashion, celebrated

> the mysteries of the Good Goddess, when the flute spurred on their loins and, under the dual effect of trumpet and wine, the raving Maenads of Priapus shook their hair about, howling and screeching. What a burning need for embraces impelled them then! What cries did their ardent desire make them utter! What a torrent of old wine poured along their drenched legs! (Juv., 6, 314–19)

These Mother-worship or Dionysiac taints did not only affect an unstable and mobile polytheism, whose measure is hard for us to grasp, and whose variants largely elude us. Installed in a variety of milieux in the *Urbs*, Christianity was not exempt from suspect infiltrations that verged on spreading confusion. At least, the Gnostic sects, so fervently combated by the Fathers of the Church, and the warnings of the Councils, who for a long time to come would remind the faithful of the ban on sacrificing to the 'demons', testify that certain converts did not always resolutely break with the old world of beliefs and idolatry.

In the time of the Severi, the priest of Rome Hippolytus criticised these ill-assorted compromises between paganism and the Scriptures. The Naassenians harked back to Assyrian, Egyptian, Eleusinian, Samothracian and Phrygian mysteries to explain the Old and New Testament. They even assiduously took part in the cult of Cybele (Hipp., *Ref.*, 5, 9, 10), without however castrating themselves like the galli. They recognised in Attis the perfect Man, the 'pastor of the twinkling stars' – in other words, the Sun – celebrated in a hymn that appears to have been sung at the theatre (ibid., 7–9).

In fact, they worshipped only the snake (ibid., 12) – *naas* in Hebrew – like the Perates (ibid., 17, 1–2), who incorporated Greek astrology and mythology in their theosophy, or the Sethians who made much of Orphic literature (ibid., 20, 4). Are we to picture this cult of the snake from an alabaster bowl on which the figures of naked men and women stand around the coiled serpent? It is known, too, that initiation into the mysteries of Sabazius involved a gilded serpent (perhaps artificial) slithering across one's breast (Firm., *Err.*, 10, 2; *cf.* Clem. Alex., *Protr.*, 2, 16, 2; Arn., 5, 21).

The Gnostic Justin (Hip., *Ref.*, 5, 26) introduced the exploits of Heracles into the economics of salvation, Elohim having chosen the Alcides to fight the twelve angels of Eden (which correspond to the twelve Labours), and this same heretic went as far as identifying the Creator of the universe with Priapus, the ithyphallic god of Roman gardens! Jerome Carcopino believed he could decipher in the very composite decoration of the underground tomb of the *Aurelii*, in Viale Manzoni, references to the Naassenians' doctrine – erroneously, in my opinion. Two centuries later, the story of the deeds of Hercules was shown alongside great biblical themes in the catacomb of the Via Dino Compagni – which does not mean to say that Justin's disciples were occupying it around 360 AD. But one must not imagine that in Rome orthodox Christians lived on one side and dyed-in-the-wool pagans on the other. Until the end of Antiquity, there were intermediate fringes between them, very difficult to pin down, but stronger and more tenacious than was thought.

Having quoted two problematic instances of funerary sites, I must put on record the numerous colleges linked with the cult of the dead under the patronage of the gods. These societies often placed themselves under the protection of a deity whose temple was near at hand and who was thought to watch over the area, though without having any particular connection with the usual worship of their members. At Lanuvium, near Lake Nemi, worshippers of Diana and Antinous (*ILS*, 7212) paired the goddess of woods and chastity with Hadrian's famous darling, who drowned in the Nile (like Osiris), probably through sacred self-immolation for the well-being of the emperor. In Rome itself, Antinous was not really the object of a cult (the Pincio obelisk likening him to Osiris comes from the Villa Hadriana), although a dedication from the *Iseum Campense* (*IGUR*, 98) has him sharing 'the throne' of the Egyptian gods. The college of Lanuvium held a celebratory banquet on the anniversary of the temple of Antinous (under the portico of which the regulations were posted up) and the temple of Diana. But there is no evidence that these cults had any direct effect on the forms of homage to the dead, or beliefs concerning an after-life.

More significant is the hypogaeum on the Appian Way where, near the catacomb of Praetextatus, the burial-places of Mithraists, a priest of Sabazius and his wife (*CIL*, 6, 142) neighbour on Christian tombs. In the Sabaziasts' *arcosolium* frecoes show us Vibia successively carried off by Pluto, brought before the tribunal of the underworld gods in the presence of three 'Fairies' of destiny (*Fata divina*), and lastly led by her 'Good Angel' to a banquet of the blessed chosen by the 'judgement of the Good', among whom the dead woman is already pictured. Another scene shows her husband Vincentius presiding at the banquet of the 'seven pious priests'. But this same Vincentius, whose incription finally extols his piety of heart and mind in the performance of the 'holy ceremonies', leaves his survivors a message of hedonism as ordinary as those on many an epitaph:

> Eat, drink, enjoy yourself and come to me; as long as you live, have a good time: that is what you will bring away with you!

As for the Mithraist priest, buried in a tomb close by, he claims to have given his 'foster children' (foundlings, sometimes adopted for immoral purposes) 'kisses, pleasure and frolics', which rather clashes with the idea one has of the strict, if not ascetic, morality taught in the caverns of the Persian cult.

Speaking of the Christians whom Nero made scapegoats in order to quash the rumour accusing him of having ordered the fire of Rome, Tacitus (*An.*, 15, 44, 5) writes that their 'loathsome superstition' had burst upon the city 'where every horror, every infamy from everywhere converged and attracted the crowds.' The statement, which in this instance targeted stories of anthropophagy (and the murdering of children) imputed to the Christians, held good for a number of shady fraternities, like those denounced by Juvenal and the heresiologists.

This 'confluence' of religions in the capital of a supranational and multicultural empire encouraged two apparently contradictory happenings: the diversification of innumerable cults and confusion of the gods. Modernists have, however, somewhat overestimated the effects of syncretism, which is supposed to have laid the way open to monotheism. In Rome, as elsewhere, it has certainly been possible to identify such and such a deity with another (or at least recognise equivalences), but without ever denying topical, functional and iconographic specifics. Jupiter *Dolichenus* may well have borne the same titles 'Most Good Most Great' as Jupiter Capitolinus, but he was still distinct from him, as he was from Serapis, with whom he was associated and put on an equal footing. The same remark is valid for Juno *Dolichena*, who is doubled by Isis without being confused with her. Isis was invoked as she who 'being one is all' (*CIL*, 10, 3800), and Apuleius (M, 11, 5, 1) makes her say that she is 'the uniform image of the gods and goddesses'. But all those *numina* whose synthesis she was deemed to form preserved their own cult, their name and their followers.

The intellectuals' syncretism had but little influence on daily and positive religion. Even if many pagans showed a preference for this or that deity, bordering on henotheism, they would take great care not to neglect the others. On this point, Romans of the senatorial aristocracy did not depart from tradition, despite the philosophical currents that tended to recognise in the gods the various powers of the supreme God. The widow of Agorius Praetextatus (d. AD 384) paid homage to the learned piety which honoured 'the multiple power of the gods': *divumque numen multiplex doctus colis* (CLE, 111, 15).

In fact, like several of his co-religionists of his class in the late period, he was not only augur, pontiff of Vesta, pontiff of the Sun, quindecemvir, curial of Hercules, but also an initiate of the mysteries of Liber, hierophant of Eleusis, 'neocor' (thus attached to the temple of Serapis), consecrated by the blood of the taurobolium and 'father of fathers' in the Mithraic hierarchy. So Macrobius (S, 1, 17, 1) was able to hail Praetextatus as the 'choregos of all cults', *sacrorum omnium praesul*, with this genuinely Roman title designating the one who conducted the Salian dances. This was more or less the time when Themistius was explaining to the emperor Valens that the Hellenes had 300 forms of belief, and that such pluralism had the consent of the deity (Socr., *HE*, 4, 32). Polytheism was by nature dedicated to that infinity:

> One path alone is not enough to attain such a great mystery. (Symm., *Rel.*, 3, 10)

By defending in this way (with the altar of Victory) the raison d'être of *religiones*, Symmachus still reveals in AD 384 the thoroughly Roman concern to win over all the gods:

> May you be preserved, Augustine, by all those subordinate gods whose mediation helps us to reach the communal Father of gods and men, whom all the nations of the earth honour and pray to in a thousand different ways but with one accord. (Aug., *Ep.*, 16, 4)

What an old pagan of Madaurus thus wrote to the future bishop of Hippo around AD 390 clearly shows that, for some of his contemporaries, monotheism in theory did not rule out polytheism in practice.

CHAPTER 5

Conclusion: The impact of Christianity

Religions wear out. They do not always continue to respond to the innermost or doubt-filled questionings of their own followers, even though the routine of ritual allows them to carry on from day to day. But official or ambient terrorism, of the law or activists of a new and soon dominant religion, also assumes the mission of persuading the last recalcitrants by forceful means.

The conqueror of Maxentius in October AD 312, Constantine did not celebrate a triumph, and quite rightly, as his enemy was not external to the *orbis Romanus*. However, an arch was erected in his honour in AD 315, not 'of triumph' strictly speaking, but with a frieze which, instead of evoking the traditional procession of booty, captives and animals pledged to a sacrifice of homage to Jupiter Capitolinus, details for us the stages of a march on Rome that terminated in the battle of the Milvian Bridge. Strangely, though, through the use of reliefs recovered from ancient buildings, the decoration of this composite monument incorporates scenes of sacrifices to several pagan gods: Silvanus, Diana, Hercules and Apollo.

Already converted to Christianity, Constantine did not celebrate the Secular Games in AD 314. Slightly less than two centuries later, the historian Zosimus (2, 7, 1) holds this omission responsible for the ruin of the Empire invaded by the Barbarians and for 'the unhappy state which at present overwhelms us' (ibid., 2). For the tenth anniversary of his proclamation, in July AD 315, Constantine did not go up to the Capitol to give thanks to Jupiter, or for his *Vicennalia* in 326 (ibid., 29, 5). The traditionalist Romans were deeply offended.

In March AD 313, the Edict of Milan recognised the right of everyone to practise the religion of his choice (Lact., *Mort.*, 48, 2–6; Eus., *HE*, 10, 5, 2. 4–5. 8). Constantine and Licinius were apparently reviving the very Roman concern of ensuring for the Empire the favour of mysterious forces beyond human measure:

so that all that is divine in the celestial region may be propitious and benevolent to ourselves as to all those who are dependent upon our authority. (Lact., *Mort.*, 48, 2; Eus., *HE*, 10, 5, 4)

In fact, the two Augusti speak only of *divinitas*, like the dedication on Constantine's arch which ascribes his victory first and foremost to 'the inspiration of divinity' (*instinctu divinitatis*). The edict expressly takes into account only the powers on high, therefore excluding from imperial toleration the gods down below, of the night and the subterranean world: those such as Hecate or Mithras, who were worshipped in shadowy caverns, and also, quite naturally, the demons solicited by magicians, but with which Christians generally lumped together all pagan gods. Indeed – and on this point even the Neoplatonist Porphyrus agrees with Christians – the demons and underworld gods were believed to enjoy nocturnal and bloody sacrifices, condemned throughout the fourth century by emperors who had been won over to the new faith.

Nevertheless, their legislation did not immediately and radically prohibit acts of idolatry themselves. Constantine wanted to convert the pagans and, according to Eusebius of Caesarea (*VC*, 2, 60), he at first envisaged abolishing the cult linked with the 'power of the shadows'. But although he forbade governors (ibid., 44) to take part in any sacrifice, and prohibited 'the abominations of idolatry' (ibid., 45) or certain occult rites (ibid., 4, 25) – which seemed to be aimed, among others, at Mithraic mysteries – Constantine remained faithful, all in all, to the letter of the Edict of Milan. He ruled out the use of a haruspex for private individuals (*C. Th.*, 9, 16, 1–2) but authorised it in the case of public buildings struck by lightning (ibid., 16, 10, 1) or when it was a matter of obtaining good harvests, or healing the sick (ibid., 9, 16, 3). Whereby, as chief priest, the first Christian emperor did not depart from Roman tradition.

True, the inventory of the temples, motivated by the state's need for precious metals in order to mint the money indispensable for paying the troops, caused revulsion among the pagans, above all when those carrying out the survey emptied the idols of their macabre relics to expose them to the ridicule of Christians (Eus., *VC*, 3, 57, 2; Ruf., *HE*, 2, 24). Moreover, certain sanctuaries were despoiled to benefit the decor of the new Rome – Constantinople. But Constantine in no way overturned liturgies that were traditionally celebrated (Lib., *Or.*, 30, 6), and Rome, chiefly, seems to have been relatively spared.

Constantine's successors, however, broke with that policy, beginning with Constans, the only one of his three sons to be baptised. In AD 341 a law laid down 'that superstition must cease'. It radically ruled out 'the passion for sacrifices' (*C. Th.*, 16, 10, 2). *Cesset superstitio*: henceforward it was not just a matter of foreign religions; the entire ancestral cult was officially accused of 'superstition'. The cultural revolution began with these words and their acceptance. It was a way of conditioning public opinion. The apologist Minucius Felix (38, 7) had pointed the way a century earlier.

The Roman population, however, remained very attached to certain forms of festive paganism and, the very next year (342), Constans had second thoughts and stated precisely:

> Although all superstitions must be abolished, we desire however that the temples situated outside the walls should suffer no damage, for several of them were at the origin of circus games or other competitions, and it is not right to destroy that which assures the Roman people of the solemnity of their traditional amusements. (*C. Th.*, 16, 10, 3)

Exactly which 'temples' did he mean? Were the *circenses* in question those of the circus of Maxentius on the Appian Way? At all events, a Christian emperor's solicitude for the crowds' diversions, even tainted with the original vice of idolatry (Tert., *Spect.*, 4, 3; 5, 4.8; 7,1), makes us wonder. In fact, chariot races would continue to be all the rage in the time of Theodoric (sixth century) and, although Constantine had banned gladiator fights in AD 325 (*C. Th.*, 15, 12, 1), the poet Prudentius (*C. Symm.*, 2, 1116) was still beseeching the emperor Honorius to abolish *tam triste sacrum* in AD 403; this he did in AD 404.

From the material point of view, Christian Rome was starting to be built and on occasion got in the way of the exercise of pagan worship. Thus the construction of the basilica consecrated by Constantine to St Peter not only affected the pagan necropolis discovered under the Vatican Caves, but also interrupted the taurobolic ritual of the *Phrygianum* situated in front of the present baroque facade of Paul V Borghese, or nearby. The inscription on an altar (*IGUR*, 127) exhumed from the foundations of a neighbouring building laments the long 'night' of twenty-eight years – between AD 322 and AD 350 – during which it had been impossible to perform the sacrifice of the bull and the ram, 'symbol of felicity'. In AD 350 the usurper Magnentius revoked the ban on nocturnal sacrifices (see *C. Th.*, 16, 10, 5), which helped the Mother-worship cult which was distinguished by a 'midnight' (*CIL.*, 13, 1751).

But Constantius II defeated Magnentius at La Batie-Montsaléon AD 353, and imperial legislation immediately increased repressive measures, sometimes repeating them, which in fact reveals their ineffectiveness (or non-application): closing of temples with the threat of the 'avenging sword' (*C. Th.*, 16, 10, 4); prohibition of nocturnal sacrifices (ibid., 5); capital punishment inflicted on anyone sacrificing to or worshipping idols (ibid., 6), which in AD 356 answered the wishes of the apologist Firmicus Maternus (*Err.*, 29, 1–2).

However, the visit that Constantius II made to Rome in AD 357 earned a kind of respite for the polytheism of the *Urbs*. The Christian ruler discovered his monumental heritage, which impressed him enough to shift his attitude towards tradition. Although he had the altar removed where the senators burned incense before the statue of Victory (Ambr., *Ep.*, 18, 32),

> he looked at the sanctuaries with a calm expression, read the gods' names inscribed on their pediments, inquired about the origins of the temples and showed his admiration for those who had had them built and, although he was a follower of another religion, he preserved ours for the Empire. (Symm., *Rel.*, 3, 7)

After Julian's pagan reaction (361–3), Jovian and Valentinian I adopted a neutral attitude which in Rome afforded polytheism almost a new lease of life. Besides, and from AD 357, the medalliions known as 'contorniate' (with a deep groove round the rim) circulated a festive imagery in which gods and pagan emperors occupied pride of place. Valentinian I still banned nocturnal prayers, services or sacrifices (*C. Th.*, 9, 16, 7), but at Praetextatus's request consented to an exception in the case of the Eleusinian mysteries (*Zos.*, 4, 3, 3).

However, in AD 381 Theodosius (*C. Th.*, 16, 10, 7) also banned sacrifices in broad daylight if they were for divinatory purposes, and we know that every Roman sacrifice called for an examination of the victim's entrails. The following year, Gratian (who had refused the title of 'pontifex maximus' in AD 379) had the altar of Victory removed from the hall in which the Senate held its sessions, although it had been replaced after the departure of Constantius in May AD 357. What is more, he did away with the salaries hitherto paid to the Vestals and pagan priests, allocating the money to the unkeep of the imperial postal service. Funds formerly devoted to festivals were diverted to the public treasury and the prefect of the praetorium. Lands belonging to the temples, the virgins of the sacred fire and the great priestly colleges became the property of the tax administration (Symm., *Rel.*, 3, 11–13).

Symmachus's protests in AD 384 went unheeded, and the legislation of Theodosius gradually tightened the screws of a repression that was increasingly well defined: in AD 385, the threat of death for those guilty of reading entrails (*C. Th.*, 16, 10, 9); in AD 389, the abolition of days off work for pagan solemnities (ibid., 2, 8, 19); in AD 391, a ban on 'killing an innocent victim', entering a temple and worshipping the idols there (ibid., 16, 10, 10–11); lastly in AD 392, the prohibition of all domestic cults (ibid., 12).

But all these measures did not apply *de facto* in Rome, where the polytheistic aristocracy retained a large part of its prestige and influence. The people of the *Urbs* were very fond of their games, festivals and *fasti*. In AD 359, when a storm threatened the safe arrival of African wheat, it was by sacrificing to the Dioscuri, protectors of shipping, that the prefect Tertullus was held to have saved the situation (Amm., 19, 10, 4). Apparently, people continued well into the fourth century to celebrate the procession of the Great Mother to the Almo every 27 April (ibid., 23, 3, 7). To read the peaceable and almost timeless letters of Symmachus, one could well believe that nothing changed, despite the bitterness of a comment made almost in passing (*Ep.*, 1, 51): 'These days, to be absent from the altars is a way of paying one's respects.'

The pontiffs met and took decisions (ibid., 1, 36; 47– 8; 51; 2, 36; 9, 147– 8). *Ostenta* were atoned for with sacrifices, which had to be repeated as long as no encouraging signs were forthcoming (ibid., 1, 49):

> Indeed, an eighth immolation did not propitiate Jupiter, and it was in vain that, by means of many victims, an eleventh homage was paid to Public Fortune.

A Vestal broke her vow of chastity; as at other times, the priests investigated the affair. They extracted the truth from her, and she confessed, together with her accomplice (ibid., 9, 147–8). Was she buried alive, according to the ritual? It is most unlikely, although Symmachus recalls the example of its ancient severity. She was not the Great Vestal whose name is hammered on a base dated AD 364 and found in the *atrium Vestae* (CIL, 6, 32422). The virgin's name began with a 'C', and brings to mind a Claudia who left the service of the public hearth to become a Christian in the church of St Laurence-outside-the-Walls, (Prud., *Perist.*, 2, 526 f.).

Prefect of the city, in AD 367 Praetextatus had the portico of the twelve *Di Consentes* restored, at the foot of the Capitol (CIL, 6, 30692), those who, literally, 'are together': six gods (Jupiter, Mars, Apollo, Neptune, Vulcan and Mercury) and six goddesses (Juno, Minerva, Venus, Ceres, Diana and Vesta). In Varro's time (*RR*, 1, 1, 4), one could see their statues in gilded bronze, which Praetextatus must have had restored. It is in memory of this same Praetextatus (it seems to me) that, around AD 390, the Symmachi and Nicomachi had an ivory diptych engraved extolling his piety and that of his wife Aconia Paulina[1]. For another member of the aristocracy who furnished a Mithraic cavern at his own expense,

---

1. R. Turcan,'Coré-Libera? Eleusis et les deniers païens', *CRAI*, 1996, pp. 745– 67.

the costs of piety are worth more than gain: is one not enriched by sharing one's modest inheritance with the inhabitants of the sky? (*CIL*, 6, 754)

Such constancy and loyalty to the ancestral cults, however, could only exasperate the opposing side. If Rome's pagans feigned unawareness of the legislation targeting them, militant Christians had no compunction about applying it in their own fashion, even getting a head start. In AD 377, the prefect of the city Furius Maecius Gracchus 'ordered the removal of the gods' images' (Prud., *C. Symm.*, 1, 563) and ransacked a *Mithraeum*, over-turning, breaking and setting fire to the 'monstrous simulacra' (Jer., *Ep.*, 107, 2), among which one may imagine the Lion-headed statue. This over-zealous candidate for baptism had probably never read Seneca (*Const.*, 4, 2): 'Those who destroy temples and melt down idols cause no harm at all to the deity!'

In the Sta Prisca cavern, the paintings were lacerated, torn down, attacked with knives, and the stucco group in the chancel hacked to pieces with an axe. Then it was filled in and the entry stopped up with a pile of bricks, broken bottles, funeral debris of pagan and Christian origin, transported from a cemetery on the Ostian road, at the foot of the Aventine. In Rome as elsewhere, the heads of the gods were attacked, methodically decapitated or disfigured, as if those faces of evil demons needed to be exorcised by swift destruction. The Christians' relentlessness expressed another form of belief in the obscure power of those despicable idols.

True, the immediate vicinity of a Christian church established above the *Mithraeum* directly exposed the latter to the commando groups of wreckers. This was also what happened at San Clemente, where the Mithraic complex extended beneath the nave-end of the lower basilica, the level of the palaeo-Christian church of which St Jerome speaks. The altar of the Persian cult bears the traces of several assaults. Broken up on a first occasion and restored, it was again mutilated and robbed of its capping; then it was dragged out of the nave the better to deliver this prey to the iconoclastic frenzy, for it represented Mithras slaying the bull. The remains of the capping were found being reused in a later paving. The *Mithraeum* excavated beneath Sto Stefano Rotondo had suffered the effects of a no less violent devastation, as is evidenced by the fragments of a painted stucco group (with the gilded head of Mithras) found scattered over the statue of the petrogeneous god which had been overturned on the floor near the chancel.

Obviously, it was necessary to conceal oneself to worship the Invincible Sun. In 1883, in a Roman house on the Via Giovanni Lanza, about four metres below the current street level, was found one of the rare *Mithraea* to have escaped the fanatical depredations.[2] It had been installed in a cellar to which access was gained, after crossing the door of a lararium, by two flights of nine and seven steps respectively, separated by a landing where two niches housed the statues of Cautes and Cautopates. In the cavern itself, the cultic relief was still in place, on a marble shelf which still bore the remains of seven torches of tarred fir used to illuminate the bull-slaying god. An Ionian capital fixed upside down on a moulded pillar took the place of an altar. In that district the Christian community of the *Titulus Equitii* (San Martino ai Monti) assembled at enough distance not to upset the clandestine Mithraists, whose cult had therefore died out without any violence.

It goes without saying that we know very little about this paganism which one dare not term 'of the catacombs'. The idolaters sometimes put statues and sculpted marbles in a safe place, but there is nothing to prove that the gods represented were ritually worshipped where they were discovered.

In Rome itself, in the fourth century AD, what is called the 'Syrian sanctuary of the Janiculum' may have housed the religious offices of a syncretic and secret polytheism.[3] Away from the city centre, the site of the Villa Sciarra has yielded various pieces of evidence relating to the cult of the Levantine gods, as they were worshipped between the end of the Antonine era and the middle of the third century. But in its final state, the 'sanctuary' no longer had any direct link with Jupiter Heliopolitanus and his partner, the Syrian Goddess. Its strange structure seems to have been derived from no known or well-identifiable model.

Access was through a closed central courtyard opening on one side into a sort of temple with a triple *cella*, preceded by a vestibule flanked by two chapels; and on the other side, on to an equally tripartite main building, but where two pentagonal chapels alone allowed acess to an octagonal room. In the temple with the triple *cella*, beneath the niche of the apse where a Jovian or Serapian type of god was enthroned, a rectangular cavity contained the skullcap of a human cranium. At the other end of the 'sanctuary', in the centre of the octagon, a triangular container held the bronze statuette of a man enfolded in a kind of shroud; a serpent entwined him in seven coils, and its jagged crest loomed over the idol's hooded head. A dried root served

---

2. D. Gallo, 'Il mitreo di Via Giovanni Lanza', in U. Bianchi (ed.), *Mysteria Mithrae*) (*EPRO*, 80), Leiden, 1979, pp. 249–58.
3. M. Mele (ed.) *L'area del 'santurio siriaco del Gianicolo'*, Rome, 1982; F. Duthoy and J. Frel, 'Observations sur le sanctuaire syrien du Janicule' in G. M. Bellell and U. Bianchi (ed.), *Orientalia Sacra Urbis Romae Dolichena et Heliopolitans*, Rome, 1996, pp. 289–301.

him as a necklace and there were seeds scattered on his chest. Seven hen's eggs were placed between the reptile's coils. The hall's apsidal niche held a statue of pharaonic appearance, and probably represented Osiris.

In one of the pentagonal chapels, the mutilated group of a triple feminine deity (three Hours or triple Hecate?) was discovered and, buried in the ground, a marble statue of Dionysus. In 1803 a triangular base (of an altar?) was unearthed, and is today preserved in the Louvre where it has been improperly restored as a candelabrum. Its three faces bear respectively the picture of the Sun, the Moon and a bull. The dedicant – *Doryphorus pater* – must have been a Mithraist. The dominant ternary feature of the architecture and furnishings probably had some significance which eludes us; and the other elements of this discovery are no less problematic.

This irregular and strange material rules out the possibility of attributing the use of this place to a specific cult. Its very disparity reminds one of the obligingly pluralist piety of the last pagans. The exoticism and peculiarity of the rites implied by both the unusual structure and the sectioned human skull, or the mummy-like statuette in its triangular tomb, were equally no longer incompatible with late Roman polytheism, in an era when Egyptian mysteries, Chaldaean oracles and theurgy often haunted the fairly confused imagination of Neoplatonist theosophers.

The section of skull refers us to the magico-religious techniques of 'telestics', for the consecration of statues; this was a procedure deemed to attract a portion of the divine potential into the idol, by way of the inclusion of organic substances, such as the bones brought to light when the inventory of the temples was carried out in Constantine's reign. As for the mummiform idol, this recalls the images of Osiris carved on Graeco-Egyptian intaglios. A small gem supposed to have come from the site or nearby represents a figure of the same type. Now, the *Book of the Dead* predicts that at the end of time the sole survivors will be 'Osiris completely spiritualised, by virtue of the transfiguration rites that accompany mummification, and Atum, the demiurge who will be retransformed into a serpent'.[4] The bronze idol had its big toes cut, a treatment applied to the pharaohs' concubines in their tombs, to prevent them from fleeing. It was bound by the coils of the snake, thus magically and symbolically fixed in the triangular tomb. It did actually escape the Christians' devastation, unlike the other divine images.

The consecration of the idols of Jupiter erected in the Alps in the face of Theodosius's armies (Aug., CG, 5, 26) was not enough to hold them back

---

4. A. Delatte and P. Derchain, *Bibliothèque nationale. Cabinet des Médailles et Antiques. Les intailles magiques gréco-égyptiennes*, Paris, 1964, pp. 74.

and ensure victory to Nicomachus Flavian's pagan side in AD 394. On the other hand, the one that stood at *Rhegium* was supposed to have prevented Alaric from crossing into Sicily (Olympiod., fr. Phot., *Bibl.*, 80, 58 *a*). In AD 408, in a Rome besieged by that same Alaric's Goths, haruspices from Umbria claimed to have saved Narni by applying the rites of the *Etrusca disciplina* to divert lightning on to the Barbarians. The prefect of the city spoke of it to pope Innocent who, in these dramatic circumstances, was willing to turn a blind eye to pagan rites, provided they were performed in secret. But for the haruspices, the rites were effective only if carried out in public; following traditional form, the Senate must go up to the Capitol and there, as in all the town's large piazze, perform the appropriate offices. However, 'no one had the courage to take part in the cult according to ancestral rules' (Zos., 5, 41, 3). It was thought preferable to buy peace by stripping the gods' statues, whose adornments consecrated by 'holy ceremonies' (telestics) 'guaranteed the city eternal felicity' (ibid., 6). They even went as far as melting down the gold and silver idols, notably that of *Virtus*:

> Once that statue was destroyed, everything courageous and virtuous about the Romans disappeared. Such was the prophecy made at that time by those concerned with divine matters and ancestral devotions. (ibid., 7)

It makes one think of an hermetic book, *Asclepius* (24), where the ills preceding the end of the world are ascribed to the abandonment of all religious practices, imposed by 'so-called laws' (*quasi a legibus* – obviously, those of the Christian emperors.

Clandestine polytheism would still have a hard time; at least so Zosimus (around AD 500) and Procopius (under Justinian) let us understand. The first, chiefly, belonged uncompromisingly to the pagans, and delighted in showing that, even when beaten, the gods took their revenge if they were offended. Before Alaric's sack of Rome, the wife of Stilicho – whom Rutilius Namatianus (2, 52) accused of having burnt the Sibylline Oracles – Serena, who was also a niece of Theodosius, had the temple of Cybele on the Palatine opened so that she could view the statue of the goddess. But she removed its necklace to put it round her own neck; seeing this, an elderly Vestal, the last survivor of the college charged with guarding the flame, openly reproached her for her impious act. Serena answered her with insults, having her driven out by her attendants; but some time later she died, strangled, in other words, to match her sin (Zos., 5, 38, 3–4).

Definitively banned in AD 394, the gods remained present in image in large houses, in mosaic floors and costly tableware, as the Parabiago dish so brilliantly testifies, or the marriage casket of Projecta in the treasures of the

Bibliography

– General works, collections of studies –

Altheim, F., *Römische Religionsgeschichte,* 3 vol., Berlin, 1931–3; re-ed. 2 vol., Baden-Baden, 1951–3; Fr. trs. H. E. Del Medico, *La Religion romaine antique,* Paris, 1955.

Bayet, J., *Croyances et rites dans la Rome antique,* Paris, 1971.

Bayet, J., *Histoire politique et psychologique de la religion romaine,* Paris, 1957 (1969²).

Boissier, G., *La Religion romaine d'Auguste aux Antonins,* 2 vol., Paris, 1874 (1909⁷).

Boyancé, P., *Etudes sur la religion romaine,* Rome, 1972 (CEFR, 11).

Dumézie, G., *Cultes indo-europèens á Rome.* Paris, 1954.

—— *La religion romaine archaïque,* Paris, 1966 (1974²).

—— *Idées romaines,* Paris 1969.

—— *Mythe et épopée,* III, *Histoires romaines,* Paris, 1973.

Fustel De Coulanges, N. D., *La Cité antique,* Paris, 1864 (numerous re-editions).

Grenier, A., *LES Religions étrusuqe et romaine,* Paris, 1948, pp. 81–233 ('Mana', *Les Religions de l'Europe ancienne,* III).

Latte, K., *Römische Religionsgeschichte,* Munich, 1960 (*Handbuch der Alertumswissenschaft*).

Magdelain, A., *Jus Imperium Auctoritas. Etudes de droit romain,* Rome, 1990 (CEFR, 133).

Marquardt, J., *Le Culte chez les Romains,* Fr. trs. M. Brissaud, 2 vol., Paris, 1889–90.

Momigliano, A., *Saggi di storia della religione romana,* Brescia, 1988.

Montanari, E., *Identià e conflitti religiosi nella Roma repubblicana,* Rome, 1988.

—— *Mito e storia nell'annalistica romana delle origini,* Rome, 1990.

Ogilvie, R. M., *The Romans and their Gods,* London, 1969.

Pighi, G. B., *La religine romana,* Turin, 1967.

Schilling, R., *Cultes, dieux et rites romains,* Paris, 1979.

Wagenvoort, H., *Pietas. Selected Studies in Roman Religion,* Leiden, 1980.

Wissowa, G., *Religion und Kultus der Römer,* Munich, 1912² (*Handbuch des klassichen Altertumswissenschaft,* V, 4).

– Iconography –

Fless, F., *Opferdiener und Kultmusiker auf stadtrömischen historischen Reliefs*, Mainz, 1995.

Hesberg, H., von 'Archäologische Denkmaler zu den römischen Göttergestalten', *ANRW*, ii, 17, 1, 1981, pp. 1032–199.

Martin, H.G., *Römische Tempelkultbilder*, Rome, 1987 (1933²).

Ryberg, I. S., *Rites of the State Religion in Roman Art*, Rome, 1955 (*Mem. of the Amer. Acad. in Rome*, 22).

Turcan, R., 'Religion romaine', in *Iconography of Religions*, XVII, 1, 2 vol. (1. *Les Dieux*; 2. *Le Culte*), Leiden, 1988.

– Vocabularies –

Benveniste, E., *Le Vocabulaire des institutions indo-européennes*, 2 vol., Paris, 1960.

Lexikon iconographicum nythologiae classiace, 8 double vol. Zurich, 1981–97.

Radke, G., *Die Götter Altitaliens*, Münster, 1965.

– Monographs or articles concerning various gods –

Bayet, J., *Les Origines de l'Hercule romain*, Paris, 1926 (*BEFAR*, 132).

Brouwer, H.H. J., *Bona Dea. The Sources and a Description of the Cult*, Leiden, 1989 (*EPRO*, 110).

Bruhl, A., *Liber Pater. Origin et expansion du culte dionysiaque à Rome et dans le monde romain*, Paris, 1953 (*BEFAR*, 175).

Capdeville, G., *Volcanus. Recherches comparatistes sur les origines du culte de Vulcain*, Rome, 1995 (*BEFAR*, 288).

Champeaux, J., *Fortuna. Le Cult de la Fortune à Rome et dans l'Empire romain*, I–II, Rome, 1982–7 (*CEFR*, 64).

Combet-Farnoux, B., *Mercure romain*, Rome, 1980 (*BEFAR*, 238).

Dorcey, P. F., *The Cult of Silvanus*, Leiden, 1992.

Dury-Moyaers, G. and Renard, M., 'Aperçu critique de travaux relatifs au culte de Junon' *ANRW*, II, 17, 1, 1981, pp. 142–202.

Fears, J. R., 'The Cult of Jupiter and Roman Imperial Ideology', *ANRW*, II, 17, 1, 1981, pp. 3–141.

Gagé, J., *Apollon romain. Essai sur le culte d'Apollon et le développement du 'ritus Graecus' à Rome des origines à Auguste*, Paris, 1955 (*BEFAR*, 182).

—— 'Apollon imperial, garant des "Fata Romana"', *ANRW*, II, 17, 2, 1981, pp. 561–630.

Girard, J.-L., 'La place de Minerve dans la religion romaine au temps du principat', *ANRW*, II, 17, 1, 1981, pp. 203–32.

—— 'Domitien et Minerve: une prédilection impériale', *ibid.*, pp. 233–45.

Holland, L. A., *Janus and the Bridge*, Rome, 1961.

Jaczynowska, M., 'Le culte d'Hercule romain au temps du Haut- Empire', *ANRW*, II, 17, 2, 1981, pp. 631–61.

Kajanto, I., 'Fortuna', *ANRW*, II, 17, 1, 1981, pp. 502–58.

Krause, B. H., *Iuppiter Optimus Maximus Saturnus*, Mainz, 1984.

Le Bonniec, H., *Le Culte de Cérès à Rome des origines à la fin de la République*, Paris, 1958 (*Etudes et commentaires*, 27).

Le Gall, J., *Recherches sur le culte du Tibre*, Paris, 1953.

Mackay, L. A., *Janus*, Univ. of California, 1956.

Mellor, R.,'The Goddess Roma', *ANRW*, II, 17, 1, 1981, pp. 950–1030.

Piccaluga, G., 'Fides nella religione romana di età imperiale', *ANRW*, II, 17, 2, 1981, pp. 703–35.

Pouthier, P., *Ops et la conception divine de l'abondance dans la religion romaine jusqu' à la mort d'Auguste*, Rome, 1981 (*BEFAR*, 242).

Schilling, R., *La Religion romaine de Venus depuis les origines jusqu'au temps d'Auguste*, Paris, 1954, 1982[2] (*BEFAR*, 178).

Scholz, U. W., *Studien zum altitalischen und altrömischen Marskult und Marsmythos*, Heidelberg, 1970.

Skovgaard-Jensen, S., 'Silvanus and his Cult', *Anal. Rom. Inst. Denici*, 2, 1962, pp. 11 ff.

Turcan, R., 'Janus à l'époque impériale', *ANRW*, II, 17, 1, 1981, pp. 374–402.

Winkler, L., *Salus. Vom Staatskult zur politischen Idee*, Heidelberg, 1955 (*Archäologie und Geschichte*, 4).

– INTRODUCTION –

Basanoff, V., *Les Dieux des Romains*, Paris, 1942 (*Mythes et religions*, 11).

Bloch, R., *La Divination. Essai sur l'avenir et son imaginaire*, Paris, 1991, pp. 67–95, especially 'La divination par les signes'.

Bouché-Leclercq A., *Histoire de la divination dans l'Antiquité*, Paris, 1882, pp. 180 ff.

Calderone S., 'Superstitio', *ANRW*, I, 2, 1972, pp. 377–96.

Festugière, A. J., 'La religion des Romains d'après un ouvrage récent', *Rev. bibl.*, no. 65, 1968, pp. 78–100.

Fugier, H., *Recherches sur l'expression du sacre dans la langue latine*, Paris-Strasbourg, 1963.

Le Bonniec, H., 'Un témoignage d'Aronobe sur la cuisine du sacrifice', *REL*, 63, 1985, pp. 183–92.

Macbain, B., *Prodigy and Expiation: a Study in Religion and Politics in Republican Rome*, Brussels, 1982 ('Latomus' series, 177).

Sachot, M., 'Religio-Superstitio. Historique d'une subversion et d'un retournement', *RHR*, 208, 1991, pp. 355–94.

Scheid, J., *Religion et piété à Rome*, Paris, 1985.

Sordi, M., 'L'*Homo romanus*: religione, diritto e sacro', *Trattato di antropologia del sacro* (dir. J. Ries), 3, *Le civiltà del Mediterraneo e il sacro*, Milan, 1992, pp. 285–337.

Wagenvoort, H., 'Wesenszüge altrömischer Religion', *ANRW*, I, 2, 1972, pp. 348–76.

Warde Fowler, W., *The Religious Experience of the Roman People from the Earliest Times to the Age of Augustus*, London, 1911 (1922[2]).

—— *Roman Ideas of Deity in the Last Century before the Christian Era*, London, 1914.

– RELIGIONS OF THE FAMILY AND THE LAND –

Aronen, J., 'Il culto arcaico nel *Tarentum* a Rome e la gens Valeria', *Arctos, Acta Philologica Fennica*, 26, 1989, pp. 19–39.

—— 'Iuturna, Carmenta e Mater Larum. Un rapporto arcaico tra mito, calendario e topografia', *Opusc. Inst. Rom. Finlandiae*, 4, 1989, pp. 65–88.

Boëls-Janssen, N., *La Vie religieuse des matrones dans la Rome archaïque*, Rome, 1993 (*CEFR*, 176).

—— 'L' interdit des *bis nuptiae* dans les cultes matronaux', *REL*, no 74, 1996, pp. 47–66.

Bömer, F., *Ahnenkult und Ahnenglaube im alten Rom*, Leipzig, 1943.

Borda, M., *Lares. La vita familiare romana nei documenti archeologici e letterari*, Rome, 1947.

Bulard, M., *La Religion domestique dans la colonie italienne de Délos*, Paris, 1926 (*BEFAR*, 131).

De Marchi, A., *Il culto privato di Roma antica*, 2 vol., Milan, 1896–1903.

Déonna, W. and Renard M., *Croyances et superstitions de table dans la Rome antique*, Brussels, 1961 ('Latomus' series, 46).

Dubourdieu, A., *Les Origines et le développement du culte des Pénates à Rome*, 1989 (*CEFR*, 118).

Dumezil, G., *L'Oubli de l'homme et l'honneur des dieux*, Paris, 1985 (pp. 162–9 on Pilumnus; 170–9 on the *genius*).

—— *Mariages indo-européens*, followed by *Quinze questions romaines*, Paris, 1979.

Harmon, D. P., 'The Family Festivals of Rome', *ANRW*, II, 16, 2, 1978, pp. 1592–1603.

Jacobsen, J. P., *Les Mânes*, Fr. trs., 3 vol., Paris, 1924.

Jobbé-Duval, E., *Les Morts malfaisants: 'Larvae, Lemures' d'après le droit et les croyances populaires des Romains*, Paris, 1924.

Köves-Zulauf, T., *Römische Geburtsriten*, Munich, 1990 (*Zetemata*, 87; detailed commentary by R. Turcan in *Gnomon*, no 66, 1994, pp. 9–13.

Kunckel, H., *Der römische Genius*, Heidelberg, 1974.

Marquardt, J., *La Vie privée des Romains*, Fr. trs. V. Henry, 2 vol., Paris, 1892–3.

Nilsson, M. P., 'Roman and Greek Domestic Cult', *Opuscula selecta*, III, Lund, 1960, pp. 272–85.

Orr, D. G., 'Roman Domestic Religion: the Evidences of the Household Shrines', *ANRW*, II, 16, 2, 1978, pp. 1557–91.

Richard, J.-C., 'Le culte de *Sol* et les *Aurelii*: à propos de Paul. Fest., p. 22 L.', *Mélanges J. Heurgon*, II, Rome, 1976, pp. 915–25 (*CEFR*, 27).

Schilling, R., 'Les Lares Grundiles', *Mélanges J. Heurgon*, I, Rome, 1976, pp. 947–59 (*CEFR*, 27).

– URBAN RELIGIONS –

Basanoff, V., *Evocatio. Etude d'un rituel militaire romain*, Paris, 1945.

Bloch, R., 'Religion romaine et religion punique à l'époque d'Hannibal *minime romano sacro*, in *Mélanges J. Heurgon*, I, Rome, 1976, pp. 33–40 (*CEFR*, 27).

Bouché-Leclerco, A., *Les Pontifes de l'ancienne Rome*, Paris, 1871.

Brind'amour, P., 'L'origine des jeux Séculaires, *ANRW*, II, 16, 2, 1978, pp. 1334–417.

Catalano, P., *Contributo allo studio del diritto augurale*, I, Turin, 1960.

Champeaux, J., 'Pontifes, haruspices et décemvirs. L'expiation des prodiges de 207', *REL*, no 74, 1996, pp. 67–91.

Cirilli, R., *Les Prêtres danseurs de Rome. Etude sur la corporation sacerdotale des Saliens*, Paris, 1913.

Dumézil, G., *Fêtes romaines d'eté et d'automne*, followed by *Dix questions romaines*, Paris, 1975.

Freybruger, G., 'La supplication d'action de grâces sous le Haut-Empire', *ANRW*, II, 16, 2, 1978, pp. 1418–39.

Gagé, J., *Recherches sur les jeux séculaires*, Paris, 1934.

Guittard, C., 'Tite-Live, Accius et le rituel de la *devotio*', *CRAI*, 1984, pp. 581–600.

Guizzi, F., *Aspetti giuridici del sacerdozio romano. Il sacerdozio di Vesta*, Naples, 1968.

Halkin, L., *La Supplication d'action de grâces chez les Romains*, Paris, 1953.

Heurgon, J., 'Le *ver sacrum* romain de 217', *Latomus*, no 15, 1956, pp. 137–58; *Trois études sure le 'ver sacrum'*, Brussels, 1956 ('Latomus' series, 26).

Künzl, E., *Der römische Triumph. Siegesfeiern im antiken Rom*, Munich, 1988.

Le Bourdellès, H., 'Nature profonde du pontificat romain. Tentative d'une étymologie', *RHR*, no 189, 1976, pp. 53–65.

Le Gall, J., 'Evocatio', in *Mélanges J. Heurgon*, I, Paris, 1976, pp. 519–24 (*CEFR*, 27).

Linderski, J., 'The Augural Law', *ANRW*, II, 16, 3, 1986, pp. 2146–312.

Michels, A. K., *The Calendar of the Roman Republic*, Princeton Univ. Press, 1967.

Piccaluga, G., *Elementi spettacolari nei rituali festivi romani*, Rome, 1965.

Piganiol, A., *Recherches sur les jeux romains*, Paris-Strasbourg 1923.

Porte, D., *L'Etiologie religieuse dans les* Fastes *d'Ovide*, Paris, 1985.

Sabbatucci, D., *La religione di Roma antica: dal calendario festivo all'ordine cosmico*, Milan, 1988.

Scheid, J., *Romulus et ses frères. Le collège des frères arvales, modèle du culte public dans la Rome des empereurs*, Rome, 1990 (*BEFAR*, 275).

Scullard, H. H., *Festivals and Ceremonies of the Roman Republic*, London, 1981. Germ. trs. *Römische Feste. Kalender and Kult*, Mainz, 1985.

Sini, F., *Documenti sacerdotali di Roma antica*, I. *Libri e commentarii*, Sassari, 1983.

Szemler, G. J., *The Priests of the Roman Republic*, Brussels, 1972 ('Latomus' series, 127).

Vanggaard, J. H., *The Flamen. A Study in the History and Sociology of Roman Religion*, Copenhagen, 1988.

Versnel, H. S., 'Self-Sacrifice, Compensation and the Anonymous Gods', in *Le Sacrifice dans l'Antiquité, Entretiens de la Fondation Hardt*, 27, Vandoeuvres-Geneva, 1981, pp. 135–94.

—— *Triumphus. An Inquiring into the Origin, Development and Meaning of the Roman Triumph*, Leiden, 1970.

Warde Fowler, W., *The Roman Festivals of the Period of the Republic*, London, 1899.

– RELIGIONS OF THE EMPIRE –

Audollent, A., *Defixionum tabellae*, Paris, 1904 (Frankfurt, 1967[2]).

Beck, R., 'Mithraism since Franz Cumont', *ANRW*, II, 17, 4, 1984, pp. 2002–115.

Bellelli, G. M., Bianchi U. (ed.), *Orientalia Sacra Urbis Romae Dolichena et Heliopolitana*, Rome, 1996 (*Studia Archaeologica*, 84).

Bianchi, U. (ed.), *Mysteria Mithrae*, Leiden, 1979, pp. 69–358 (*EPRO*, 80).

Bianchi, U., Vermaseren M. J. (ed.) *La soteriologia dei culti orientali nell'Impero Romano*, Leiden, 1982 (*EPRO*, 92).

Cordischi, L., 'La Dea Caelestis ed il suo culto attraverso le iscriziono, l. Le iscrizioni latine di Roma e dell'Italia', *Archeologia Classica*, no 42, 1990, pp. 161–200.

Cramer, F., *Astrology in Roman Law and Politics*, Philadelphia, 1954.

Cumont, F., *Les Religions orientales dans le paganisme romain*, Paris, 1929[4].

—— *Lux perpetua*, Paris, 1949. *Texts et monumets figurés relatifs aux mystères de Mithra*, 2 vol., Brussels, 1896–9.

—— *Les Mystères de Mithra*, Brussels, 1913[3].

Fishwick, D., *The Imperial Cult in the Latin West*, 4 vol., Leiden, 1987–92 (*EPRO*, 108).

Foucher, L., 'Le culte de Bacchus sous l'Empire romain', *ANRW*, II, 17, 2, 1981, pp. 684–702.

Frey, M., *Untersuchungen zur Religion und zur Religionspolitik, des Kaisers Elagabal*, Stuttgart, 1989 (*Historia*, Einzelschr., 62).

Gallini, C., *Protesta e integrazione nella Roma antica*, Bari, 1970.

Graf, F., *La Magie dans l'antiquité gréco-romaine*, Paris, 1994.

Graillot, H., *Le Culte de Cybèle, Mère des dieux, à Rome et dans l'Empire romain*, Paris, 1912 (*BEFAR*, 107).

Grenier, J.-C., *Anubis alexandrin et romain*, Leiden, 1977 (*EPRO*, 57).

Guidobaldi, F., 'Il complesso archeologico di S. Clemente', in *San Clemente Miscellany II*, Rome, 1978, pp. 215–300.

Halsberghe, G. H., 'Le culte de Dea caelestis', *ANRW*, II, 17, 4, 1984, pp, 2203–23.

—— 'Le culte de Deus Sol Invictus à Rome au IIIe siècle ap. J.-C.', *ANRW*, II, 17, 4, 1984, pp. 2181–201.

Hesberg, H. von, 'Archäologishce Denkmäler zum römischen Kaiserkult', *ANRW*, II, 16, 2, 1978, pp. 833–910.

Hörig, M., 'Dea Syria-Atargatis', *ANRW*, II, 17, 3, 1984, pp. 1536–81.

—— 'Jupiter Dolichenus', ibid., pp. 2136–79.

Johnson, S. E., The Present State of Sabazios Research' *ANRW*, II, 17, 3, 1984, pp. 1584–613.

Lane, E. N., *Corpus cultus Iovis Sabazii*, II, *The Other Monuments and Literary Evidence*, Leiden, 1985; III, *Conclusions*, Leiden, 1989.

Leclant, J., *Inventaire bibliographique des Isiaca*, 4 vol., Leiden, 1972–91 (*EPRO*, 18).

Lissi Caronna, E., *Il Mitreo dei Castra Peregrinorum*, Leiden, 1986 (*EPRO*, 104).

Malaise, M., *Inventaire préliminaire des documents égyptiens découverts en Italie*, Leiden, 1972 (*EPRO*, 21); *Les conditions de pénétration et de diffusion des cultes égyptiens en Italie*, Leiden, 1972 (*EPRO*, 22).

Merkelbach, R., *Isis Regina-Zeus Sarapis*, Stuttgart-Leipzig, 1995.

Montero, S., *Diosas y adivinas. Mujer y divinacion en la Roma antigua*, Madrid, 1994.

Nilsson, M. P., *The Dionysiac Mysteries of the Hellenistic and Roman Age*, Lund, 1957 (New York, 1975²).

Pailler, J.-M., *Bacchanalia. La répression de 186 av. J.-C. à Rome et en Italie*, Rome, 1988 (*BEFAR*, 270).

Pippidi, D. M., *Recherches sur le culte impérial*, Paris, s.d. (1939).

Réville, J., *La Religion à Rome sous les Sévères*, Paris, 1886.

Ross Taylor, L., *The Divinity of the Roman Emperor*, Middletown, 1931 (New York, 1975²).

Roullet, A. H., *The Egyptian and Egyptianizing Monuments of Imperial Rome*, Leiden, 1972 (*EPRO*, 20).

Sfameni Gasparro, G., *Soteriology and Mystic Aspects in the Cult of Cybele and Attis*, Leiden, 1985 (*EPRO*, 103).

Tupet, A.-M., *La Magie dans la poésie latine*, Lille, 1976.

Turcan, R., 'César et Dionysos', in *Hommage à la mémoire de J. Carcopino*, Paris, 1977, pp. 317–25.

—— 'Culto imperiale e sacralizzazione del potere nell'impero romano', *Trattato di antropologia del sacro* (dir. J. Ries) 3, Milan, 1992, pp. 309–37.

—— 'La promotion du sujet par le culte du souverain', *Subject and Ruler: The Cult of the Ruling Power in Classical Antiquity*, Ann Arbor, 1996 (Suppl. *Journ. of Rom. Archaeology*). 'Le culte impérial au IIIᵉ siècle', *ANRW*, II, 16, 2, 1978, pp. 996–1084.

—— *Héliogabale et le sacre du Soleil*, Paris, 1985 (1997²).

—— *Les Cultes orientaux dans le monde romain*, Paris, 1989 (1992²). Eng. trs. 'The Cults of the Roman Empire', Oxford, 1996.

—— *Mithra et le mithriacisme*, Paris, 1993².

—— *Numismatique romaine du culte métroaque*, Leiden, 1983 (*EPRO*, 97).

Ulansey, D., *The Origins of the Mithraic Mysteries*, New York-Oxford, 1989.

Vermaseren, M. J., *Corpus cultus Iovis Sabazii*, I, *The Hands*, Leiden, 1983 (*EPRO*, 100).

—— *Cybele and Attis. The Myth and the Cult*, London, 1977.

—— *Corpus cultus Cybelae Attidisque*, III, *Italia-Latium*, Leiden, 1977 (*EPRO*, 50).

—— *Mithriaca IV, Le monument d'Ottaviano Zeno et le culte de Mithra cur le Célius*, Leiden, 1978 (*EPRO*, 16).

Vermaseren, M. J. and Van Essen, C. C., *The Excavations in the Mithraeum of the Church of Santa Prisca in Rome*, Leiden, 1965.

Vidman, L., *Sylloge inscriptionum religionis Isiacae et Sarapiacae*, Berlin, 1969.

—— *Isis und Sarapis bei den Griechen und Römern*, Berlin, 1970.

Wunsch, R., *Sethianische Verfluchungstafeln aus Rom*, Leipzig, 1898.

– Conclusion –

Aronen, J., 'I misteri di Ecate sul Campidoglio? La versione apocrifa della legenda di S. Silvestro e il drago riconsiderata', *Studi e Materiali di Storia delle Religioni*, NS, 9, 1985, pp. 73–92.

Boissier, G., *La Fin du paganisme*, 2 vol., Paris, 1891 (1894²).

Briquel, D., *Chrétiens et haruspices. La religion étrusque, dernier rempart du paganisme romain*, Paris, 1997.

Chuvin, P., *Chronique des derniers païens*, Paris, 1990.

Goodhue, N., *The Lucus Furrinae and the Syrian Sanctuary on the Janiculum*, Amsterdam, 1975.

Guarducci, M., 'L' interruzione dei culti nel Phrygianum del Vaticano durante il IV secolo d.Cr.', *Soteriologia dei culti orientali nell'Impero Romano*, Leiden, 1982, pp. 109–22; 'La scomparsa di Cibele', ibid., pp. 123–5.

Momigliano, A. (ed.), *Il conflitto tra paganesimo e cristianesimo nel secolo IV*, Turin, 1968.

Stern, H., *Le calendrier de 354. Etude sur son texte et sur ses illustrations*, Paris, 1953.

Turcan, R., 'Les motivations de l'intolérance chrétienne et la fin du mithriacisme au IVᵉ siècle ap. J.-C.' *Actes dur VIIᵉ congrès de la FIEC*, Budapest, 1983, pp. 209–26.

Wytzes, J., *Der letzte Kampf des Heidentums in Rom*, Leiden, 1977 (*EPRO*, 56).

A guide to further reading
J. E. Reeson

The student new to the subject may be daunted – and reasonably so – by the vast wealth of literature on Roman religion. The following is intended as a brief entrée.

Broad and accessible introductions are provided by R. M. Ogilvie *The Romans and their Gods* (London, 1969) and K. Dowden *Religion and the Romans* (London, 1992). The established heavyweights on the subject are still worth dipping into: W. Warde Fowler *The Religious Experience of the Roman People* (London, 1911) and, for students with German, G. Wissowa *Religion und Kultus der Römer*, 2nd ed. (Munich, 1912). Studies frequently take a diachronic approach, charting change and development in Roman religion, and suggesting reasons for that change: among the most well-known of these is J. H. W. G. Liebeschuetz *Continuity and Change in Roman Religion* (Oxford, 1979); see also A. D. Nock 'Religious developments from the close of the Republic to the reign of Nero', *Cambridge Ancient History 10* pp. 465–511 (Cambridge, 1934), and, on the earlier period, G. Dumézil *Archaic Roman Religion* (Chicago, 1970).

The first volume of M. Beard, J. North, S. Price *Religions of Rome* [2 vols., *text and sourcebook*] (Cambridge, 1998) continues that diachronic approach, but also rigorously examines the act of interpreting religious change and, in particular, argues against the specifics of Dumézil's methodology. The second volume, a sourcebook of both literary and non-literary documents, arranges the material synchronically, by theme, and includes a convenient glossary of technical terms. The two volumes together provide a full and lively account, and include an extensive bibliography for the student wishing to venture further afield.

Several studies are aimed at more specific aspects of religion in daily life. The standard work on Roman public ceremonies is H. H. Scullard *Festivals and Ceremonies of the Roman Republic, with 88 illustrations* (London, 1981); useful appendices include maps of religious sites in Rome, and tables setting out the annual calendar. Students interested in the Roman calendar may wish to read the *Fasti*, a poem by the Roman poet Ovid (43 BC–AD 17/18), either in the original Latin (E. H. Alton et al. *P. Ovidius Nasonis Fastorum Libri Sex* (Leipzig, 1988)) or in translation (J. G. Frazer *Ovid's Fasti* (Loeb Classical Library, London, 1931)); but be aware that, while for a long time Ovid's *Fasti* was studied mainly as a mine for esoteric snippets of information on specifics of Roman festival, recent scholarship has placed it in a wider historical (e.g. G. Herbert-Brown *Ovid and the Fasti: an historical study* (Oxford, 1994)) and literary (e.g. C. E. Newlands *Playing with Time: Ovid and the Fasti* (Ithaca, 1995)) context. For the relationship between Roman religion and Roman literature in general, see D. C. Feeney *The gods in epic: poets and critics of the classical tradition* (Oxford, 1991), and the same author's *Literature and religion at Rome: cultures, contexts and beliefs* (Cambridge, 1998).

On art and architecture as sources for Roman religious life, see I. Scott Ryberg *Rites of the State Religion in Roman Art* (Rome, 1955; = *Memoirs of the American Academy in Rome* 22), and R. Turcan *Religion Romaine* (Leiden, 1988); for the latter a knowledge of French is desirable, but not essential, as the photographic plates can speak for themselves. E. Nash *Pictorial Dictionary of Ancient Rome* (London, 1961–2) and L. Richardson *A New Topographical Dictionary of Ancient Rome* (Baltimore and London, 1992) will guide the student around the religious monuments of Rome.

The beginner-friendly sourcebook on 'everyday' Roman life, as studied through mainly written sources, J.-A. Shelton *As the Romans Did* (Oxford and New York, 1988), contains a useful section on religion (pp. 360–437).

Index